LOVE CEMETERY

"The Keepers of Love." Nuthel Britton (left) and Dorris Vittatoe (right) in front of Ohio Taylor headstone. Oil on canvas by Janet McKenzie.

LOVE CEMETERY

UNBURYING
THE SECRET HISTORY
OF SLAVES

CHINA GALLAND

HarperOne
A Division of HarperCollinsPublishers

HarperOne

True success is circular, therefore, a percentage of royalties for this book goes to key non-profit organizations who helped make this work possible: the Center for the Arts, Religion, and Education at the Graduate Theological Union, the Tides Foundation, the Hedgebrook Women Writers Center, and the Harrison County Historical Museum, on behalf of the Keepers of Love's black history project, Marshall, Texas.

Photo credits can be found on page 275.

FIRST EDITION
Designed by Joseph Rutt

Library of Congress Cataloging-in-Publication Data is available upon request.

ISBN: 978–0–06–077931–3
ISBN-10: 0–06–077931–4

07 08 09 10 11 RRD(H) 10 9 8 7 6 5 4 3 2 1

To my husband, Corey Fischer

Contents

Prologue

———— •◆• ————

*To find a common future together, we must reconstruct our
common past.*

      —Manning Marable,
      The Great Wells of
      Democracy

People said that Mrs. Newton kept Negroes in her attic, that
her abandoned house was haunted. Those were rumors cir-
culating in Highland Park in the mid-1950s, in the days before
it became such an exclusively wealthy white township of comfortable homes inside the city of Dallas. I was about ten when I
first heard whispers of Cosette Faust Newton's story. My return
as an adult, to research her story for an article, set me off on a
path that eventually led me to the story of Love Cemetery, a
small, rural, African American burial ground in East Texas.

Cosette named her house the "Miramar," after her street, a
few blocks from my grandparents' home in Highland Park. The
front yard of the Miramar was surrounded by a barbed-wire-
topped chain-link fence. Heavy jail-bar doors and barred windows hung throughout the house, inside and out, and were
clearly visible from the street. The rest of the block was filled

with large, well-landscaped homes.[1] Instead of a neatly trimmed lawn like her neighbors', Cosette had scattered thirteen open red-and-white metal umbrellas, anchored in concrete blocks, around the front yard. As a finishing touch, she had hand-lettered a sign stuck in the front yard that read: "For Sale to Negroes Only."

When I was sixteen, I finally worked up the nerve to try to sneak in and up to the third-floor attic, where she supposedly kept Negroes imprisoned, to see if there were still any chains there. Just as my girlfriend, my accomplice of the moment, and I started up the third-floor stairs, we heard footsteps. We froze, convinced that the house was really haunted. But when we turned around, we saw two uniformed Highland Park police officers. We were arrested and taken down to the station and booked on charges of trespassing. My mother came and bailed us out. Cosette pressed charges. We made our court appearance and escaped punishment by swearing that we would never again go in the Miramar.

I kept the promise I'd made to the judge that late summer day in Dallas and forgot about the Miramar until I was an adult, a writer living across the country. Then, one night, a poem I was reading, called "Abandoned Places," brought that house back to me—that battered, abandoned, bizarre place out of my childhood.[2] I went back to investigate, discovered the other side of the story, and wrote about it.[3]

It wasn't a ghost story; Cosette, a Ph.D., M.D., and a former Dean of Women at Southern Methodist University with half a dozen more degrees, had kept a prisoner in her attic. In a front-page story in the *Dallas Morning News* of July 30, 1938, was a photograph of Cosette and her African American gardener,

Mickey Ricketts, just after he had been rescued by the police. Mickey's face was wrapped in medical bandages with only a large opening for his mouth. He had been captive in her attic; no one was quite sure for how long, less than a week it seemed. I tracked down Chief Gardner, the retired police officer who had arrested her for kidnapping. Chief Gardner had carried the weakened Ricketts down three flights of stairs. When I asked the officer why Cosette would have kidnapped Mickey, he assured me that Mrs. Newton was just crazy.

Then I went looking for Mickey Ricketts. I wanted to hear his side of the story. He could have still been alive when I started my research in the 1970s, so I plunged into the black community to find him. As I started to ask questions, I heard a different narrative than the one reported by the officer or the press. I found the sister of William Earl Harrison, Cosette's chauffeur, one of the African American men Cosette employed to help kidnap Mickey. Harrison's sister told me that Cosette knew exactly what she was doing; she wasn't crazy. She wanted him for sex.

I had entered another side of the story.

A different African American woman with whom I spoke claimed that Dr. Frank Newton, Cosette's husband, knew about and tolerated Cosette's sexual use of Mickey. Dr. Frank never said no to Cosette. She told me that Cosette bathed Mickey, perfumed him, dressed him in satin pajamas, and that Mickey was utterly terrified of her. Mickey ran away from Cosette. He wanted out. That's why she had him kidnapped.

Cosette claimed that Mickey had stolen a valuable jade ring from her and that what went on in the attic was simply an interrogation, with the help of a former FBI agent, to get the "truth" out of Mickey. In the end, the charges against Cosette were reduced to a misdemeanor. Mickey Ricketts settled out of court for $500 and left town.

But there was another crime here, a murder. According to Harrison's sister and others in the African American community, William Earl, Cosette's chauffer, had stepped forward to testify on Ricketts's behalf and got shot for it by one of her lawyers. In fact, there were newspaper accounts that one of Cosette's attorneys had killed a "Negro" man who entered the office. The attorney claimed self-defense and was never charged for Harrison's murder, even though Harrison's death certificate listed "homicide" as the cause. Harrison, unarmed, had been shot three times in the neck and head, in the attorney's office. Harrison's family sued for damages. But it was the white attorney's word against a dead black man's in Texas in the 1930s. The suit went nowhere.

I kept looking. I found out that there was a black newspaper published in Dallas in the 1930s. Founded in 1892, the *Dallas Express* had a different perspective on Cosette's story than the *Dallas Morning News*, the mainstream white paper. It echoed the points of view I had heard in the black community, while the *News* painted Cosette as merely eccentric and intimated that Mickey must have done something wrong to have gotten himself into such a position. The *Dallas Express* gave credence to the idea that there was more to the story and that Harrison, who was about to talk, had been murdered to keep him quiet.

Though I found no proof of the nature of Cosette's relationship with her gardener, I did find the court records, the newspaper stories—largely from the white perspective—and William Earl Harrison's death certificate.

Over the years, as I continued the lines of research that Cosette's story had started me on, I discovered a history full of lynchings, of Ku Klux Klan and Citizen's Council violence, of black disenfranchisement, and I understood that this history was part of a larger narrative that continues to unfold today, like a troubling, transparent overlay on the map of the United States, especially the map of Texas—East Texas, where my great-grandparents on my mother's side settled in 1900 and where the story of Love Cemetery begins.

Note

In order to protect the resting places of the dead and the privacy of the living, certain names of people and places in this book have been changed. For anyone looking for lost relatives thought to be buried in Harrison County, contact the Harrison County Genealogical Society at the Harrison County Historical Museum in Marshall, Texas, or the Marshall Public Library.

www.easttexaskin.com
www.harrisoncountrymuseum.org
www.slaves.8m.com
www.txgenes.com/txharrison/index.htm

ONE

Getting into Love Cemetery

They are not powerless, the dead.
—Chief Seattle,
Suquamish and Duwamish
Native American leader

The road that leads to Love Cemetery is deeply rutted red clay and sand, and it winds for well over a mile through open fields and stands of East Texas pine until it arrives at a ten-foot-high chain-link gate just a couple hundred yards from the graveyard. On a chilly late winter morning in March 2003, the fence seemed impenetrable, with heavy metal chain woven around the steel end-poles clamped shut with a big brass combination lock. Mrs. Nuthel Britton, guardian and caretaker of Love Cemetery, had been given the combination, but the lock would not yield. This was a new fence, a new gate, and a new lock, and therefore, Mrs. Britton suspected, a new owner too. The 3,500 acres surrounding the old, overgrown cemetery, which she had rediscovered in the mid-1990s, had been cut up and sold off again. Whoever bought this parcel had fenced the cemetery in. The combination Nuthel had been given must have been for an old lock on the *outer* gate, the first one we'd come to. There was no fence attached to it; that one was just a free-standing gate. The deep ruts around it indicated that the fence had been taken down years ago. We drove past that first gate and continued on until this second gate stopped us. Now Nuthel stood there with Doris Vittatoe, who also had ancestors buried in Love Cemetery, and me, trying to solve this puzzle. This second gate was big enough for an East Texas logging truck to drive through—if you had the combination. We didn't.

A manganese blue sky shone through the pines and the bare branches of a few red oaks that still grew here. The bright sun took the chill off the air. The quiet of the morning was broken by the resonant calls of mockingbirds, mourning doves, and a warbler. The familiar *rat-a-tat-tat* of a red-headed woodpecker echoed from deep in the woods.

We shook our heads, thwarted by the new lock. At seventy-nine, Nuthel—as she insisted we call her—was still lean, tall, and active. Doris, about twenty years younger, had an elegant oval face with big dark eyes. Like Nuthel, she mowed her own yard and worked in the garden, staying trim and fit. Nuthel wore a long-sleeved red sweatshirt and an army camouflage hat. As secretary of the Love Colored Burial Association, she was "the Keeper of Love." Nuthel had wanted to show us the cemetery, but she was blocked this morning. Legally, she had every right to be there, and so did Doris. The land belongs to the dead in Texas. Cemeteries cannot be sold or transferred. In 1904 a local landowner named Della Love had deeded this 1.6 acre parcel to the Love Colored Burial Association. In turn, the Burial Association secured a permanent easement to use the road to the cemetery. Someone from the timber management company that once owned the larger, surrounding parcel had given Nuthel the combination to the lock some years before, but the property had changed hands many times in recent years—from a timber company to an insurance conglomerate to whomever the current owner was.

Last Nuthel knew the timber was owned by an East Coast insurance company. "It must have changed hands again," she said, matter-of-factly. That would explain the fancy new fence and new lock. "Whatever they got in there, they don't want it to get out, that's for sure," she said with a chuckle.

She pulled up her sweatshirt to get to her pants pocket and fished around. With a straight face and a solemn air, she pulled out a small strip of paper with the combination number written on it, glanced at it, then shot us a smile. Nuthel had an inscrutable face that I was only learning to read. She was a great tease. "Hmmm," she said, shaking her head and chuckling, puzzled, "I see here that I put in the right *numbers*," she paused. "Only thing is, it's the wrong *lock*."

A rifle shot cracked in the distance and startled me, a city dweller. Nuthel and Doris paid it little attention.

"Somebody's back in there huntin', I bet," Nuthel remarked with another big smile, as Doris nodded. "It's nothing. You're just not used to it," they assured me. Hunting was still a way of life here. We had passed a deserted duck blind and an empty hunting camp on the dirt road coming in.

"Look," I said, "I'm going to get some folding chairs out of the trunk of my car. You can sit here in front of this locked gate; I'll take your picture and interview you right here. The picture alone will tell a big part of the story."

But when I brought the chairs back, I noticed that there was something strange about the gate. It didn't look right, it wasn't straight—something was awry. "Wait a minute," I said. I looked at the hinge on the right and—sure enough—the gate had been lifted off its hinges and opened from the side. Maybe someone had slipped inside and was poaching. That would explain the rifle shots we had heard even though hunting season was over. I pointed out this opening to my companions.

"Since you have family buried back there, you two have a right to go in," I said, "at least that was how the attorney explained it to me."

They considered this a moment. Then Nuthel grinned and clasped her hands together, "And you're with us, China," she said, "so you can come too."

"Well, that would be my logic," I said, laughing.

Doris nodded in agreement. "Of course."

We picked up the gate and inched it open just wide enough for us to slip in one by one. We laughed like schoolgirls, excited by our unexpected adventure. As soon as we were on the other side we pushed the gate back just as we'd found it, so close to the pole that it *looked* all the way shut.

Nuthel assured us that the cemetery wasn't that far anyway— straight down the road we were on, close enough that she could almost see its boundary from where we stood. She tried to point out a railroad cross-tie that marked the corner, but everything was so overgrown and covered with vines that I couldn't distinguish the dark brown of a cross-tie from a tree trunk. Doris couldn't either.

"Come on," Nuthel said and started ambling down the road with Doris walking next to her. I hung back a little out of respect. This was their burial ground and these were their ancestors. I was there only because Nuthel had asked for my help.

A solid bank of young pines, ten to fifteen feet tall, continued on our right as we strolled. On our left, the woods were mixed, the pines thinning up to a row of elms. That was where the cemetery started, Nuthel informed us triumphantly.

"Keep lookin' for that cross-tie," she instructed us. "My sons put one in at each corner of the cemetery and set them in concrete so they couldn't fall over."

The road we were walking down was in much better condition than the logging road we had driven earlier in the day. This road was even-surfaced and well drained, largely sand and weeds flattened by tire tracks. About two hundred yards from the gate, Nuthel pointed out the dark wood of the railroad tie.

"Now look at this," she called happily and stopped walking. "This is it," she said, punctuating her remark by pointing her index finger in the air, tapping it like a teacher would a chalkboard. "See that row of trees on your left? Those trees are the northern boundary of the cemetery. Come on now," she said and took off from the road to clamber up a sandy embankment into a dense web of leafless vines.

Doris and I followed. "Go slow now," Nuthel said. "This old wisteria'll get you. Watch your feet or you'll get all tangled up." She pushed aside shoulder-high dry weeds and proceeded twenty or thirty feet, then stopped and looked around. She hadn't been here for nearly five years and she was disoriented. "We've got to go back," she announced. The vines and underbrush were too thick to get through. She couldn't see any headstones. We retraced our steps to the road and continued walking toward the woods. Sure enough, farther down, the road turned left along the southern border of the cemetery. We found a duck blind and an easier entrance where the underbrush hadn't grown so high.

Within ten feet of the entrance, we began to see flashes of pale headstones through the sinuous, interwoven loops of brown, green, and gray vines. We went over to investigate, pushing aside the vines and overgrowth.

"See, there they are," Nuthel said. We stopped a minute to brush aside the dirt and fallen leaves and read two granite headstones: "*Albert Henderson, born April 16, 1865, died May 22, 1929* and *Mattie Henderson, born October 29, 1875, died March 16, 1951.*" Doris went on by herself, deeper into the underbrush. She had caught glimpses of more headstones and kept going.

Nuthel and I made our way to her, as the vines snapped and wild rose and blackberry thorns raked our pants. Doris had stopped and was bent over a large headstone. She read the inscription to us slowly: "Ohio Taylor, died 1918. 84 years old."

"Do you have a pencil to write that down?" Nuthel asked me with the mock sternness of the schoolteacher she had been. I told her I did and reminded her that I'd promised to write down everything. Breaking into a smile, she said, "Good, 'cause I didn't bring a pencil or nothin'."

"This is amazing," Doris said quietly, as Nuthel and I made our way closer to the granite headstone she was standing in front of. "Ohio Taylor," she repeated. Then, suddenly, she drew her breath in sharply, "Why, he's my great-grandfather!" she said. "I didn't even know he was back here."

The air was still cool, not a breeze stirring. I leaned over to read the inscription. "If he was eighty-four," I said, "that means he was born in 1834." I said slowly, "He lived through slavery."

"Okay," Doris said matter-of-factly.

I knew enough to avoid calling someone a slave. *People* were enslaved. Being enslaved by someone was a condition, a degraded position, not a category of being. Calling people "slaves" was a way of denying that they were human beings first. Still, I had to stop and think and choose my words to reflect an understanding that did not come naturally growing up in northeast Texas. The region from Dallas to Scottsville—the part of Texas where I grew up—was part of the cotton-growing, plantation-holding South, not the mythic West that most people imagine Texas to be.

Nuthel, Doris, and I walked around Ohio Taylor's rectangular headstone and discovered large stone pieces scattered around it on the ground.

"These pieces belong to this headstone," Nuthel announced authoritatively. "Now look at this," she said, pointing to the outline of a rectangle on top of the headstone, indicating where a rectangular-based piece had once sat. I got down on my hands and knees and dug through the dead leaves. I felt something hard. Brushing away the leaves I found a small footed granite bowl. Its bottom matched the shape on top of the headstone. Then I saw two three-foot-high fluted columns lying nearby at odd angles on the ground, but they were too heavy to pick up. I couldn't budge them. We found another piece of stone, the delicately carved plinth that must have crowned the columns when the marker was assembled. The plinth had an ornate letter T for Taylor carefully incised in it, with an oak leaf pattern trailing down one side and ivy on the other.

"What Taylor is *this?*" Nuthel asked. She had moved to the grave next to Ohio.

I squatted down to make out the letters on the foot-high white marble headstone, and read: "Fr. Anthony Taylor." I asked Doris who he was, but Doris wasn't over her elation and amazement in finding Ohio Taylor's headstone. She would not be distracted.

"I tell you now, at that time, back then, for 1918, that is a *nice* tombstone," she said. "Honey, they paid good money for that, a long time ago. It has lasted all this time."

Ohio Taylor had been a person of means. Later, I would learn from Doris's brother that Ohio had owned maybe two hundred acres of land or more. This was especially interesting because he had survived slavery. I had read historian Randolph Campbell's work on Harrison County, *A Southern Community in Crisis*, as well as *Grassroots Reconstruction in Texas, 1865–1880.* Thanks to Campbell, I had some appreciation of the obstacles that Ohio Taylor might have had to overcome to become a landowner. Whatever land he had came from what he and his family were able to acquire *after* June 19, 1865, when federal troops arrived in Galveston, finally bringing Emancipation to Texas.

Though Lincoln had signed the Emancipation Proclamation in 1863, a good two years earlier, Texans ignored it until after Lee's surrender, when Major General Gordon Granger and his Union troops arrived in Galveston to enforce the proclamation and to protect those newly freed. Granger gathered a crowd on the street and read the Emancipation Proclamation aloud on June 19, 1865. Only then did Texans, stubborn to the end, begin to acknowledge the new legal status of freed men, women, and children. From that day forward, there was no more enslavement of African Americans in Texas. The word spread swiftly in the enslaved community, producing a tide of joy and bewilderment. Some people stayed put, others left immediately—to get away from former owners, to find family members who had been sold off, to go North, to leave the country. Some came back, some never returned. It was a tumultuous time. African Americans had only first names, and for the most part, they had no money and no land. After slavery ended on that June day, people made up names, took the names of former owners if they had been decent, or used someone else's if they hadn't. It wasn't until the 1870 census that African Americans were officially listed with first and last names.

Ohio Taylor and others buried here in Love Cemetery had managed to acquire parcels of farmland. Taylor would have been thirty-one years old in 1865. The fact that he became a land-owner was remarkable in itself, but to think that he might have held on to his land after Congressional Reconstruction ended in 1870, and kept it through the White Citizens' Party rise to power in 1878, when they "redeemed" Harrison County, and after, was also significant. When the federal troops left Harrison County in 1870, all hell broke loose. The Citizens' Party set out to again disenfranchise African Americans and put an end to the sub-stantial progress they were making in political and civic life, especially in education. Much of the white community was terri-fied and angry at finding themselves outvoted at the ballot box and, in some cases, actually represented in the state legislature by black men who had only recently been enslaved by them. Women, of course, no matter what their color, were not allowed to vote until 1920.

Granger's arrival in Galveston is the event celebrated on the holiday Juneteenth.[5] Now, as we stood before Ohio Taylor's damaged grave, the era of Emancipation seemed so real, and so close. Nuthel suggested that the damage must have been caused by the wind. I took that to be her way of avoiding the possibility that someone had intentionally desecrated the headstone out of racism or wanton vandalism. To me, white racism seemed obvious; I assumed that was why the community had been locked out of Love Cemetery to begin with. But I followed Nuthel and Doris's lead and did not broach the subject. Instead, I asked Doris what it was like for her to see her great-grandfather's grave for the first time.

"I am *elated* to be able to come back here!" she said, "I am sixty-one years old, and this is the first time I've been able to get back here to see this. This is *amazing*."

"Do you have children?" Nuthel asked her.

"Yes," said Doris.

"Well, you bring your children back here so they can see this," Nuthel said.

"Oh yes," Doris replied.

"Here's another one," I called out. I could make out a nearby headstone in the shape of a lamb at rest, underneath more vines.

"You know these ancestors are happy to see us back here today," Nuthel said.

I hadn't noticed any wisteria on the drive out to the cemetery, but suddenly I was in the thick of it. Some of the graceful woody gray vines were as thick as your finger, some were as thick as your wrist, it had been growing back here so long. In East Texas people say wisteria takes over so fast you can hear it growing. According to unverified family lore, it was my forebearers who introduced wisteria into East Texas in the 1920s. My great-grandfather started a nursery business here in 1900, after moving his large Catholic family from Chicago to Scottsville. An older cousin told me that wisteria was not native to East Texas, that it was originally from China and that the family imported it and now it grows everywhere here. When I was a child, that sounded distinctive, but as an adult, I grew to doubt it. Whether it was native, non-native, a tall tale, or true about where this wisteria came from, it didn't change the fact that I'd never seen such a tangle of it.[6] As I stood there looking at the twisting, balled up, overgrown vines that blanketed these graves, Nuthel explained the connection.

Doris Vittatoe.

"Some of these people used to work for your family, at the nursery. They brought wisteria cuttings over here from the nursery and planted them to decorate the graves, it was so pretty." She herself had even worked for my family's nursery at one time, she said. The Ancestors must have been laughing indeed. "My, when this is all bloomed out, you ain't never seen anything like those purple blossoms. They smell so good. Sweet. It's so peaceful out here, so quiet," she said. "It's the most beautiful place in the world."

"I tell you," said Doris, "I have you to thank for this, Mrs. Britton—somebody had to know *how* to get back here." Doris said she was going to have to call family, "This is something."

"You know if we come back with machetes and spray the roots, we can clear this," Nuthel told us. I didn't want to talk about toxins, and I was too overwhelmed by the magnitude of forty years of overgrown wisteria. If we cleared it, it wouldn't be with herbicides. I changed the subject.

"When were you made the Keeper of Love?" I asked her.

"Oh, I don't know, I just got out here and started working. First I had to find out who owned all this property and get a key to the gate—that first gate we drove *around* today. One of the county commissioners helped me track it down. Once we were able to get in the gate, it still took us three days of looking and traipsing around back here to find this cemetery, it was so overgrown. You just couldn't see it. The man who helped me find it again, after I moved back here from Ohio, told me to put posts around so I could always find it. I had my sons dig holes and put those railroad ties in vertically, in concrete, so they couldn't get knocked over. They dug down deep, put one at each corner of the cemetery. I found only one today, I guess the other ones are still covered up. My sons helped me out here until they got transferred to the Middle East—Kuwait and Iraq."

Nuthel had been married to a career military man herself and had lived away from East Texas for over thirty years. She met her husband at the Tuskegee Institute, where she had gone for a college summer session.

"I'm a road lizard," she told me. She liked to get out and go. She finished her bachelor's degree at Bishop College in Marshall, Texas, and after living in Taiwan, where her husband was stationed during the Vietnam war, completed her master's degree in Ohio after they moved back to the States. Eventually Nuthel came back to the area to take care of her grandmother Lizzie Sparks's nearby farm.

"You've got people buried back here too," I said to Nuthel. "Shouldn't we visit them?"

"If you want to," she said. "We've got to work our way around here," pointing to the thickest part of the wisteria and grapevine.

The vines didn't look as bad over by the big pond that bordered the cemetery. If we walked toward it and then cut along the edge between the water and the wisteria, we reasoned we could zigzag back into the underbrush when we drew parallel to Nuthel's family graves. As we got closer to the water, I could see that what I had thought was a pond was more like a small lake. We couldn't tell how big it was because of the trees that edged the perimeter and curved away from the clearing we were in. The water continued out of sight—a hundred yards, a mile? No way to tell.

As we made our way toward the pond, Nuthel said, "You know, some of these graves used to have little bottles on them," and told me to keep an eye out.

Doris suddenly exclaimed, "No way! Here's Harvey Johnson—he was one of my dad's uncles!"

I spied another stone and made my way over to it, as I called out to Doris, "There's another marker by the Hendersons. Are those your people too, Doris?"

"No," she said. After a few more steps, she told us that she'd found another one. "Look, Sidney Johnson. Died in 1963."

Then Nuthel called, "Look here—Bettie Webb, 1840 to 1923."

Bettie Webb's stone was knocked over, flat on the ground, but it wasn't broken. It was a traditional white marble stone with a rounded top. "We will meet again" was incised under her name and dates. I moved to Nuthel's side. Ten feet farther we found another Webb headstone, Claude Webb's. It was a nicely shaped concrete stone with an engraved brass plaque giving his name and the year of his death, 1954.

I paused to take notes on the graves we had found. I drew the markers as quickly as I could in a small notebook while Doris and Nuthel kept going.

"Wait up, please," I said. I told them I was trying to draw a map but I was disoriented. "Which way is north?"

"That's a good idea," Nuthel said, "We're on the west side of the cemetery. Let me see ... no ... no ... this is east. By the water. We're going north."

Finally we got to Nuthel's relatives: Daily and Oscar Sparks, her uncles, buried side by side under a double headstone. A few feet away we found Daniel Sparks, another uncle, his traditional headstone buried in vines. Lizzie Sparks, Nuthel's grand-mother—that's the grave she wanted to look for. Nuthel kept a small garden for tomatoes and onions at her house in Marshall, but she raised the corn and other crops at Lizzie Sparks's out here in Scottsville, in the country, where there was room—thirty-three acres.

Nuthel remembered that there was no headstone for Lizzie Sparks, and I didn't see how we'd ever find her grave in the thick growth of vines. Nuthel stared at the ground and then pointed.

"See that glass jar sunk in the ground?" Nuthel said. I saw— barely—a thin circle of glass in the leaves. "That's it," Nuthel said grandly. "That is Lizzie Sparks's grave." A jar as a grave marker? I would have walked right by it.

Doris and I crouched down to look. I ran my hand through the dead leaves on the grave, and sure enough, within a foot or so was a small, rusted, blue metal funeral home marker on a stick—a temporary marker—protruding six inches or so from the ground. The glass cover on the marker was broken and the slip of paper with the name was missing. Nonetheless, someone had written on the soft metal inside the marker: "Lizzie Sparks d. 1964, 100 yrs."

"This is my grandmamma," Nuthel said proudly. "She was Indian. She was real Cherokee."

She used the word *Cherokee* as an adjective. I asked her what she meant. Was she from the Cherokee tribe?

"I mean she was *Indian*. I'm not sure which tribe she was from: Cherokee, Caddo, I can't remember. I've got a portrait of her I'll show you back at the house."

Lizzie Sparks was Native American *and* black. The Caddo were the indigenous people of this part of the world. They flourished in East Texas, Louisiana, and southern Arkansas as early as 600 CE. But the Native American presence in East Texas, at least to a white person like me, had been particularly elusive. Years ago I had tried, unsuccessfully, to find a member of the Caddo tribe to speak with. Local black history, much of it, lies forgotten or buried, but local Native American history has been virtually obliterated.

"Who told you about Love Cemetery, Nuthel?" I asked, as I stood up again.

"Oh, my grandparents, and my parents," she said. "I *always* knew about Love," she laughed.

Again, I asked her if she knew how the community had been locked out in the first place.

"I think when the farming went bad," Nuthel replied, "when the farmers sold their land, they just got up and went. Everybody left, and they forgot about this place. And the ones was here, they just don't seem to know anything about it," she said with a shrug of her shoulders.

"If nobody told you about this cemetery," Doris said, "you wouldn't have known Love was here."

"That's right," Nuthel nodded.

Doris looked around, trying to orient herself. Lizzie Sparks's grave, where we stood talking, was on the pond side of the cemetery, the eastern edge.

"Somewhere near here was my grandmother's house," Doris told us, "on the other side of this pond. When I was little my mother was still coming back out here and planting cotton. I probably wasn't ten years old. My mom used to say, 'Love Cemetery's back there,' but I never did see it.

"Richard Taylor and Irene Taylor," she continued. "That's their names—my grandparents, the ones who lived on the other side of this pond. We didn't see their graves today, but they're back in here somewhere," she said, looking around again. "We need to watch out for them." Then another memory surfaced. Doris told us, in low tones, how her mother had never been able to get back into this cemetery to clean her mother's grave before she died. By the time Doris moved back in the 1980s, the community was locked out. "Mother was so sad. She never got over not being able to clean her mother's grave. It was awful," she said, frowning. "I tried to help her when I moved back here, but we were locked out. That's all there was to it."

"Could not come back," Nuthel said softly, like a refrain.

Doris, like Nuthel, had moved away and lived in Seattle and Los Angeles until the 1980s, when her mother became ill and she returned to help care for her.

Geese honked overhead as they flew in a V toward Caddo Lake. Nuthel spied dewberries coming out. The rain forecast for the day had never arrived.

"You can see the little buds coming," Doris said. "Look, everything's going to pop—the wisteria, the grapevine, elderberry, all going to be taking over again, any time now, it's coming."

I asked Doris and Nuthel if the cemetery had *ever* been cleaned up before.

They both started talking at once. "They used to keep it up," Doris began rapidly. Nuthel overtook her in slow, measured tones, contrapuntally. "This was the prettiest place...."

"My mom used to come back here," Doris continued, "and clean off her parents' graves."

"They had a tool shed back here," Nuthel recalled, "where they kept all their tools for cleaning up. Once a year—and it was in August—and there'd be so many peoples out here, the men would come and clean the graves, and the wives would come and bring ..."

"Food!" said Doris.

"Food!" Nuthel said. "It was a real good time. Now you talking about cookin', they cooked! Mmhmm. There was fried chickens, pies—berry pies, lemon, cherry—you name it, greens—all kinds—beans, collard greens, squashes, and onions, the little pearl kinds, and peas, fresh peas, oh it was all fresh, ham, barbecued beef, corn on the cob...."

"How many people would come?" I wanted to know.

"I would say around fifty," Nuthel answered, "it was like a church out here, lots of people would come. People everywhere for grave-cleaning day."

It was time to go. We needed to start back while the sun was still high. After we made it to our cars, we still had well over a mile and a half on a logging road full of ruts and low points of red boot-sucking sand-and-clay muck.

It took us a good half-hour to work our way back through the vines to the first road, the well-drained one to the gate, tiptoeing and pushing dry shoulder-high weeds. We had just emerged from the cemetery and stepped back out onto the road when a huge crash stopped us in our tracks.

"What's that?" I asked, looking at Doris and Nuthel. Nuthel didn't look the least bit startled.

"Must be one of those big elms coming down," Doris said. "Those wisteria vines are so strong they can pull a whole tree down over time."

But Nuthel just smiled sweetly and shook her head. "That's just the Ancestors lettin' us know that they've seen us," she said, "and that they're happy we're here."

———— • ◆ • ————

TWO

How We Got to Love

"The Ancestors are the ones who take your prayers to God."
—Sobonfu Somé
on the Dagara belief
about the Ancestors

I didn't start out trying to get into Love Cemetery. The journey that eventually brought me there was more roundabout. It had started ten years earlier, quite innocently, when I was back in East Texas for a short family visit. My great-grandfather, Stephen John Verhalen, had bought 2,800 acres of land in rural Harrison County to raise peaches but quickly found he needed a variety of crops. His nursery business branched out into narcissus bulbs, rugosa roses, Cedars of Lebanon, Voorhees cedars, American holly, and a wide variety of nursery stock, including crepe myrtles and wisteria. His brothers George and Ray were also in the business, which grew to the point where they shipped a million narcissus bulbs by rail to one grower in Florida alone. I was only following up on a snippet of family history and the history of the nursery they once owned. During the course of that brief trip I made a shocking discovery, and it haunted me for years.

A cousin, hoping to help me with my research, referred me to an elderly local historian, Lydia Drayman Ball. Lydia and I became friends. Tall and slender, still an elegant woman in her late seventies, she was also active, bright, and completely devoted to local history, especially her own family's, which went back to the 1840s in Harrison County. Though Lydia lived in an apartment when we first met, she still owned the original thousand acres of Blossom Hall, a former plantation built in 1847. There were other stately antebellum homes in the area, but ownership had changed hands as the land was either parceled off or sold out of the builder's family. Blossom Hall had remained intact, and at that time, in 1993, it was probably the last former plantation in the county that had been owned and occupied continuously by the family that had it built.

Lydia couldn't drive anymore, so one day my favorite older cousin, Jack Verhalen, and I took her out to the woods to search for an abandoned graveyard that belonged to her relatives. In a sunlit grove within a pine forest, she found six headstones standing in a circle, with names and dates of distant family. She was elated to find them after years of unsuccessful searching. Lydia told us that cemeteries were an invaluable source of information—sometimes, as one goes further back in history, the information carved onto a headstone may be the only record of that person's life. And in this matter she was an expert. A childless widow, she had traveled to the Eastern seaboard for her family research, going through church records and cemeteries everywhere she went, writing it all down in an even, curving hand to give to each of her nieces and nephews.

Lydia returned the favor we had done for her that day by inviting me to go on a tour of Blossom Hall, her graceful white

Greek Revival plantation home. Lydia was so comfortable in the past, particularly in the nineteenth century, that she kept two of the bedrooms in Blossom Hall just as they had been in the late 1800s. The house was just a home to her, but to me it was a living history museum. In the hallway downstairs hung a striking family tree, carefully calligraphed in her uncle's precise hand.

The dark, heavy mahogany furniture in her uncle's upstairs bedroom had come up the Mississippi River, the Atchafalaya, the Red River, and Twelve-Mile Bayou by paddle steamer from New Orleans, arriving at Swanson's Landing on Caddo Lake, less than ten miles east, or Jefferson, farther north, in the days when long shallow-draft paddle steamers plied the waterways between Caddo Lake and New Orleans.

The bed that had belonged to Lydia's great-grandmother was still covered with the striking red, yellow, and green "Star of Texas" quilt that she had stitched while traveling overland by ox-cart to Texas as a thirteen-year-old girl. A box of watercolors from Paris lay on a table by the window, a remnant of the days when imports from France were not uncommon in the wealthier households of Harrison County. Ball gowns, wedding dresses, and crystal chandeliers from Paris were shipped upriver from New Orleans between the 1840s and 1890s, until Caddo Lake finally became too shallow for the paddle steamers to make the runs that connected the eastern part of Texas to the rich, cosmopolitan, Creole culture of New Orleans, with its French, Haitian, African, Spanish, Native American, and Caribbean influences.

After the informal tour of Blossom Hall, we drove down the pink crepe myrtle–lined drive to Drayman Road. We were headed back to town, but at the point where we should have turned right—the way to town—Lydia told me to turn left and continue down Drayman Road. I followed her instructions.

"Pull over, here, on the right," she said, after a moment. "I want to show you something." We got out and walked a few steps to a rusted barbed wire fence that ran alongside Drayman Road.

"Honey, look here," she said, pointing something out to me, her soft, white hair framing her finely wrinkled face. I couldn't see what she was pointing to. "My daddy never let anybody plow this end of the field," she said matter-of-factly. "The slaves are buried here."

The slaves are buried here. I had no idea how to respond to this news. I looked again; I peered for headstones, wooden crosses, something that would indicate a grave, even just one. I told her that I couldn't see any graves.

"That's right," Lydia said. "You can't see them because they're not marked."

"Not marked?" I asked. "This is an unmarked burial ground?" I had never heard of such a thing. "Why, yes," she said. She was looking back over the field as though there were nothing unusual about having an unmarked burial ground of slaves on one's property.

I stood dumbfounded. Why had she told me this? Did she believe that her father's refusal to let this ground be plowed was a way of honoring the dead? Or that, by telling me, she would establish or preserve her family's honor? I saw Blossom Hall in a new light, like a night landscape suddenly illuminated by a lightning strike that pulsed for seconds, streaked across the sky, blazed, and then all was dark again. All the artifacts of nineteenth-century life in her home that had charmed me marked her connection to a past that was inseparable from slavery. East

Texas in those days was shaped by the profits from cheaply produced cotton: it created riches for some whites—the big planters—and threatened to break not only the backs but the souls of
enslaved blacks who worked the fields. On this beautiful afternoon in the countryside that had been home to my family too, the
burial ground reminded me that slavery had never really been
resolved here or, for that matter, anywhere in this country. That
cemetery had been left where it was for more than a century,
unmarked but known to her family, a secret history just under the
surface.

Lydia rattled on sweetly: "Our cook, Sally, was so afraid to
walk past this place when she went home at night that Mother
always made one of the Negro men walk with her. Sally was superstitious—she swore this curve on the road was haunted." Her
blue eyes glistened. Lydia chuckled and turned away to look out
over the field again. She looked so innocent.

"That Sally! She was a big old woman and sweet, sweet as she
could be, but my, she was superstitious. Mother always told us
Negroes were like that and we shouldn't believe such talk, so I
didn't."

I was so taken aback by her revelation that I could scarcely
speak.

In that moment I understood why I had grown up hearing stories during my visits about not going down Drayman Road. The
black community said Drayman Road was haunted—and it was.
When whites called truth "superstition," the reality of slavery
and the racism that persists could be circumvented, glossed
over, ignored, and dismissed. For a time. Sally's story gave me a
different map, and I was learning to read it as clearly as any
road sign.

"But Lydia," I finally managed to get out, "don't you think the people whose ancestors are buried here would like to know about them too?" I reminded her how much her family history meant to her and how much she had learned from visiting family cemeteries. I mentioned the family tree she'd pointed to with pride in the hallway at Blossom Hall. There must be people living right nearby who have ancestors—relatives—buried here.

She listened, then slowly nodded her head. "Why honey," she said, "I suppose that's true."

"Lydia, don't you think it's time to mark this burial ground?" I asked her. Her eyebrows shot up in surprise, her blue eyes opened wide.

"Why honey, I just never thought about *that*," she said, smiling as she paused. "Maybe you're right."

I was surprised by her openness. As fond and respectful as I was of Lydia, I knew that she was a daughter of the Old South; her world was filled with racial stereotypes that she hadn't begun to recognize, and yet she seemed to appreciate my concerns. We shared an understanding of the importance of history, and perhaps that understanding could become a bridge over our differences.

In that moment of possibility, a fully formed vision of a ceremony of reconciliation blossomed in my imagination. I saw people, blacks and whites together, performing a rite of healing. First, a stone would be laid to mark this burial ground of nameless enslaved beings. Then I remembered the old "planter's journal" I'd seen at another nearby plantation. The word *journal* disguised what it really was: an inventory of property and record of every enslaved person "owned" by the plantation, listed by first name, the only name they had. Chances were that Blossom Hall had such a journal too. It would contain the names of the dead in these graves. The names could be read aloud, and we would dedicate this ground to them. There would be prayers and songs, old-style gospel hymns. Our marker stone would signify the laying down of a new covenant to remember the people enslaved here and to tell their history. We would put to rest the ghosts that haunted this land by finally acknowledging their existence, their personhood.

Lydia interrupted my reverie. "Honey," she said slowly, "there's just one problem. I don't own Blossom Hall anymore. I deeded this place over to one of my nieces, Mary Ann Drayman Birch, in Natchitoches."

My vision collapsed and disappeared in the afternoon breeze. Lydia went on to tell me how that thousand acres of land had gotten to be just too much for her to care for alone. She had moved into town, at peace with the idea that Blossom Hall would be cared for by someone who loved the place as much as she did.

I would have to call Lydia's niece and get her permission before anything could happen. "I'm not saying she wouldn't do it," Lydia tried to reassure me. "She's a lovely person. But I don't know, honey. I think it would be best if you talked to her in person."

Seven years passed before I telephoned Lydia's niece, Mary Ann. That was in April 2000. By then, Mary Ann and her husband had left Natchitoches and were living year-round at Blossom Hall. I introduced myself. She already knew of me through Lydia. I told her who my family was; she knew several of my cousins. She promptly invited me for coffee the next morning.

It took a while to get through the pleasantries—how I liked my coffee, what a beautiful spring day it was, still not too hot—and the sorting out of relations: who was kin to whom and who was once-removed. It was all a southern ritual, a form of greeting, and a favorite pastime. Finally I told Mary Ann and her husband, Howland, that Lydia had brought me here years earlier and showed me the unmarked burial ground. I explained that, as a writer, I was fascinated by the historical significance of this discovery. Mary Ann seemed to sit up a little straighter and Howland cleared his throat.

I took a deep breath and said that I thought the burial ground needed to be marked and that I was writing a story about it. After a short silence, Mary Ann said, "Well, I suppose we could think about that." She turned toward her husband, who said softly, "That's right." He smiled. "We could take it under consideration." Having gotten that far without a breach of civility, I asked them to show it to me again, explaining that I wanted to be sure of its exact location. They did not hesitate, southern hospitality was so ingrained in them. I understood their dedication in a new way, the commitment to making a guest comfortable above all else, and I was grateful for it.

At the burial ground, the Birch's graciously allowed me to take snapshots of them next to the tree that marks one boundary of the cemetery. Before I left, they promised to think about my proposal. Of course, they would have to talk to the rest of their family, which was large and far-flung. And there was one other issue. Mary Ann didn't own this land anymore; she'd deeded the parcel with the burial ground to a sister of hers in Beaumont. It wasn't clear when she had done this or why. Still Mary Ann promised to talk to her sister about the burial ground and to get back to me. She wasn't comfortable letting me phone or write her sister directly. I would need to be patient.

The next time I returned to Scottsville, six months later, we went through this same ritual of hospitality. Again they politely fended off of my attempt to reach an agreement with them. I tried to appeal to their self-interest. I explained that if Drayman Road were to be straightened out or widened by the county, something they told me they never wanted to see happen, they could prevent that by marking this burial ground. Otherwise the cemetery could be paved over. And though I didn't say it, I tried to convey the idea that marking the ground wasn't an issue of color but an issue of being human.

They politely sidestepped my argument. "Won't you have more coffee?" they asked. "We'll have to think about that. We still haven't been able to discuss it with everyone involved. It's so complicated. We have to consult with the others because they own land around that parcel too." Another twelve people at least were involved.

After the third or the fourth visit, I realized that the Birches would always be polite and they would always put me off. I had to take a new approach.

Following the suggestion of a friend, I went to some spiritual leaders in the community for guidance, starting with my own family's pastor at St. Joseph's Catholic Church in Marshall, Father Ron Diegel. Yes, this matter needed to be attended to, he agreed, and he suggested that I gather other pastors and ministers and lay leaders from the community and form a committee to address it. He would work with us. He suggested the pastor at Trinity Episcopal Church, Father Steve Sellers. Steve quickly agreed to join the group, and he suggested Rev. James Webb, the pastor at the historic black Bethesda Baptist Church. We soon had a small committee, and without giving any thought to its composition, we had formed a remarkably balanced group that was black and white, male and female, ordained and lay.

At our first meeting, we were joined by Gail Beil, a tall and willowy woman with big blue eyes, who was a fount of local history, especially black history. She was the incoming president of the East Texas Historical Society and a member of the Historical Commission for Harrison County. Gail had spent years working as a reporter for the *Marshall Messenger*. She and her husband, Greg Beil, were active members of the Methodist Church; it was in response to a church request that they had moved to Marshall three decades earlier. Greg helped set up the science program and taught physics at Wiley College, the liberal arts college founded in 1873 by the Episcopal Methodist Church and the Freedman's Bureau. Wiley was the first historically black college west of the Mississippi. Gail ran the Head Start program for the city of Marshall.

There were two other laypersons at the meeting, Doris Vittatoe and Nuthel Britton. I had met Doris only once before this meeting: several months earlier, I had finally followed Lydia's advice to seek her out for her historical knowledge of the area. Doris Vittatoe was the secretary of Shiloh Baptist Missionary Church, the closest black church to Blossom Hall. Like Bethesda Baptist Church, Shiloh dated back to 1867.

I had not yet met Nuthel, though. Doris invited her. When we went around the table that night, Nuthel Britton introduced herself as a farmer and as "the Keeper of Love." She explained that Love was a black cemetery in the Scottsville area that the descendant community had been locked out of for over forty years.

Of course this was before any of us knew the story of Love Cemetery. I was so completely focused on Blossom Hall that not much of what she said about this other cemetery got through. We agreed to look into Love Cemetery after we had taken care of the matter at hand, Blossom Hall

After each person had spoken about why he or she was there, I laid my dilemma in their hands. This was their community. Did they think the burial ground at Blossom Hall should be marked? Was this important?

Their answer was unanimous: yes, it was very important and long overdue. We should work together to get it marked.

But despite the good will and enthusiasm of our committee, we made no headway marking the ground at Blossom Hall. A small group of us met with Mary Ann and Howland Birch; again, they were unfailingly polite, but again they had reason after reason why we needed to wait. Meanwhile, at our second committee meeting—in March 2003 Nuthel brought up Love Cemetery again. This time she had brought the original handwritten 1904 deed of 1.6 acres by a local landowner, Della Love, to "the Love Colored Burial Association." That little parcel was only a few miles from Blossom Hall, as the crow flies. Nuthel asked Doris and me to go with her the next morning to see Love Cemetery. "It's so peaceful out there," she explained.

That was how I got to Love Cemetery for the first time on that Saturday when Nuthel and Doris and I slipped through the gate. It was my first visit to the place that would become the center of my life for the next four years. But even then, I didn't understand the scope, or the difficulty, of the project that lay ahead.

In May 2003, we had the third meeting of our burial ground committee at Gail Beil's Victorian home in Marshall, and I reported on our lack of progress at Blossom Hall. Doris and I had visited the Birches together, but to no avail.

By that May meeting, I had been to Beaumont and tracked down Mary Ann's sister and met with her for hours myself. Elizabeth Drayman Simmons had no objection to marking the ground and suggested the possibility of donating the land to mark it properly as a cemetery, but at the end of our talks, she put the issue back in the lap of the Birch family, since they actually lived near the burial ground. She would not act without their agreement. And so I returned yet again to meet with Mary Ann and Howland Birch. By then, the buffer of good manners was wearing thin, and relations were becoming tense. Howland in particular was testy, insisting that any historical marker the county might put up to mark the ground would surely be torn down overnight, though he didn't know who would commit such vandalism. But it was quite clear that the Birches would not willingly allow the burial ground to be marked or named or understood as the powerful symbol it was.

Leaving our meeting at Gail's that balmy night, I walked Nuthel back to her car. As we descended the many steep steps from the front porch to the walk, I held her right arm to steady her and felt how frail she was getting. Nuthel would be eighty that summer, she told me. "I would sure like to see Love cleared up before I die," she said.

This time, I knew what she was talking about. I had been to Love Cemetery and seen the powerful effect that the rediscovery of an ancestor's grave had on Doris and Nuthel. When that unseen tree had fallen as we left, I had felt the truth of Nuthel's explanation: "That's just the Ancestors lettin' us know that they've seen us, and that they're happy we're here."

I told her I'd do whatever I could to help. She asked me to track down the timber management company that oversaw the land and find someone who could give us the combination to the lock on the gate. Nuthel wanted us to have grave-cleaning days like they used to have to keep the Ancestors happy and restore Love Cemetery to its proper state. Her calls to the timber company in Louisiana had gone unreturned for months.

I opened her car door and helped her inside. She talked all the while. "I would surely be happy to see people coming back to Love to have those reunions with their families and remember who their ancestors are and do some cleaning up," she repeated. The door clicked shut. "I would really like to see that before I die."

I stepped back up onto the curb. Nuthel started up her engine and drove off, then made a U-turn. As she turned, I noticed that she'd failed to turn on her headlights, so I dashed out into the street, calling for her to stop. "Lights! Nuthel, turn on your lights!" I said when I caught up to her. She gave me a big smile, turned them on, and drove off. I stood there in the middle of the street watching her red taillights fade into the darkness.

I was being presented with a choice that humid East Texas night. As I drove away from that meeting at Gail's house, I recalled a story I'd first heard many years ago not too far from here, fifteen miles north, over at Caddo Lake, from an elderly woman named Mabel Rivers. Mabel told me about her husband Leon's grandfather, Sam Adkins, who used to live with them. He'd grown up in slavery. As a boy of eight, Sam had been brought upriver from New Orleans and put on the auction block and sold away from his family. As a child, he staved off hunger by sweeping up the spilled flour on the floor around the master's barrel to make rough biscuits for himself. In his later years, young Mabel helped take care of him. She told me that no matter how hard his life had been, there was nothing in Sam Adkins but sweetness. In those days she worked as a maid in a fishing camp on Caddo Lake. One day she came home from work and slammed the door, yelling, "White people can sure enough be mean. I hate white people!" Sam rose up from his rocking chair, his tattered Bible in his hands, and holding it up like a cup, offered some simple, unexpected advice. "You got to choose love, Mabel," Sam told her. "You got to choose love when there's reason to hate. Choose love, Mabel. Hate dries you up—makes your heart bitter. Choose love, Mabel. Choose love."

Yes, I thought, that will have to be the way for me too. That's what I need to do, let go of Blossom Hall and choose Love Cemetery. And I could start immediately.

During my visits to East Texas, I used to stay at the home of my cousins Jack and Agnes Verhalen. The house, built by my great-grandparents, was actually two houses built Spanish-style around a central courtyard with a red tile-covered walkway that connected the two sides. When I got back to Jack and Agnes's house that night after our meeting at Gail's, all the lights were off on their side of the house. But my cousin Philip, Jack and Agnes's son, lived on the other side with his wife, Carolyn, and they were still up. Philip was the person I needed to talk to.

Philip Verhalen was a retired navy officer and pilot. He was also a popular chemistry teacher at a nearby college. Most important for me, Philip was a Boy Scout troop master. Would the scouts be willing to help us clean up Love Cemetery, I asked? Philip said he would check with them at their next meeting.

Some days later, they sent their answer: yes. There was no merit badge for a service activity like cleaning up a cemetery, but they wanted to help anyway. We set the date for our first cleanup on a Saturday in July, one week before Nuthel's eightieth birthday. Perfect. I surprised her with the scouts' offer of help and she was delighted.

There was just one hitch: we still didn't have the combination for the gates.

We'd been lucky back in March, when the fence was down and we drove around the first gate. The second gate being left ajar was a fluke. But in Texas, the land belongs to the dead; descendants have a right of access to their deceased family members, regardless of how much private property they have to cross. An attorney assured us that we had the law on our side. Even so, this time we would have scouts and the larger descendant community with us for the cleanup, along with all the volunteers. The owners of the surrounding property needed to know what we were up to. And we needed the numbers for their locks.

No matter what Texas cemetery law says, no matter what rights are accorded to the families of the dead, the descendants of Ohio Taylor, Lizzie Sparks, and the others had been locked out of Love Cemetery for roughly forty years. As I worked to track down the combinations to the locks that currently blocked their entry, I discovered that there was no simple explanation for why they had been barred from Love for so long.

To unravel the mystery, one had to understand the past. Subtract 40 years from 2003 and the year is 1963—which meant that the descendant community got locked out during the civil rights era, a particularly volatile, tumultuous period in Marshall, the Harrison County seat. The magnitude of racism in Harrison

County had been well known, and a committed civil rights community had risen up in response.

There were actually two historically black colleges in Marshall in the 1960s: Wiley College, as noted, and Bishop College, founded 1881 by the Baptist Home Society. (Bishop later moved to Dallas; Wiley remains in Marshall.) Students at both colleges helped spark the civil rights movement in Texas with their demonstrations and sit-ins.

Born and raised in Marshall, and a Wiley graduate, James Farmer Jr. became one of the principal leaders of the Civil Rights movement, along with Dr. Martin Luther King Jr., Bayard Rustin, Dorothy Height, John Lewis, Rev. Ralph Abernathey, and Roy Wilkins, to mention only some of the best known—there were so many. In 1942, Farmer was one of the founders of the Congress of Racial Equality (CORE), one of the country's most important civil rights organizations, in Chicago. He also helped organize the Freedom Rides of the 1960s. In him, the Marshall students, especially those from Wiley, had a towering home-grown example of someone powerfully committed to justice and freedom.

Both Wiley and Bishop students demonstrated in the 1960s at the Harrison County courthouse. Their attempts to integrate Woolworth's and the local movie theater became legendary as they persisted despite a storm of open hostility. The entire nation was shocked to see photographs splashed across the front pages of drenched students blasted by fire hoses and threatened by dogs.[8] The situation was so explosive that when Rev. Martin Luther King Jr. came to Marshall to address the students at Bishop College and Wiley, he did so under the cover of darkness and quietly slipped out of town before the white community even knew he'd been there.

I was tempted to write off the lockout as an outgrowth of the rampant racism of those days and to think no more about it. But there was only circumstantial evidence to support that conclusion. Neither Nuthel nor Doris could give me a specific date or year for the start of the lockout. Neither one lived here at the time.

Certainly no event has a single cause; events take place within a context, and causation is dynamic and complex. In truth, it could have been a land sale that set off the lockout. As I looked more deeply into the rights of the Love Cemetery families and the rights of those who owned the surrounding land, I found a Byzantine tangle of laws that was as unruly and persistent as wisteria: private property laws, easement allowances, Texas cemetery law, U.S. corporate law. To interpret these laws and apply them to Love Cemetery, one relied on antiquated county records that required special training to use and were sometimes incomplete or conflicting.

The process was made more complex still by the increasingly rapid turnover of East Texas timber properties, a trend that had started some years ago and would soon swell into the largest sale of privately held forests in the United States—nine million acres across the nation in 2006.

In 1907, Professor Herman Haupt Chapman from Yale's School of Forestry took the train to East Texas with several students to investigate virgin longleaf pine forests and evaluate the forests' marketing potential for the timber industry. He found that the vast standing forests of pines and hardwoods in East

Texas were extremely valuable, especially the pines—longleafs and loblollies. Some of the preferred longleaf pines were 350 and 400 years old. With the abundance of rivers and navigable waterways and the expansion of the train system, there were few limits on getting logs to market. The commercial timber industry was already in full swing. Those 350-year-old pines had a girth of fifteen feet. Today it would be hard to find a sawmill in East Texas that could take a tree over fifteen inches in diameter.

Soon the longleafs were gone. The loblolly, prized for rapid growth, quickly took over, and dominates the landscape to this day. The wildness was gone from the land. Its forests were compromised and, with them, the habitats they had provided. Jaguars, panthers, black bears, red wolves, black wolves, honeybees, the ivory-billed woodpecker, and even bright yellow, red, and green parakeets, all once native to East Texas, then disappeared.[9]

Nearly a hundred years later, here, about seven miles east of Marshall, the Scottsville-Leigh area that surrounds Love Cemetery was increasingly riddled with clear-cuts, burn-offs, and rows and rows of obedient, genetically manipulated loblollies. I was told by a man near Love that periodically there was a process for the "releasing of the pines," which he found amazing. "The releasing of the pines" was an aerial spraying of pesticides that was meant to kill everything *but* the pines. The fact that his property adjoined what was, at the time, one of the nation's largest paper company's tree farm was no problem to him, for they "released the pines" only when the wind wasn't blowing.

I discovered that the same multinational paper company started selling off 1.5 million acres of East Texas woodlands in 2001. The land was sold to other timber interests, independent operators, and real estate developers. In 2006, another 900,000 acres of East Texas woods were sold to private interests. Decisions made in corporate headquarters—in Boston, Singapore, Dubai, the Bahamas—and decisions made by the Texas State Legislature in Austin not only generally ignored the impact of sales on wildlife habitats, the carrying capacity of the land, or the state of the soil and water that sustained its use—the environment itself—but they trumped the right of Love Cemetery descendants to have access to ancestors buried on a 1.6-acre plot that had been established, marked, legally deeded, registered, and recorded at the courthouse since 1904.

Nuthel had given me the name and phone number of an agent at a timber management company in Shreveport. The timber management company handled the property for the owner, John Hancock Insurance in Boston. At that time, their holdings didn't include Love Cemetery itself, but they did include some of the thousands of acres of land along the road leading to the cemetery. Nuthel had dealt with this agent years earlier, when she and her sons had gotten a permanent easement through the property that surrounded Love Cemetery. The timber manager had been agreeable and helpful, respectful and easy to work with. Then he was gone. A year went by with no return phone call; then she asked me to help.

I phoned the company, and my call was returned within twenty-four hours. Now the land was handled by a different timber manager from an entirely different company. Another multinational company was unloading its timber stock. This manager too was a cooperative and helpful man. He immediately gave me the combination and faxed a map detail to me showing that the cemetery had been held out of the sale because it had been properly designated on their maps. Later, when I met him in person, he gave me deeper insight into the complexity of the situation surrounding Love Cemetery.

It was one thing to have an easement on the road to the cemetery, he explained, but it was another matter to track down the property owners whose land the road crosses. As parcels changed hands in greater numbers and with greater frequency, the land was being divided into smaller pieces. And as time went on, fewer and fewer people from the community knew that the cemetery was there. Older folks who still knew where Love Cemetery was, like Nuthel, couldn't physically get back there. You needed a pickup. And even with a pickup, depending on the weather, you still risked getting stuck in that infamous red East Texas mud. I began to see how this lockout might have evolved over time.

A lot of owners and managers might not want to bother with the claims of a few community members, he said. By himself, he managed tens of thousands of acres in two states and had to deal with hundreds of easements. It simply wasn't practical, he suggested, to devote close personal attention to each of them.

The timber manager also helped me track down the man who now owned the land immediately surrounding the cemetery. He was from out of state. He'd turned the land into a private hunting preserve, and he was the one, ultimately, who had put Love Cemetery behind the new, second, locked gate.

I called the owner and congratulated him on having such a historic cemetery on his property. I explained that the local Historical Society, the Boy Scouts, the families of the people buried in Love Cemetery, various friends and volunteers, my cousin, and I were excited to have assembled a group to clean it up. I put all my cards on the table: I told him that I was writing a story

about our cleanup efforts, and I let it be known that I was familiar with Texas cemetery law and the right of access for family
members. But before I was able to muster much indignation, he
disarmed me by saying that he'd always known that someone
would come back to tend to that cemetery. He said that the cemetery was the prettiest place on the property when the wisteria
bloomed. And he was happy to give me the combination to his
gate's lock.

He did express one concern about our visit: he had stocked
the reserve with elk and deer. He'd raised the elk himself and
gotten pretty attached; even with the hefty price he was able to
charge to kill an elk, he found it difficult to let them go.

"Just don't let my elk out," he asked. "We'd never catch
them." I assured him that we wouldn't.

———— •❖• ————

THREE

The First Cleanup of Love Cemetery

A great people is made not by its blood but by its memory,
by how well they transmit wisdom from the elders to the
youth.... A people is its memory, its ancestral treasures.
                                        —Robert Pinsky

"That's why I am here *today*," Joyce Schufford told us when we met outside the first of the two gates we had to pass through to get to Love. "To keep those graves clean, like we used to. That's what I want." It was July 31, 2003.

We were waiting for my cousin Philip, Doug Gardiner, the assistant scoutmaster, and the scouts they were bringing with them for our first cleanup.

Joyce, dressed in a short-sleeved yellow shirt, with her hair pulled tight off her neck, was ready for the July heat. Her sister, Clauddie Mae Webb, wore her signature tri-cornered straw hat as well as a long-sleeved purple shirt and work pants. Rev. Marion Henderson, well into his eighties, was the oldest member of the descendant community to go in with us. Though he claimed he couldn't work much, he was dressed in old denim coveralls and looked like he wasn't going to let age stop him from trying. Two of

the scouts from Troop 210, Luke Girlinghouse and Ulysis
Bedolla, had ridden out with me. Nuthel was there, of course,
along with R.D. Johnson—Doris Vittatoe's brother—and Willie
Mae Brown, a relative of the Johnson family. Altogether six members of the descendant community had come for this first communal cleanup. Three were over seventy, and two were in their
late sixties. Nuthel would be eighty the following week. As she
had said in March, we needed to get the oldest people—the
keepers of the group memory—to come with us to identify
graves.

Nuthel looked like she was ready for combat in the army fa-
tigues that her career military son had sent her, but she was
smart, for no matter how hot it got—it was already ninety-five
degrees and climbing at eight in the morning—it was important
to stave off the poison ivy, nagging brambles, and thorny blackberry vines. I wore long sleeves and long pants too. Nuthel had
brought a machete, as well as several cases of cold drinks for the
scouts, she so appreciated their coming.

A rifle shot went off in the distance, then three more in quick
succession. Hunters—but this time I didn't jump. Mourning
doves called down from the trees.

While we waited, I asked everyone to form a circle under the
pines so the descendant community and the scouts could meet
one another. I asked Nuthel to fill in the scouts on the history of
the cemetery, but she insisted that R.D. do the talking.

R.D. was a big man in his early seventies, six-foot-two with
a wide girth and grizzled white hair, dressed simply in a white
t-shirt and denims. His voice was deep and fairly boomed a
greeting into our circle. "I'd like to say good morning to all of
you. I am the grandson of Richard Taylor—Poppa, we called

him, my mother's daddy. I was born in 1932, Poppa died around 1940."

The descendant community stood together, listening solemnly. Luke and Ulysis, the scouts who drove out with me, stood in rapt attention behind Joyce while R.D. told us a little about Love Cemetery.

"Katie Taylor was my mother. All her uncles and aunties were buried back there," he said, pointing back over his right shoulder with his thumb, "but since they fenced this place in and you had to find somebody to let you in here, we just bypassed this place. Other words, we didn't think about going back in there, trying to keep it clean. But we always remembered Love Cemetery because all our ancestors were buried back there: Ohio Taylor, Richard Taylor, the Jacksons, the Browns, the Webbs, Nuthel's people—they're all back here.

"I'd like to say I am very proud of you, trying to get back in here and line it out where we can keep this cemetery alive. So in loving memories of our foreparents, if they were here, you would get the credit for fixing it where we can go back and check on it. And I'm so proud of these young men coming to try to help us to get it clean because I am seventy-one years old now. I can give a little advice and help here and there, but when we get young men who are willing and able to come back and help us, we the Ancestors of Love Cemetery appreciate everything you all are doing. I think God will bless you and may God ever keep you in his care. Thank you."

The circle began to break up just as Doug and Philip showed up in their pickups with two more scouts, Tony and Adam Harmon, two hefty brothers, one sixteen, the other seventeen. Doug wore a wide-brimmed white straw cowboy hat and a faded gray t-shirt and jeans. Doug, like my cousin Philip and R.D., stood about six-two. Unlike Philip, Doug wore a neatly trimmed full beard and black wraparound sunglasses. We had another quick round of introductions and then sorted ourselves into the various pickups and drove in.

The scouts fanned out and were quickly swallowed up in a sea of summer green. Soon the sounds of machetes cutting through heavy vines—*thwack, thwack*—rang through the woods. Since Nuthel, Doris, and I were there four months earlier, the wisteria vines had grown seven or eight feet and even more in places. They were draped over bushes and entwined around trees. The scouts popped up and down in the undergrowth, disappearing as they got down on their hands and knees to look for headstones, standing up again when they'd had no luck and needed to get oriented. Luke was the easiest to spot, with his tall lanky frame topped by a red baseball cap and red-and-white striped t-shirt. It was Luke who first called out, from underneath a mountainous tangle of wisteria and chinaberries, "Hey, I found one!" He read out: "J-A-C-K-S-O-N" from a small, rusted metal marker. This was one of the few temporary funeral home markers that still had a name visible. Others were twisted back on themselves or blank or entirely missing the small, neatly typed card that had been placed under a little rectangle of glass.

"Did you get that, Ms. China?" Luke asked as he spelled the name out again, making sure I had written it down. Everybody was Mrs., Ms., or Mr. to the scouts, from Rev. Henderson on down. We were all their elders. And so we worked through the morning, finding grave after grave, many of them with no name left to read.

The familiar drone of cicadas in the trees filled the air, their chorus rising and falling, throwing me back into a treasured childhood summer day when my mother and grandmother put me on the train to East Texas from Dallas at the old Highland Park station. "All aboard!" the conductor called. "All aboard!" At ten, I couldn't wait to get to East Texas for another hot July

Assistant scoutmaster, Troop 210, Doug Gardiner (standing), with Tony Harman (l), Luke Girlinghouse (m), and Ulysis Bedolla (r)

full of the outdoors and always someone to play with; I had at least a dozen cousins who lived near my great-grandmother's house.

As I pushed vines aside or pulled them up to cut, I stopped to make a note of stone markers we found. I followed the path Ulysis opened up with his machete and felt deliciously at home.

In a burst of gratitude and pride, I called out to Philip to thank him for his willingness to jump in and for bringing these eager scouts to help. He laughed and spoke in his simple, understated way. "I'm not doing anything special. Mrs. Britton, Mrs. Vittatoe, Mr. Johnson, Mrs. Brown, Ms. Webb, Mrs. Schufford, Rev. Henderson—these people are part of our community. They're my neighbors. The people buried in here in Love were their relatives, this was their cemetery, this is just what you do when your neighbors ask for help."

After a good hour of hunting and clearing, Ulysis popped up again. "Hey, I found one, a big one," he announced, and disappeared from sight again. He'd stooped down to read the letters and whatever date he could find. Moments later he stood up and called out, "Ohio Taylor, died 1918." He had rediscovered the headstone that Nuthel, Doris, and I had found in March. It was Doris and R.D.'s great-great-grandfather, only now the summer growth had swallowed up the tombstone. We had a big job ahead of us to free it from the vines and bushes.

R.D. made his way through the thicket to Ulysis, calling out, like a surgeon, "Bring me some long-handled clippers!" Philip worked his way over with an ax. I found the clippers R.D. needed in the back of Philip's truck, and by the time I waded out to them, R.D. was using Philip's ax to chop down a young chinaberry. *Thwack!* It was down in two blows.

Philip took his ax back from R.D. and cut down a chinaberry in front of the headstone. Doug, red-faced from the heat, his gray t-shirt dark with perspiration, clipped the vines that had bound the small chinaberry trees together and dragged them off to the side. Once those chinaberries were down, we could see Taylor's headstone, an age-darkened, streaked granite rectangle with a flat, smooth top.

"Cut those vines right here," I heard R.D. tell Ulysis as I headed back to the trees. He was guiding Ulysis around Ohio's headstone. "See what I say," he said with an edge of frustration in his big, gravelly voice, "they knocked over *all* these tomb-stones—Ohio Taylor, Richard Taylor. Ohio's was tall as I was; now these pieces are laying around here on the ground. Look here at that lamb they knocked off"—another piece we had found in March—"that's from another Taylor grave."

"Somebody got in here and cut some of those big pine trees down and knocked these tombstones all over. See the stump here?" he said, pointing to a nearby stump that had emerged from Philip's clearing. "It got cut down about four or five years ago, you can tell by its condition. Now hand me those long clip-pers." Whoever stole those trees, they had done it in the last four or five years, he was sure. That was wrong, he said—those trees belonged to the cemetery.

"When they dragged those big pines out, that's what tore up this cemetery. These things here," he said, gesturing at the fluted columns and the plinth on the ground, "they were sitting on top of Ohio's grave, my great-grandfather. We need to put this back together."

I went back to where Nuthel and the other women were sit-ting—except for Clauddie Mae, who was out of sight somewhere on the burial ground, determined to find the headstone marking the grave of her father, Claude Webb, and the row of five Webb family members that lay alongside him. Nuthel had put her machete away and was sitting in the shade on the Hendersons' tombstone. It was 102°F and still climbing; she wouldn't be able to take the heat much longer.

We watched as R.D. bent over and picked up one of the fluted columns and carefully placed it where it belonged, on one side of Ohio's headstone. The metal anchor inside the column had been sheared off by whatever hit it. I had tried to lift one of those columns when Doris and Nuthel and I were here in March, but I couldn't budge it in the slightest. I could hear R.D. breathing hard. Nonetheless he got the other column as well and carefully laid it on the other side. He knew how to pivot the weight to put those columns in place with the kind of grace that comes only from experience. Then he got Ulysis and Luke to help him with

R.D. Johnson (l.) and Philip Verhalen (r.)

the plinth—the graceful, elegantly engraved triangular stone, incised with ivy and oak leaves, that rested on top of the two columns. Heavier than the columns, it took all three of them— the two scouts and R.D.—to get it securely balanced in place.

Ulysis Bedolla Clearing Ohio Taylor's Grave

From where we sat, Ohio Taylor's grave marker emerged like a ship on the horizon, low in the water, weighed down with memory. It was balanced precariously, but it stood now as it had stood for over three-quarters of century.

"My, oh my," Nuthel said, "now look at that."

After the excitement of seeing Ohio Taylor's grave put back together, Joyce joined Nuthel, sitting back-to-back on the Henderson headstone. We were dripping and wiped our faces with bandanas or tissues, whatever we had. Willie Mae wore a cool, beltless purple dress with white embroidery, and seemed to have fared the best with the heat. I sat on the ground on my day pack, trying without much success to avoid poison ivy.

Willie Mae Brown

I needed to tell Nuthel what I had found out about Della Love, the mysterious woman who deeded this cemetery to the Love Colored Burial Association in 1904. Nuthel had given me a copy of the original 1904 deed and told me that Della Love was a white woman, part of the Scott family. The Scotts had been the largest landowners in the eastern part of the county; Scottsville was named after them. Old man W. T. Scott brought in the railroad and ran it due east from Marshall past his cotton gin in Scottsville and over to nearby Caddo Lake, where they could load the bales onto paddle steamers that ran downriver to the Cotton Exchange at New Orleans.

The Scotts were also the biggest slaveholders in the county. My great-grandfather had bought the land from them in 1900 for what became the Verhalen Nursery business. Next to their original plantation in Scottsville was the historic white Scott cemetery, boasting elegant marble statuary and a Gothic-style stone chapel with stained-glass windows. Beyond that cemetery, another mile or so up the road, there was a well-populated black Scott cemetery. There was an endless mixing of blood in slaveholding families, with many African American children fathered by white slave-owners. I was surprised to see it as open and public, if not acknowledged, as it seemed to be in the white and black Scott cemeteries down the road from each other. There was also the black Rock Springs Cemetery just on the other side of the fence from the white Scott cemetery. Some say that Rock Springs began as the burial ground for enslaved people on the Scott plantation. It continues to be used and maintained to this day, like the Scott cemetery.

Before this cleanup, I told Nuthel and the others, I'd gone down to the Harrison County Historical Society Library to find out what I could about Love Cemetery. The librarian, Edna Sorber, brought out an unusual homemade book devoted to the Love family, *The Love Line*.[11] The book included a photograph of Della Love that made it clear Della was black, not white. Nuthel's eyebrows shot up in surprise. So did Joyce's and Willie Mae's. All three of them exclaimed "Ohhhhhh...!" at the same time.

Della Love Walker, 1883–1920

According to the Love family history, Della Love's father, Wilson Love, was half-white. His brother, Nat Love, went west and became the famous black cowboy "Deadwood Dick." Wilson's father, Robert Love, was a white plantation owner from Ireland. Wilson's mother had been Robert's household slave, and Wilson was apparently one of those rare free black men in 1860s Marshall. Free African American men were not welcome in Texas. They were considered a threat to the institution of slavery, and it was against the law for them to enter Texas. As historian Randolph Campbell writes in *An Empire for Slavery*: *The Peculiar Institution in Texas*, there were only about 350 free blacks in the entire state of Texas in the 1860s, just before the Civil War broke out. Wilson Love's upbringing as a free black man would have made him a lonely anomaly in Harrison County, where virtually all African Americans were enslaved until after the Civil War. Prior to Emancipation, an "owner" had to petition the Texas State Legislature if he or she wanted to free someone they held in slavery, for in the eyes of the state, "Negroes were fit only to be slaves."

Wilson married an African American woman, had a family, and divorced, then married Della Love's mother, who was also black. Despite Wilson's astuteness in buying more than two hundred acres of rural land in the county, either by himself or with business partners, he was declared mentally incompetent in 1882 and a guardian was appointed by the court. He was only fifty years old. Wilson Love died the following year, 1883. Compounding the mystery of Wilson's mental condition is the fact that the records of the lawsuits that ensued over Wilson's estate, according to one Love family history, seem to remain missing from the Harrison County Clerk's office.

Had Della inherited land from her father—is that where this cemetery for the Love Colored Burial Association came from? Had she bought it herself? Della married, had several children, and moved to Oklahoma with her husband. In the self-published history, the text following the photograph of the attractive, alert woman said that Della died on an Indian reservation in Oklahoma, probably after being poisoned, in 1920.

A chorus of sighs greeted this news. The women shook their heads. None of us knew how to respond to these seeming non-sequiturs. Lawsuits. Indian reservation. Death by poison. I explained that I felt that I'd reached a dead end with my research on Della, at least for the moment.

The mood changed when Nuthel said decisively, "We got to clean up Love, now ain't that the truth? No matter how it came to be here, if this was all cleared, you'd really see something. It's a beautiful place." Everyone agreed.

I noticed that R.D. was sitting nearby on a big tree stump, taking a break too, drinking ice water and wiping his face with a kerchief. Most of his white t-shirt was soaked through and sticking to his chest. The scouts were still out clearing and burrowing under the vines looking for more graves. They labored on, unfazed by the sun, unimpeded by age, propelled by the unfamiliar excitement of finding graves. Doug worked with a broadax to cut high vines, while Philip was in the thick of it, chopping down trees whenever he could, the sound of his ax echoing in the woods.

"How you doing, R.D.?" I asked. He allowed that he was enjoying his break but was planning to get up and work a little more before we left. A breeze stirred under the trees shading the stump he sat on. "Now that feels good, mighty good." He took another big drink of ice water. "Soon as I'm done restin' up a bit, I need to get over there and tell those young boys to be on the lookout for some things might not come to mind too easy, they bein' so young and not familiar with our ways."

He explained that everyone who was working on the cleanup needed to be aware that graves might be marked in all sorts of ways.

"A lot of these folks out here, they didn't have money for no headstone," R.D. said, as Nuthel and the others leaned in to listen. "They were all farmers back here. They just used what they had. Plates, crocks, plow points, churns. Just put something on the grave so they know who was buried where."

"Old lamps," Nuthel added.

"That's right," R.D. said, "and plenty of them, old kerosene lamps."

I later learned it was an African tradition to put a lamp on a grave, to guide the soul of the deceased and light their way.

"Even a sewing machine, or part of one," Nuthel said, "if somebody'd been a seamstress."

"Uh-huh," R.D. said. "You would be surprised. Could be an old pipe, anything connected to that person."

Just then, Clauddie Mae returned and told us that she and Joyce had found the grave of their father, Claude Webb, and several more relatives. She was very happy but had to leave early to take Rev. Henderson back to his house. His wife was in the hospital and it was time for him to get changed and go for a visit.

Nuthel, R.D., Willie Mae, and Joyce switched from cataloguing types of grave markers to rattling off more names of people they knew who were buried out here: Taylor, Brown, Sparks, Webb, Jackson, and Henderson. The gentle talk, the shade of the trees, the comfort of ice water to drink, the sound of a woodpecker drilling into a tree nearby all coalesced into a sense of deep peace. Nuthel was right. This was a beautiful place.

I checked my notebook for some other names of people I'd been told we would find here: the Jenkins, Kings, and Johnsons—more of R.D. and Doris's relations—and the Brooks, Mineweathers, Samuels, and Woodkins.

There had hardly been any air movement, but suddenly a breeze whooshed through the trees. It made me think of the tree that had crashed here months earlier when Doris was with us, when Nuthel explained that it was the Ancestors. I asked R.D. what he believed about them.

"My belief is the Ancestors come back, in a sense, because if you will notice you can come to a place like this and if it gets late in the evenin', you hear a noise," he said authoritatively, elongating his words, pausing, pacing himself, as if he were telling us a story around a fire. "Sometimes you will hear a fox howl. Or a treetop fall. That's a noise they're making to let you know that they know you're here. That's really true.

"They know we're out here working today," R.D. continued, "and they are proud of us cleaning this cemetery back up. They know we're here. They're smiling on us right now."

"And they know why we're here," said Nuthel.

Now even the scouts were almost done. Philip, still out in the sun in the middle of the cemetery, called out that he was "just about warm" and thought it was time to head back to the house. Philip's wife, Carolyn, would have hot dogs waiting for us, so we could all have lunch together. It was well after one in the afternoon.

"Do you think we could do a little singing and praying before we leave here today?" I asked R.D., feeling that the end of this first cleanup day needed to be marked.

"I will do anything for the upbuilding of God's kingdom," he replied with a big grin.

I called to the others: "Why don't we all circle up. R.D.'s going to lead us in a prayer and a song."

The scouts gathered respectfully, taking their hats off, and stood in a rough circle with the rest of us. R.D., still sitting on the stump, started singing: "Guide me over, great Jehovah, pilgrim through this barren land; I am weak but Thou art mighty, hold me with Thy power hand; bread of heaven, feed me till I want no more...." He stood up. Willie Mae, Joyce, and Nuthel joined him singing, and it was clear they had been singing like this all their lives. R.D.'s deep and gravelly voice kept the pulse of the song while the long, extended *ummmhhmmms* of Joyce, Willie Mae, and Nuthel were moans that sent shivers through me.

I listened, all the white folks listened, but none of us could follow to the country where the singers lived in this moment, a far country filled with the Spirit. That's where that song was coming from—"under the water," an African phrase, and the pain of being dragged in chains to this country. It was humbling just to hear it, sung out here in the woods on the burial ground. The scouts bowed their heads and held their hats with hands crossed in front of them.

Then R.D. began to pray, rhythmically, erasing any line between speech and song. "Our Father in heaven ..." Nuthel, Willie Mae, and Joyce kept humming the melody they'd been singing while R.D. prayed right over them.

"Father, we give thanks for thy many blessings. Our Father, we give you thanks because your name is worthy to be praised, thank you, Father, for what our eyes have seen and our ears have heard, thank you again our Father for those who turned away from their busy schedules and come over today trying to help us reestablish this cemetery. You know our hearts, you know our heart's desires, *hmmhmm*, we thank you, Father. We love you because you first loved us. We continue to hold up this blood-stained banner, and we pray, our Father, that you will bind us together in one band of Christian love. You said in your words, our Father, there is no chain stronger than its weakest link. We are weak, Father, but we know you are strong. And we ask you to hold us and keep our heads about us, Father, as we all head home. In the name of Jesus we pray, for his sake. Amen."

All together we answer: "Amen."

"Now let us be dismissed," R.D. says, "and may the peace of God that passes all understanding keep our hearts and minds on Jesus Christ our Lord. Let us all sing now," he said, and began "'Til We Meet Again," a hymn that was easy to follow.

"'Til we meet again, 'til we meet again, God be with you, 'til we meet again...."

"There're hot dogs on the table, buns, mustard, and relish," my cousin Carolyn, Philip's wife, said to the scouts, R.D., Mrs. Britton, Doug, and me, when we got back to my family's house. Willie Mae had had to leave early, but the rest of us were hot, dirty, hungry, and thirsty. Carolyn had been cooking all morning, but when we arrived she seemed the picture of coolness. She greeted us with the screen door open. She was wearing a red, white, and blue American flag silk blouse and American flag earrings; her dark, curly hair was perfectly coiffed.

"Get your food in here and then you can bring it back outside to the picnic table," she instructed as we filed in to wash our hands and get lunch. We got our plates of homemade beans and coleslaw and plucked hot dogs from a boiling pot of water on the stove and went outside. The lawn was grassy and shady under the massive pecan tree in back. There was a picnic table and, most importantly, a breeze.

Carolyn was used to entertaining with flair after years of being an officer's wife and living in Europe, where Philip was stationed in the navy. She loved being a hostess and was good at making people of many backgrounds and nationalities feel welcome and comfortable. We ate lunch and drank iced tea, then enjoyed the brownies she'd baked; we relaxed and talked over what we'd seen at Love Cemetery, and the work that still needed doing.

Philip, Doug, and R.D. sat at the picnic table making plans to get out to Love again on Saturday—two days away—with a tractor and a brush hog, a machine with spinning blades that would clear out anything above ground level. They would use the tractor to tow it around the perimeter where there weren't gravestones and markers that could be destroyed. For the foreseeable future, the work among the gravestones had to be done by hand. Some of the markers we found were little temporary funeral home markers only six inches high. Some headstones were only a foot high. At least one had been knocked down and was flat on the ground, and there could be others. R.D. assured us that there were a lot more graves back there; we'd only cleared a small part of the cemetery. We had to work carefully. He suggested waiting awhile before coming in with the heavy equipment.

The clearing we'd made by hand around Ohio Taylor's gravestone would soon be reclaimed by the vines if we didn't get back out there and keep cutting back the wisteria and pulling it out as much as we could. Philip had impressed on me that, when left wild, the East Texas wisteria could envelop and slowly pull on a seventy-foot pine until one day it would topple to the ground. Now that we'd started the job, they agreed, we had to keep after it.

In that moment I had a great hope: If we could work together like we had, side by side, if we could sweat out the pain of it, if we could sing together and pray together as we helped reclaim this graveyard for the Ancestors and their descendants—and for the larger community—then there was a chance we could begin to transform some of the mistrust and lack of understanding that has gotten in our way for more than 200 years. And if we could re-establish Love in this community, it would be possible anywhere.

FOUR

Borderlands, Badlands, and the Neutral Ground

So long as Texas is not seen as a Southern state, its people do not have to face the great moral evil of slavery and the bitter heritage of black-white relations that followed the defeat of the Confederacy in 1865. Texans are thus permitted to escape a major part of ... the burden of Southern History.

—Randolph B. Campbell,
An Empire for Slavery

Stories rise out of a landscape as surely as plants grow out of the earth. History is made of stories, as are lives. All are grounded in the soil and the waters below. The landscape is our first context, the actual ground upon which our stories take place. So it's time to understand the landscape of Harrison County out of which the story of Love Cemetery and the lives of Nuthel, Doris, R.D., and so many others have grown.

This place was given its character by the presence of Caddo Lake and its labyrinth of sloughs and bayous and by the vast pine forests that once blanketed this landscape. East Texas is part of the Gulf Coastal Plain and was once covered by warm shallow seas. Moreover, more than 65 million years ago, during the Cretaceous period, an enormous shallow sea stretched from the Gulf of Mexico to the Arctic Circle, submerging what is now Texas, as well as the middle section of what is now the United States and Canada. Long after those seas disappeared and the continents took on their current shapes, this small bit of land called East Texas produced enormous stands of pine forests; on the sandy ridges were longleaf pine, with loblolly and shortleaf pine below, then oak, hickory, and finally cypress and water tupelo in the bottomlands.[13] Underneath it all was a sandy red clay and loam soil that would prove to be fertile ground for growing cotton. Below the sands and clays were limestones, shales, and deeper sands full of fossilized and compressed remains from those earlier millennia that could be extracted as coal, gas, and oil.

The earliest known inhabitants of the area were the tribes of the Caddo Confederacy, a matrilineal society of highly developed agriculturalists who lived in settled villages along the Red and the Sabine rivers, in what is now East Texas and Louisiana. The Caddo Confederacy was made up of about twenty-five tribes, of which the main three were the Natchitoches, the Hasinai, and the Kadohadocho. They were part of the ancient mound-building culture that flourished in the Mississippi and Ohio river valleys, stretching from Central America and Mexico up through Louisiana and Texas into the Midwest and as far north as Illinois and Minnesota.

The Caddo people had been living in northeast Texas, southwest Arkansas, and western Louisiana for roughly one thousand years at the time of the first contact with whites, when it was estimated that 200,000 Caddo people flourished in the area. Spanish explorers came through East Texas in the sixteenth century, hoping to find gold and the mythical passage to India. Traveling from Florida into northeast Texas with Hernando De Soto, who died en route, Luis de Moscoso, the leader who took over his expedition, came face-to-face with the Caddo in 1542. Moscoso's party also seems to have come upon Caddo Lake, "Laguna Espanola," and chose to travel south of the lake rather than attempt to cross it.

What looked like open, unoccupied land to the Spanish and to the immigrant communities that followed them was often land that had been carefully managed for over 1,000 years or, according to some estimates, for 1,500 to 3,500 years. Agriculturalists like the Caddo—river Indians famed for their fertile lands and abundant harvests—knew what crops to grow to add to the soil and when to stop growing to prevent soil depletion. They understood river bottomlands, animal habitat, migration, and space requirements for different species. They knew to leave enough land uncultivated to provide what we now call wildlife corridors and ranges—the stretches of land that animals need in order to thrive. To incoming white immigrants, the open land might have seemed uncultivated and free, there was so much of it. Some respected the boundaries of Indian villages, farms, and hunting grounds, but for the most part, whites continued the pattern of stealing land from Native people who laid the groundwork for this country and supported it for centuries.

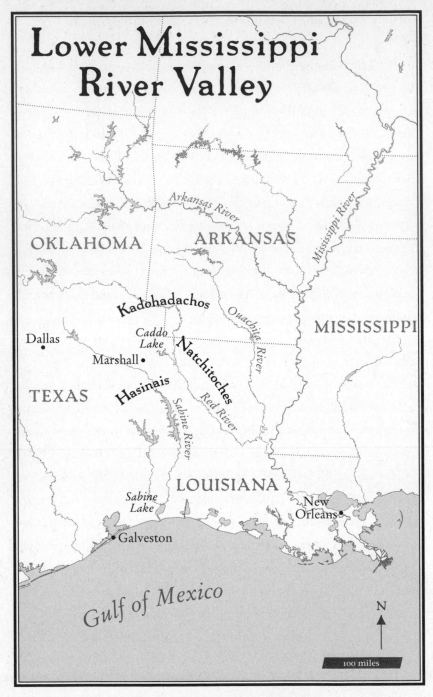

Lower Mississippi
River Valley

Arkansas River

Mississippi River

OKLAHOMA   ARKANSAS

Kadohadachos

Caddo
Lake   *Ouachita River*   MISSISSIPPI

Dallas
•

Marshall •   Natchitoches

TEXAS   Hasinais   *Red River*

Sabine River

LOUISIANA

Sabine
Lake   New
Orleans•

• Galveston

Gulf of Mexico   N
↑

100 miles

Map of seventeenth-century Texas and
the Mississippi River Valley

By 1760, France and Spain were fighting over land that belonged to neither power. The French had taken over enormous areas east of the Red River that would become the Louisiana Purchase of 1803. On the other side, the Spanish had claimed what would become Texas. The Caddo and other Native American tribes were caught between the two military powers. The Caddo were already fluent in French and were skilled traders. One of their main villages was at Natchitoches, on the Red River, where the French built an outpost. Across the river was New Spain. The constant shifting of boundaries between the Spanish and the French left a large swath of land over which neither government had jurisdiction.[14]

In the meantime, in 1803 Napoleon sold Louisiana to the United States, to finance his renewed war against the formerly enslaved people of what would become Haiti. The successful slave revolt that had begun in 1791 continued for twelve years. Napoleon attempted to take back the country and reestablish slavery, and was finally defeated in 1804. The rebels, formerly enslaved people, had won a huge and costly victory. They renamed the island Haiti, the original name the indigenous Arawak Indians had given it. No rebellion of enslaved people on this scale had ever succeeded before in North or South America. Slaveholders throughout the hemisphere were on notice.[15]

The United States became increasingly entangled in the border disputes between France and Spain. Finally, in 1806, a tacit agreement was reached: Spain would not allow its troops north and east of the Sabine River, and the French and the Americans would accept the Red River as their western boundary. In this way, a forty-mile-wide buffer zone, to be inhabited by no one, was created.

The Neutral Territory, as it was called, was an ill-defined, anarchic, ungovernable area that included Caddo Lake and Harrison County. It became known as the Badlands. The boundaries of the Neutral Territory were vague and constantly subject to renegotiation. The area soon attracted criminals on the run, horse thieves, land speculators, and pirates like the infamous Jean Lafitte, who smuggled African slaves into Louisiana through Galveston, Texas. There were law-abiding families who came just to find a place to live and who worked hard and were not criminals, but by and large the politics of the territory and the justice administered was catch as catch can, on the fly, and often settled by gunfights. Given that this was to have been a no-man's-land, there weren't laws to be administered and upheld. The letters GTT—"Gone to Texas"—were hand-lettered on notes and nailed up on many a door across the South. Such a note indicated to all, families and creditors alike, that the signer had skipped out on any and all obligations. To say that you had "gone to Texas" meant that you had gone beyond the law, to a foreign country where the laws of the United States did not apply. You were free from everything but the weight of your conscience. Faked deed purveyors poured into the territory and mixed with the Caddo tribes who had lived there for centuries. Vigilante justice ruled.

Meanwhile, the major cotton planters along the Atlantic Seaboard and in the Deep South were discovering that years of intensive cultivation was depleting the soil. East Texas with its rich, fertile land provided a tantalizing opportunity. Conventional white opinion held that chopping and picking cotton in the southern heat was too much for white people to bear. Still subscribing to that idea a century and a half later, Lydia Ball had told me that day at Blossom hall, "Why, honey, white people just can't tolerate that heat!" She added that dark-skinned Africans, however, were made for such labor.

By the early nineteenth century, as a result of nearly three hundred years of European rationalization and a sixteenth-century mistranslation of the Biblical description of Noah's son Ham as "black," the enslavement of Africans had become acceptable, even "Christian."[16] Thanks to the towering work of English abolitionists like William Wilberforce and his band of Quakers, the African and Caribbean slave trade was outlawed by England in 1807, and even by the United States in 1808. Nonetheless, the institution of slavery was still legal.[17] As the voices of abolitionists in the United States began to be raised, the issue of whether new states entering the Union would be "slave" or "free" became a central one. The admission of Texas in 1845 was not without controversy, given its unsavory reputation.

Randolph B. Campbell explains in *An Empire for Slavery* that New Spain had tolerated the ownership of slaves, but that Mexico, at least officially, did not. Shortly after gaining independence from Spain in 1821, the Mexican government outlawed slavery. Even though Texas was still part of Mexico, this territory was so large that laws against slavery could not be enforced effectively. Land grants continued to be given to settlers bringing slaves into Texas. In an attempt to increase Texas's slave population and thereby enlarge its economy, Stephen F. Austin's colony on the Brazos River gave immigrants eighty acres for each additional slave they brought in. This meant that in 1822, for example, one man was assigned 7,200 acres on the Brazos solely on the basis of his bringing ninety slaves with him from Georgia. He couldn't occupy all the land he was given by Austin's colony, it was so extensive.[18]

Another new arrival to what was still Mexico in 1834 was a man from Louisiana, W. T. "Buck" Scott, who would eventually give his name to Scottsville. Scott was attracted by the Neutral Territory's "flexible" legal system, the good soil, and the ease with which he could claim 25,000 acres of land in the northeast quadrant of what would become Harrison County. One can surmise that Love Cemetery was once part of the land Scott claimed. He built his main plantation home—a wood frame house—on the site at Rock Springs where it stands to this day. Scott, like the rest of the people who poured into Mexican Texas, grabbed what he could. The fact that he had no title to the land didn't stop him from building on it. He created his own fiefdom of five plantations, produced twelve children, and enslaved somewhere between one hundred and seven hundred people.

A year after Scott's arrival, on July 1, 1835, the Caddo chief, Tashar, dispirited, hungry, and continually pushed back by whites like Scott and the hundreds who had preceded him, signed the Treaty of Cession selling the United States one million acres of Caddo land in Louisiana for $30,000. It's not hard to imagine the chief's despair. With the overwhelming influx of whites, there was less and less land for farming. Hunters had to travel longer and go farther afield, often for months at a time, to find bison, leaving the remaining tribe members increasingly vulnerable. Why not salvage something, he reasoned to the members of his tribe and the other elders. The Caddo way of life was being destroyed. Soon they would have nothing. The remaining Caddo accepted his decision. The Caddo too had a Trail of Tears.

Though it was thought that all the Caddo were forced onto a reservation in Oklahoma in 1859, in fact a handful remained at

Caddo Lake and intermarried into the local population. Their descendants remain there to this day.

The 1835 treaty took place only months after Captain Albert Shreve, a steamboat builder and captain who gave his name to Shreveport, Louisiana, had completed years of dynamiting and breaking up enough of the Great Raft on the Red River to allow steamboat traffic through. The 160-mile log jam had blocked the waterways between Caddo Lake and the river for hundreds of years, making navigation impossible.

Shreve's dynamite not only blasted a path through the log jam but also ensured the end of Caddo culture in East Texas. With news of the Red River being opened up for steamboat navigation, a new wave of white immigrants surged into Texas from the Old South like water bursting a levee. Not only was Texas land fertile, plentiful, and cheap, but now there was a waterway to transport goods to New Orleans.

Era No. 10, *a nineteenth-century paddle steamer*
loaded with cotton. The Era *traveled back and*
forth between Caddo Lake and New Orleans.

From this obscure part of Texas, Caddo Lake, boats traveled down the connecting Twelve-Mile Bayou out onto the Red River, briefly onto the Atchafalaya and, finally, onto the Mississippi River and on down to New Orleans. Within a few short years, the combination of rail and river transportation, bumper crops of cotton in the 1850s, and the stolen labor of slaves built the wealth of Marion County on the north shore of Caddo Lake and Harrison County on the south.

A year later, in 1836, after the Battle of the Alamo, when Texas declared itself a republic independent from Mexico, the constitution that was drafted legalized slavery but prohibited foreign slave trade. Planters from the South, as we've seen, were encouraged to bring with them the people they had enslaved. Free blacks could not live in Texas without the consent of the new Congress of the Republic of Texas. Years of war with Mexico followed. In fact, a new look at Texas history and the legendary Battle of the Alamo shows that the Texas fight for independence from Mexico had much more to do with the question of slavery than previously acknowledged. It was not the only reason for the break from Mexico, but it was a major factor.

The Republic was viewed with great suspicion by many. British abolitionists railed in the British parliament against granting the Republic of Texas diplomatic recognition. One of them, Benjamin Scoble, in 1837, called Texas "that robber state ... settled by hordes of characterless villains, whose sole object has been to re-establish slavery and the slave trade."[19]

In 1839, Frédéric Gaillardet, a French writer sympathetic to *l'aristocratie* and the new Republic, pointed out that Texas, with its rich soil and "location at the southern end of the American Union," was indeed becoming a haven for slaveholding planters from the upper South: "In the enjoyment of this position lies the germ of Texas' future greatness. It will become in the more or less distant future, the land of refuge for the American slaveholders; it will be the ally, the reserve force upon which they will rest.... If ... that great association, the American Union, should be one day torn apart, Texas unquestionably would be in the forefront of the new confederacy, which would be formed by the Southern states from the debris of the old Union."[20]

Amid the clamor and controversy, Texas was finally admitted to the United States as a slave state in 1845, the twenty-eighth state of the Union. Mexico had long accused Texas of being a crude cover for land speculators and slave traders who sought enormous profits and wanted to reopen the African slave trade.

The tumult continued after Texas came into the Union, and in 1858 John Marshall, editor of the *Austin Texas State Gazette* (but no relation to the man who gave Marshall, Texas, its name), claimed that Texas was destined to become the "Empire State of the South," provided that the African slave trade could be reopened. Slavery was growing, but too slowly, Marshall wrote, "and until we reach somewhere in the vicinity of two million slaves, it is equally evident that such a thing as too many slaves in Texas is an absurdity."[21]

The number of people held in slavery in North America's "internal slave trade" grew from 1.5 million in 1820 to 4 million by 1860, the eve of the Civil War. It was this phenomenal growth of domestic slavery that allowed white Southerners to clear enormous tracts of land and extend the Cotton Kingdom from the Atlantic Coast across the entire South and eventually to East Texas.

By the 1840s, 60 percent of the world's cotton was provided by the South, notes David Brion Davis, the author of *Inhuman*

Bondage.[22] The cheap American cotton that dominated the world market was the result of the cotton gin, water transport, and the use of slave labor. The South supplied cotton to New England, Britain, continental Europe, even Russia.

Aside from the land itself, slaves were the major form of wealth in the South, and owning them the means to prosperity. "Large planters soon ranked among America's richest men.... By 1860, two-thirds of the wealthiest Americans lived in the South."[23] And despite the myth of the Southern slave economy as being backward and unproductive, it was, as Davis says, chillingly effective and brought in record profits during the antebellum years.

East Texas landowner W. T. Scott, the biggest slaveholder in Harrison County, was a prime example of someone who built up great wealth as a result of the international demand for cheap American cotton. Scott was one of the founders and owners of the early railroad in Harrison County, and in the late 1850s, he laid down track that ran directly from Marshall to the gin he owned seven miles to the east at Scottsville. From there, the train continued east and then turned north to Swanson's Landing on Caddo Lake, where paddle steamers were waiting. Scott had the means to move his cotton to market quickly, first by train and then by paddle steamer to New Orleans, hence his becoming the largest and wealthiest slave owner in Harrison County before the Civil War.

On one of my earlier trips to East Texas, long before I knew anything about Love Cemetery, I discovered that it was from W. T. Scott's son, Rip (R. R. Scott), that my great-grandfather, Stephen John Verhalen, had bought the acreage for his nursery. It had been one of Scott's plantations, part of the Blossom headright, a form of land grant used by the Republic of Texas based on the head of a family. I became uneasy. I wasn't sure why. Though my great-grandfather had bought approximately 2,800 acres in 1900, well after the Civil War and Emancipation, I was dimly aware that he had built a large business in this eastern part of the county during the worst years of Jim Crow,[24] the period marked by a collection of shamelessly racist laws that began to be passed around 1875 to undermine any gains made by African Americans during the years of Reconstruction immediately following the Civil War. The Jim Crow era lasted right up to the Civil Rights Act of 1964 and the Voting Rights Act of 1965.

I didn't yet know about the "store system" or debt peonage. It too was very much a part of the Jim Crow era and was often as restrictive and cruel as the institution of slavery itself.[25] "There are more Negroes held by these debt slavers than were actually owned as slaves" declared the Georgia Baptist Convention, in 1939.[26]

Only during this writing did one of my cousins tell me that the wages of field hands at the Verhalen Nursery were paid to one of the three stores in Scottsville, not directly to the workers, a common practice throughout the South. Over time, I learned the implications of this. Though some white storekeepers were known to help people and might see a farmer through a bad season, others became notorious for the ways they took advantage of people. I would hear local stories of storekeepers demanding—and getting—a deed of land as collateral for a ten-dollar loan or even burning down a house if the owner wouldn't give over a deed as collateral for seed to start the planting season. By the 1940s, the Verhalen Nursery was paying its field hands directly, breaking with the store system that had pre-vailed since the demise of Reconstruction. Were the wages fair? I have reason to doubt it, but no proof. Were wages fair anywhere for African Americans in the 1940s? I doubt that too. Injustice knows every age, including ours. Roughly forty families were housed by the nursery and employed there, receiving some form of medical care when needed. But no matter. There was no way around what one of my older cousins told me about the nursery business participating in the store system. He knew, he told me, because he wrote out the checks for the field hands. He didn't know what precipitated such a big change in how business was done, but there it was. That was about 1939.

I questioned how it was that the wages were paid to the store-keeper, not the field hands who earned it. "That's how things were done in those days," he answered, and then we put the subject aside. I put it aside. It made me uncomfortable. I couldn't assign that information a place in a moral universe, so I whitewashed it. For a time. But I couldn't forget what I'd been told. I saw how naïve I was to imagine that because no one in my family had enslaved people, somehow that meant my hands were clean. What my family did or did not do had nothing to do with me. I could no longer hide behind that excuse.

Debt peonage cropped up along with the adoption of the "black codes" of early Reconstruction. Emancipation was quickly countered by recalcitrant whites and Confederates stung by the Union's defeat. African Americans were quickly denied the abil-ity to vote, to serve on juries, and to attend school, among other things. Such was freedom after Emancipation.

The store system was part of the white reaction too, only the store system involves only debt. Debt peonage was a federal crime—it went further. It was widely used by southern whites to keep black labor and mobility under white control after Emancipation. With debt peonage, a person was physically restrained from leaving their "employer" until their debt was paid. It was debt tied to employment and to confinement. Debt peonage revolved around a person being physically restrained from leaving his or her employer until the debt was paid. The tentacles of debt peonage stretch out across the world and time. Debt peonage was, and remains today, slavery by another name. It continues to spread.[27]

To understand the real tragedy of the long Jim Crow era, you need to have a sense of the enormous hopes generated among African Americans immediately after Emancipation. For a short time after the Civil War, during Reconstruction, blacks held an array of elected offices. They served as judges, lieutenant governors, members of state legislatures and the U.S. Congress. The Fifteenth Amendment, ratified on March 30, 1870, prohibited depriving a citizen of his vote due to race, color, or condition of servitude. It essentially enfranchised black men. (Remember, no woman could vote until 1920, regardless of color.) During Reconstruction, approximately three-quarters of the registered voters in Harrison County were African Americans. Fifty-nine percent of the people in Harrison County were enslaved in 1860. They significantly outnumbered whites in the county and they voted. Marshall sent an African American state representative to the capital in Austin, as well as a black state senator, David Abner. Blacks were elected to a wide variety of offices in Harrison County too. African American children received their education in the Freedmen's Bureau Schools set up by the federal government.

Literacy was spreading, and with it, black land ownership was on the rise.

Land was a precious, hard-won commodity. The crushing story of formerly enslaved people being given "forty acres and a mule" at the end of the Civil War and then having that same land taken away from them was known throughout the South, fueling black farmers' determination to buy their own land whenever they could. Formerly enslaved people were given forty acres and a mule, briefly, thanks to General Sherman's special Field Orders, No. 15, issued in January 1865.

"Sherman's Order was temporary and did grant each freed family forty acres of tillable land on islands," the coast of Georgia, South Carolina, and the country bordering St. John's River, Florida.[28] The army also provided them with mules. After the assassination of President Lincoln, his successor, Andrew Johnson, revoked Sherman's Orders over the repeated objections of his generals. Untold thousands of former slaves had followed Sherman's march. Those who had been granted land had been living on it and working it for a year, along the coast in South Carolina and Florida, only to have their deeds taken back in one of the greatest treacheries of Andrew Johnson's administration.

As soon as federal troops withdrew their protection from Harrison County in 1870 and Reconstruction began to be dismantled, southern whites began to enforce measures aimed at again disenfranchising black voters. These actions included poll taxes and literacy tests, as well as the use of violence, especially lynching, to intimidate blacks. Though statistics show only the number of lynchings that were actually reported, thousands of African Americans were lynched across the South, effectively extending a rule of terror that reverberates to this day. Taken together, black votes in the South were effectively eliminated until the passage of the Voting Rights Act of 1965.[29]

The white Harrison County town fathers were in the vanguard of these efforts. They had grown increasingly fearful, impotent, and angry as former slaves established themselves as a dynamic political force. To some of them, the rapid advancement of African Americans was intolerable. They organized the Citizen's Party in 1876.[30] (Some sources refer to it as the "White Citizen's Party.") By 1878, they had wrested control of the ballot box—in some cases, by literally stealing it. Once again, W. T. Scott, the county's wealthiest antebellum planter and a three-term state senator during the 1850s, played a central role.

In 1936, a certain R. P. Littlejohn of Harrison County wrote *A Brief History of the Days of Reconstruction in Harrison County, Texas*. In it he explained how the white "gentlemen" of Harrison County "won" the elections in 1878. Given that white men were greatly outnumbered and that "it was impossible to defeat [blacks] at the polls by fair means," Littlejohn wrote, the former town fathers decided that "any means we could adopt to overthrow that unscrupulous, thieving ring of carpet baggers would be just and right." Formerly enslaved people were lumped into the category of northern carpetbaggers, thereby "justifying" all manner of activity.

As Littlejohn explained, "It devolved on this committee to have a watchful eye on political matters and especially elections." The Citizen's Party substituted fake ballots for legitimate ones. On Election Day they would mingle "among the negroes, ask to see their tickets and unknown to them would exchange our tickets for theirs, thus securing many votes for the Citizen's Party." After polls closed, members of the Citizen's Party would

steal the ballot box and replace it with a duplicate they had prepared.

Closer to our story, Littlejohn notes that W. T. Scott was himself "holding the election" in Scottsville. Near the end of voting
day in 1878, he didn't like the way things were unfolding so he
got word to his fellow party members back in Marshall, seven
miles west, that his "voting place was surrounded by Negroes
who demanded that the votes be counted before those holding
the election went to supper."

"Those [Citizen's Party] boys wanted a chance to swap a box
that had been prepared for the regular box and told the Negroes
they would go to supper and count the votes when they got back,
but the Negroes would not let them out [with the ballot box]. So
about fifteen of us secured an engine and caboose from the Rail-
way Company (always willing to help in cases of emergency) and
went to Scottsville."

The Citizen's Party men from Marshall got off the train a little
way up the track from Scottsville and "took the negroes by surprise and surrounded them." They freed the white men and saw
to it that they could leave for supper as they had planned, with
the ballot box. Littlejohn again: "When the votes were counted,
though that was a large Negro precinct, it developed that the
Citizens Party had carried it, by a large majority." Littlejohn
noted that "the ringleaders of the Negroes were arrested, tried,
and fined."

In the final paragraphs he tells how the Citizen's Party broke
up any "Negro meetings" they could find and added that "the
Negroes were very ignorant in those days and much leniency
was shown them on this account, but harsh measures were re-
sorted to in some instances." He said that it was easy to outvote

the Republicans of those days by "changing Negro votes" and using "fictitious ballots, and other methods ... until the majority of Negroes gave up trying to vote and finally were excluded in primary elections." His brief history, written in 1936, closes with this final note: "Negroes have made wonderful progress since the days of Reconstruction, in education, acquisition of property.... They have accepted the political situation and no longer try to interfere with a white man's government and as long as they maintain that attitude, the best element of whites bid them Godspeed."

Littlejohn's account could be dismissed as exaggeration were it not for countless other accounts that paint a similar picture. History is not a repository of lifeless archival information. It is a story and stories are alive. They keep taking hold of us until we can retell them in ways that point us toward a new understanding.

In the early 1980s, I had spent time in Harrison County, around Caddo Lake in particular, meeting and interviewing African American elders for a story I was working on. On those trips, I came to know Deacon Hagerty and his wife, Pammy, Mabel and Leon Rivers—Sam Adkins's grandchildren, who cared for him at the end of his life—and Kizzie Mae Hicks. Their stories brought to life painful terms like disenfranchisement and land theft.

Deacon Hagerty, still tall, rail-thin, and erect at ninety-seven when I first met him, told me that he didn't learn to read until World War I, when he was on the battlefields of France. There his commanding officer taught him to read by lantern light in his tent at night. He came back to East Texas a very different man. He was literate, he'd seen the larger world, he'd fought for our country. When he arrived back in Marshall in 1918, he told me, he went down to the courthouse to register to vote. He was greeted with barrels of shotguns lined up to meet him or any other black man who dared to try to vote. He knew those men and they knew him. He never forgot that, he said. Once off the battlefield, American guns were turned on him. Deacon Hagerty ended up working for the railroad and was a member of the Brotherhood of Sleeping Car Porters, the famous black labor union.

It was also Deacon Hagerty who gave me a firsthand account of the workings of the "store system" that had so troubled me when I discovered that the Verhalen Nursery had participated in it.

He told me, "The storekeeper would give you a mule, a wagon. And then, time to pay, he'd say: 'You owe me so many thousands of dollars, oh, you don't have the money, well I'll just have to take your land.' Black folks didn't understand the system and they didn't know nothing, they couldn't read and write. Storekeepers continued to take advantage of them, even after they turned 'em free. A lot of land got put together that way ... yes it did, unless you had learned to read and write. I'm strong about that," he told me. He had put his son through college. He had a daughter getting a master's degree. He had a granddaughter with three degrees. He told me, "Most colored people didn't have no one to help them at first."

Deacon Hagerty told me that he was fortunate in his family, because his father "had a good white friend, Old Man Driscoll, quite nice, and he taught him how to own the land." He let Deacon Hagerty's father have a plot of land and told him, "I'm going to deed this land to you. Now you take it and raise your family on it."

"My daddy bought the land from Driscoll cheap, two hundred acres. Driscoll set the price so he could afford it. He showed him how to do the paperwork and register a deed, how to handle and work two hundred acres of land and how to leave it for his children. Driscoll showed him how to do it, sure, that's right, mmhm. That's the way it was. When we was in the army, my brother went next to me. Driscoll told us, 'When you boys come back out of the army, you take your discharge papers and go on down to the county and get them recorded so you get your benefits.'

"Driscoll helped me and my father. Old Man Driscoll's father helped colored people too. They were some good white people, they weren't all bad.

"In three more years of living, I'll be one hundred," Deacon Hagerty said. "If I make it, I will thank the Lord. We got to get together and pull together, black and white, everybody, we got to be all one nation. I'm strong about that. We got to come together, we got to work together on one accord, we're all God's children. That's what the *Lord* said to do. He said we'd have to sit down together, reason things out. That's what the Good Book tells us ... we got to love one another."

Then, after a pause, he asked with genuine bafflement and sincerity, "What is wrong with your people? Don't white people read the Bible?"

"That's a good question, Deacon Hagerty," I said, but I had no answer.

The enormous importance Deacon Hagerty placed on education was echoed by almost all the African Americans I came to know in East Texas. Nuthel's family had been gathering college degrees for generations. Nuthel's aunt had a bachelor's degree from Wiley—that meant graduating in approximately 1896. Education—even learning to read—had for the most part been forbidden to those enslaved. During Reconstruction, the fierce hunger for education could not be stopped. Dedicated teachers came to Marshall from around the country to teach in the Freedmen's Schools—white teachers who were risking their lives to educate these children. Freedmen's School teachers were insulted, sometimes shot at, and driven out of town. They also trained African American teachers, who continued schooling their newly freed communities, risking their lives to educate their people. Young African American people walked barefoot for miles to school. They too faced harassment and danger, but they could not be stopped.

In Leigh, Texas, between Scottsville and Caddo Lake, a dozen miles northeast of Marshall, neighbors and members of the historic African American Antioch Baptist Church banded together to work the fields of their pastor, Jim Patt, so he could go to Marshall for an education in the 1870s. Patt not only became literate and learned enough property law to be able to help his community prove their ownership of the land, but in 1881 he also became involved in the founding of Bishop College. Jim Patt taught his congregants how to read and write and how to register their deeds at the courthouse, while taking care of their spiritual needs as well.

By the end of Reconstruction in 1880, historian Steven Hahn notes, "owing to their many struggles for schooling and literacy ... between 20 and 30% of African Americans over the age of ten in the former Confederate states could read and write. Between 1865 and 1880, more than fifty newspapers [were] edited, and at times owned, by African Americans." Those numbers grew rapidly over the next two decades. People were on fire with freedom.[31]

Though some people learned to read during slavery, most could not. It was illegal to teach a slave to read; in some cases, doing so was punishable by death. After Emancipation as African Americans fed their hunger for learning, they were stymied by the white colleges and universities that barred them from attending. The need to remedy the situation prompted church groups and the Freedmen's Bureau to start elementary schools, high schools, and colleges throughout the South as quickly as possible. It was specifically the Freedmen's Aid Society of the United Methodist Church that started Wiley College in 1873, in Marshall. In 1907, Wiley College was the first recipient of an Andrew Carnegie library west of the Mississippi. Ironically, Wiley had a better library than the city of Marshall.

Gail Beil, a member of our Love Cemetery Committee, knew a good deal about Wiley's surprising history through her friendship with James Farmer Jr., her involvement with Wiley, mentioned earlier, and her research for a book about James Farmer Jr. and his father. Farmer's father, James Farmer Sr., was the first African American in Texas to earn a Ph.D. (Boston University, 1918) and was a professor at Wiley. James Farmer Jr. was born and raised in Marshall and graduated from Wiley in 1938. Though his early days there would be eclipsed by his later prominence in the civil rights movement as the founder of CORE and a leader of the Freedom Rides, Farmer had been a member of the famous Wiley College debate team that, in 1935, defeated the reigning national champion college debate team, the University of Southern California. Given that, in 1935, black teams were not allowed to debate white teams, Wiley's victories became the stuff of a legend that grew from that famous victory in 1935 to their 1937 win over the Oxford University team, then on tour in the United States.[32]

The Wiley team was coached by the extraordinary Melvin B. Tolson, a poet and English professor who continued to have a deep influence on Farmer for the rest of his life. Farmer was fond of saying that after he beat Malcolm X in a debate for the fourth time, he thought Malcolm should just give up; Malcolm hadn't been trained by Tolson, whose strict discipline and ferocious preparations made Wiley's team famously unbeatable. Tolson, in turn, had been influenced by the Harlem Renaissance, spending summers in New York while finishing his master's degree at Columbia University. Tolson taught his students about W. E. B. Du Bois, Zora Neale Hurston, Langston Hughes, and other great African American and African Caribbean thinkers and artists, bringing awareness of the Harlem Renaissance and the 1930s flowering of black intellectual and artistic culture to East Texas. It's not hard to imagine that Tolson's introduction of James Farmer Jr. to Henry David Thoreau's *Civil Disobedience* could only have helped shape the course of the civil rights movement of the sixties.

Later, I would meet another member of that legendary team back in California: Rev. Hamilton Boswell, pastor emeritus of Jones Methodist Church in San Francisco and a leader in the San Francisco community, who also served ten years as the chaplain of the California State Assembly. The influence of Tolson's debate team at Wiley made itself felt far beyond Marshall.

Boswell explained how in 1935, even though blacks were prohibited from debating whites, the Wiley team was so outstanding that it was informally invited to debate the University of Southern California through their mutual ties with the Methodist Church. Boswell was present at that electrifying debate in Los Angeles and was so inspired that he left school in California to attend a tiny black college in "Prejudice, Texas," as he called it, to join the debate team with Farmer and to study under Melvin Tolson.

THE VARSITY

HOBART JARRETT   HENRY HEIGHTS   J. LEONARD FARMER JR.

The Wiley College debate team is nationally known. It has just completed a second Annual Interracial Goodwill Tour to the Pacific Coast. Wiley has engaged in 150 debates during the past twelve years, meeting most of the leading Negro colleges and several outstanding white universities. Lost only one decision debate out of seventy-five. Completion of the tentative date with Oxford in England in 1937 is expected to be announced soon.

1935 Championship Debate Team,
Wiley College, Marshall, Texas

As Gail Beil has noted, almost every Wiley debater during this period either observed or was threatened with lynching.[33] Boswell, who had become one of Tolson's star debaters by then, told me about a night when he and Farmer and Tolson found themselves driving into a lynching in progress in a little town between Marshall and Beaumont, where they had been competing.

"You see, I'm not what you might call a southerner," Boswell told me, still very alert at ninety-three. "I was reared in California, and I had a reputation for fighting. I remember the southerners, Farmer and Tolson, as we were driving along, as we began to see the crowd gathering, they knew something was up. I was oblivious, didn't know what was going on at first, until they said, 'Hamilton, you get in that backseat and keep your mouth shut and let us handle it if there's any trouble.' They had faced this situation before. I was fresh in from California. They put me in the backseat to keep quiet, and I did. Nobody bothered us. We got through town.

"After driving on for a while, though, Tolson decided to turn around so we could see what had happened. By then most of the crowd had dispersed. There were only a few, very few people around that tree then. You could see the body hanging on the tree about fifty yards from the road we were traveling on. The dismemberment of the body. It was the worst thing I ever saw in my life. I still sometimes have nightmares about it.

"They had dismembered most of his fingers, his penis, toes. People took them for souvenirs. Souvenirs," he repeated for emphasis, still shocked at ninety-three, as was I to hear this from a living witness.

"They had their children there to see the lynching. Carried them on their shoulders. Schoolchildren! The worst thing I ever saw.

"Tolson saw a man standing in the shadow, a black man. He went up and talked to him, and the man said the victim was his cousin and he would get him down. There was a relative waiting.

Someone to cut him down and care for the body. Tolson decided that it was best to get out of there now that he knew that there was somebody there to take care of the body."[34]

Rev. Boswell admitted to me that after experiences like that, he started to hate white people. It was when he realized that Jesus himself had been lynched that he was able to let go of those feelings. That's when he felt called to become a pastor.

In that tumultuous period after the Civil War—in the 1870s and 1880s—African Americans were intent on educating themselves, and for the first time in the South, they were also beginning to acquire land to farm. People like Ohio Taylor, Lizzie Sparks, the Johnsons—Doris and R.D.'s grandparents—the Hendersons, and others, maybe even Wilson Love, Della's father—managed, over time, to buy land together or adjacent to one another on the north side of Scott's main plantation. The deeper I navigated into the history of this place, the clearer it became that Love Cemetery was indeed, as Nuthel had told me, the last vestige of that thriving black farm community. There was no little irony in the fact that almost all this land must have belonged, at one time, to W. T. Scott, the former slave owner and white supremacist politician. In 1872, according to one source, Scott was "brought low" by creditors, including Pendleton Murrah, the governor of Texas, and was forced to sell off parts of his holdings.[35] This sale occurred around the time that African American farmers were buying land.

By November 1877, black farmers in Harrison County were meeting weekly. Steven Hahn, in *A Nation Under Their Feet*, notes that by 1890 the Colored Farmers' Alliance could claim 90,000 members in Texas.[36] A new militancy was growing, as African American landowners, tenant farmers, and sharecroppers took up issues ranging from low wages paid to cotton pickers to emigration to Liberia.

How did this little-noted rural activity affect the farmers around what became known as the Love place? I found no record of that, yet. But no amount of organization, education, and progress could keep out the larger forces at play. Hahn's well-taken point is that vibrant organizing, thinking, and communicating were going on in the emerging black farming communities across the South, largely unnoticed by white people.

What happened to the community of farmers around Love Cemetery? I still had only fragments. Obviously, there is no single answer to that question. Even those families that had been able to hold on to their land, like Doris, R.D., and Albert Johnson's, had not been able to keep the younger generations from seeking opportunities in large cities. The Depression and World War II had had their effect, taking many people off the farms or out of farming altogether. The difficulties of farming and bias against African Americans took their toll. And, always, there was the issue of land theft.

In contrast to Deacon Hagerty's story about Old Man Driscoll, who had helped his family buy land and made sure they knew how to *keep* it, there was a story that another friend of mine, Kizzie Mae Hicks, had told me. The consensus in Uncertain, Texas, when I met her in 1983, was that Kizzie was "the best fry cook on Caddo Lake." Over the years, Kizzie's story became, for me, emblematic of land theft. This is how she'd told it to me one day, sitting in the Waterfront Café on Caddo Lake, where she was the cook at the time.

"Strange things happen when you live around a place like this for a long time. I used to work a second job cleaning house for a man who lived nearby. One day I was there cleaning and we got to talking. My family used to have a lot of land nearby, the Hicks, and some of my cousins still do. He remarked on that. I told him this story that came down in my family.

"After Emancipation, my great-grandfather, Jeff Hicks, put together a lot of land, three or four hundred acres, some say nearly a whole section of land, even though he'd been a slave. When he died, that land passed on to his children and some of it became my grandfather's.

"Well, one day my grandmother was out plowing behind a mule and the mule ran off. She broke her leg and grandfather put her in the wagon and took her to the doctor. He had no money to pay for a doctor so he put up the deed to his land to get the doctor to treat my grandmama and set her leg. He paid the doctor off on time and went to get his deed but the doctor said my grandfather never paid his bill, so he'd just have to keep the title to his land. The doctor said he wouldn't run my grandfather off, that he could stay on his land and sharecrop.

"It was the 1930s in East Texas. It was a black man's word against a white's. So that's what my grandfather did, he became a sharecropper on his own land. Then my father became the sharecropper.

"My father hated sharecropping on that land. I will never forget the day he said he'd had enough. Said he wouldn't sharecrop no more no matter what, he didn't care, he couldn't put up with it. He would never be able to get our land back, no matter how hard he worked or how many years he tried. He piled all our belongings into two wagons and we left. He bought a little land here near the lake and built the house I live in now with my children. It's not much, but it's ours.

"I told this man I was working for this story about how my grandfather lost his land and he said, yes, he imagined it was true. 'Lotta land got put together like that. Nothin' you can do about it.'

"The strange part was we kept talking and we figured out that the doctor who stole my grandfather's land was the grandfather of the man I was talking to, the man whose house I was cleaning that day. In fact, that house I was cleaning was on the very piece of land that was stolen from my grandfather."

Kizzie Mae Hicks (r), her daughter Barbara Brooks (l),
and Barbara's children

Kizzie's story took hold of me and kept working on me through the ensuing years and my regular visits back to visit family. I started checking records. First I found her great-grandfather in the 1870 census, the first time African Americans had last names in the eyes of the law. I started checking deed records and discovered that her great-grandfather, Jeff Hicks, had indeed owned over three hundred acres, if not more. In 1983, when I first tried to understand Kizzie's story, I was naïve enough to think that black people had never owned parcels larger than a few acres. But through research, I discovered that in 1910 black Americans owned more farmland than at any time before or since—at least 15 million acres. Nearly all of it was in the South, according to the U.S. Agricultural Census. By 2000, blacks owned only 1.1 million of the country's more than 1 billion acres of arable land.

In 2001, the Associated Press carried out a remarkable investigation that included interviews with more than a thousand people and examination of tens of thousands of public records in county courthouses and state and federal archives. The report, "Torn from the Land" by Associated Press reporters Todd Lewan and Dolores Barclay, documented 107 land takings in thirteen southern and border states. In those cases alone, 406 black landowners lost more than 24,000 acres of farm and timberland. Today, virtually all of this property, valued at tens of millions of dollars and growing, is owned by whites or by corporations. Thousands of additional reports of land takings remain to be investigated. Ray Winbush, director of Fisk University's Institute of Race Relations, said the Associated Press findings "are just the tip of the iceberg of one of the biggest crimes of this country's history." And I might add, one of the least known and least understood.[37]

I ended up in the back office of a title company, where the staff let me sit for as long as I wanted with a long box of typed and handwritten index cards. One clerk told me to make myself comfortable and "have at it." I discovered that the parcel of Kizzie's grandfather, Gifford Hicks, changed hands time and time again as it was leased or sold. There was oil and gas all over East Texas, and Gifford Hicks's parcel appeared to have some of it, or at least the likelihood of it.

It was like going through geological layers in time with names and stories painted across those cards like petroglyphs on a canyon wall: one person's suicide, another family's need to sell. The most unsettling of all the cards I found was the one in which I discovered that my own great-grandfather had once, briefly, owned Kizzie's grandfather's parcel. Our lives had crossed long before we met.

I've stayed in touch with Kizzie, and I try to see her whenever I'm in the area. The last time was at the Big Pine Lodge, overlooking the lake. I could see the waitress working her way over to our table. I quickly looked at the standard lake menu of catfish, shrimp, Gulf Coast oysters, or steak. Down at the bottom of the page, enclosed in a wide black box was a discomforting official warning about the mercury content in local fish.[38] In fact, the catfish served at Big Pines Lodge and other restaurants around the lake no longer come from Caddo Lake, but are trucked in from catfish farms in Louisiana. For all its beauty, Caddo suffers from mercury poisoning. The biggest reserve of "dirty coal," lignite, in the United States, is found near Caddo Lake. It's mined and burned in nearby coal-fired plants for power generation. As beautiful as it is, Caddo Lake can no longer be described as pristine.[39]

Caddo Lake

Kizzie said that people who fish the lake, including her, don't talk about this. She has kept fishing the lake through it all—acid rain, mercury poisoning. While Kizzie fishes some for enjoyment at this point in her life, when she was growing up, she and her father fished as a necessity, hunted too, to supplement their crops. Kizzie's family was not alone in needing to hunt and fish. The lake and the woods still feed people; not everyone at Caddo fishes for sport or hunts for pleasure.

After we ordered our dinner of fried catfish, hush puppies, and coleslaw, Kizzie told me that increased fencing of land, the "Posted, Stay Out" signs, and increasing numbers of parcels designated as private hunting clubs and reserves had locked out more and more people. There were fewer and fewer places to hunt. She had seen it change in her lifetime. The commons that people depended on here had almost vanished but for this jewel—Caddo Lake.

"The fishing's not as good anymore. The lake is low now—not what it used to be. Motorboats, all that gas and oil have hurt it. When I started fishing these parts, there was nothing but wagon roads to this place, nothing paved or black-topped, and you could always catch something. This place, the Waterfront, is on what we used to call Sand Banks. Every slough and bayou had a name given to it by the old colored. We called them something other than what's on your map. We've got a whole different map of the same area—'course it's not printed up, never will be.

"I have been on and around this lake most all my life. I've cooked at most of the lodges: Waterfront, Flying Fish, Shady Glade, Curley's, and now the Big Pine. When I first started working, I never sat down like this. Couldn't take a break, not even to eat, nothin' but work, it was so busy.

"I made three dollars a day when I started, working from ten in the morning to ten at night. Did that for six days a week. After twenty years of working like that on my feet, I've got arthritis bad. I don't want my daughter Barbara to ever have to work like that. Kids today hardly know how different the world is for them."

Love Cemetery was one of the few tangible vestiges of that different world Kizzie was talking about. Here was another compelling reason to restore Love Cemetery. Kizzie said that younger generations didn't know the extent of their ancestors' suffering. They couldn't, but they could learn their history. Wasn't it just as important for them to know their ancestors' hopes, their visions? Love Cemetery's fragments and shards might be what was left of a community that had kept its connection with the land. That's what Nuthel had been trying to help me understand when she spoke of the Ancestors or when she spoke of the peace and beauty of Love Cemetery. That's what needed to be remembered and marked and protected. That's what drew Doris, R.D., Willie Mae, Albert, Clauddie May, and Joyce: that long-ago vision of community that their Ancestors offered them, and a place to remember and honor them. By reclaiming the cemetery, they could reclaim a part of themselves. Only now, it would take all of us to make it happen, young and old, all races, to get it untangled and cleared out. This was the story. This was the story that needed telling, the story of the clearing and what it takes to reclaim the ground.

FIVE

"Guide Me Over"

"... to be rooted and grounded in love."
—Ephesians 3:17

"You know our hearts, Father, you know our heart's desire," R.D. began. Doris and Nuthel joined in as we stood in a circle around Doris's coffee table in her living room. A calm came over me. I took a deep breath. Finally I was here, again being cradled in prayer.

R.D., Doris, and Nuthel sang in the old style I'd come to love and look forward to hearing. I hummed along as best I could, but it was so different from the Latin hymns that I'd been brought up with. Their song was full of feeling, and so spontaneous, that it seemed different every time I heard it, even though the words and melodies were the same. I heard echoes of old-time moans and shouts, calling on the Lord to "bring us through." They sang with intricate syncopation, enlivened by unexpected beats that shifted to long-drawn-out phrases. I couldn't tell which way the melody would move or how long to hold a note. Doris's harmonies came out of places I would never have thought to go. I was surrounded by song, the living word. I felt shy and happy, privileged to be there.

"What were you singing?" I asked when they were done. R.D. replied, "One of the 'Old One Hundreds,'" a cycle of gospel songs rarely heard these days, like 'I Need Thee Every Hour' and 'What a Friend We Have in Jesus.'

"Those are the songs that people sang," R.D. said. "I tell people, those songs were good for our Ancestors," he paused, "and they still good for us. It brought 'em through. It learned 'em how to lean and depend on Jesus."

"Yes it did, ummmhuuh," Nuthel said slowly, and Doris nodded, "Yes, that's right."

As they started up another song, I thought of the stories Doris had told me about their mother. The images and the singing seemed to come from the same grounded place. Their mother had been given a cow as a wedding present. From that one cow, she had managed to put together a herd of thirteen cows, working hard and saving as much as she possibly could. She then sold that herd and used the money to buy the land this house of Doris's was standing on. In turn, as a young woman, Doris had worked just as hard. All day, when her boys were in school, she tore down and cleared out the old buildings left on her mother's property. Digging up pipes, killing copperheads, clearing land, digging up the underbrush, clearing it with her brush ax and her machete, smoothing out the soil, composting, planting—Doris had done it all and largely by herself. Now, her voice, along with Nuthel's and R.D.'s, filled the comfortable brick house she had built while raising two children.

As they sang, I recalled one day after church at Shiloh when Doris had taken me on a drive down a beautiful small dirt road in Scottsville that I'd never seen, past well-tended pastures and open fields, past a sagging old wood barn wrapped in wisteria. The hay had just been mowed, and the sweet smell hung in the air so strongly that you felt like you'd been dipped in it. Driving along slowly with our windows down, we were surrounded by the loud drone of cicadas in the afternoon heat. "Turn here," Doris said, as we zigged one way, then zagged another. Much as I'd explored the back roads in this part of the county, I never knew these lanes were here, much less the well-tended farms Doris showed me, maybe three miles from my own family's land.

"Stop here," she said. She pointed to an open field where, she told me, their house had stood when she was growing up. "I walked this road to the school bus down on the highway, two miles each way. Every day. Before I left for school, I pumped the water for the cows by hand, filled the buckets, and toted them across the road. That's where we kept them."

Even though we were the same age, Doris had grown up without running water or electricity. She did her homework by a kerosene lamp. There was a copper bathtub in the kitchen where the family bathed in water heated on a woodstove. Doris grew up chopping cotton in the summers in a world where you learned to work alongside your family whether you liked it or not. The cotton picking came later. Driving down the road she had once walked every day to catch the school bus, Doris led me into a world I'd never seen, a world that existed alongside mine but to which I had been blind. I'd traveled the world, I'd volunteered briefly at Mother Teresa's Home for the Dying in Calcutta and her Home for the Elderly in Kathmandu. I wasn't naïve about the world—I was naïve about my own country. I knew little to nothing about the black neighborhood in Dallas two blocks from where I grew up. I knew even less about the black parts of Scottsville, where I'd been visiting my cousins for a good many years, both as a girl and as a well-traveled adult.

Without a trace of self-pity, as one friend talking to another about childhood, Doris told me about how her heart sank when she was running late for school one morning and a car with neighboring white children and their mother drove past, leaving her in the dust. She recalled getting down to the highway one morning to find the "Negro" school bus had broken down—as it often did—and then seeing the white children's new bus roar by. Through the big, clean windows, she could see the white kids laughing.

"That bus was like our books—used, marked up, pages missing. We never got new books. And that school bus of ours never seemed to stay fixed."

Even though I understood the notion of white privilege, at least intellectually, hearing these stories from a professional woman who was my contemporary brought the disparity home to me in a visceral, personal way that left a knot of pain in my stomach. The closeness between us that was growing as we worked together on Love Cemetery brought into inescapable focus the fact that the things that I took for granted growing up, that I never gave a thought to—running water, electricity, books, transportation, summers, swimming pools, sports—had simply not existed in her childhood. I knew about prejudice. I had African American friends. But I'd never had a friend give me an actual taste of what white prejudice was like in her experience, in a place that I thought I knew so well. This wasn't a newspaper account I was reading, or a television show about some other place. Doris and I were sitting in a car next to the fields where she had grown up, across from the pasture where she had carried the hand-pumped buckets of water she had to take to her mother's cows before leaving for school. She showed me where the bus stop was where she had to wait, separate from the white children, for that broken-down "colored-only" school bus.

I realized that while Doris had been chopping cotton in the summers here in Scottsville, I'd been riding the train over from Dallas to visit my country cousins on a lark. Three miles and a galaxy away from Doris, I was jumping on hay bales in the barn one day, swimming in the family lake at the nursery the next.

Suddenly I was back standing in the room with Doris, Nuthel, and R.D. Their voices fell away, leaving R.D. to begin a spontaneous sermon on the prodigal son in the Bible. Doris and Nuthel came in like a chorus with "that's right" and "yes!" while R.D. spoke in a kind of southern dialect of the Spirit. It had nothing to do with church. It had everything to do with God.

"That young man found himself feeding hogs and eating the corn husks right along with them, that's how low he was, when he suddenly woke up. (*That's right.*) He didn't have to live that way. He'd squandered his fortune on a life of debauchery, and this is what it bought him, eating corn husks with the hogs. (*Yes!*) Bible tells us that he came to himself. (*Ummhuh.*) The young man went back to his father's house in a far country, and there was great rejoicing. (*That's right.*) We're like that prodigal son (*yes*), we got to go to our Father's house (*that's right*), we got to try God, just try him. He will rejoice."

One of the reasons we had met that night was to plan the August cleanup and family reunion we hoped to organize. We'd made enough headway out at Love Cemetery to be ready to bring in more family, to invite the larger community to come see what we had done, to join us.

Could we incorporate some simple, inclusive prayer service at our big gathering in August, I asked, like they had in the old days? R.D.'s tone had been perfect that evening. He testified, he didn't proselytize. He had poured that story of the prodigal son out of his heart, because that's how he talked, that's what he believed. Doris, Nuthel, and R.D. were comfortable in their beliefs in a way I never had been. Their religion was like a pair of well-worn shoes that would carry them far, and had already taken them through countless journeys. Many of the descendants of those who were buried at Love Cemetery were church-going people. I asked if we could open and close with prayer out in the cemetery like we'd done at the first two cleanups, and then have some kind of special program at the community center potluck that would follow. Maybe one of the scouts could talk about what it had been like for them going out there with us and working. My friends agreed that we should suggest all this to the committee when we met a few nights later.

We could talk to Philip and the boys the next day. Philip was bringing his dad's fifty-year-old John Deere tractor, which he had managed to keep running, and a brush hog. R.D. was happy we'd gotten enough wisteria and overgrowth down that we could move beyond hand tools. R.D. would walk along in front of the tractor, looking for headstones and stumps, signaling to Philip where it was safe to use that brush hog.

We divided up our tasks. Doris and Nuthel were going to call more family members, and R.D. said, "I'm going to call my son and tell him to come help us."

Nuthel would try to get her daughter to drive up from Houston and see if her sons in the military might by chance be home on leave. Her son Christopher was back from Iraq. It seemed that, unbeknownst to any of us, including Nuthel, he'd driven over in March and tried to join our last cleanup but found himself locked out. He hadn't told us he was coming, and we had locked the gates behind us. We were sorry not to have him with us.

Philip would get the key to the community center. Doris and I would go to the scouts' meeting the following Tuesday evening to make a pitch for more young men to join us for the big August cleanup.

Nuthel wanted me to put up a flyer around town, even put it in the paper, she was so happy, but I begged off. We were a small group, going in with the permission of the surrounding landowners. I reminded them that the permission wasn't for the public. In fact, I had agreed to meet the owner of the surrounding property for coffee later in the week at 6:30 in the morning and would have lunch with the manager of the timber company the same day. I told the group I was nervous.

"I think the man's going to be reasonable," Doris said. "That owner's got to love somebody. If it was his wife or child buried back there, wouldn't he want to visit that cemetery? He told you that he knew someday people would want to get back into this cemetery and that's why he put the gate where it is."

On the other hand, Doris couldn't understand why the man hadn't made it easier for people to get into Love. "Why did he fence it in in the first place? If this was his relatives," she said, "how would he like this? Way it is now, wild animals can run across it, knock over gravestones, hunters traipse around in there. Somebody's cut those big pines down on it, logged it, it's not right. You're not supposed to touch a cemetery. I'm sure there are still people in the community who'd like to bury someone out there with their ancestors."

I asked if they had any suggestions about what I needed to say to the man from the timber company.

Nuthel said slowly, "I was just fixin' to say, invite him."

I was taken aback. "Invite him?"

"Ummhuh," said Nuthel, nodding. "That's right. Invite them both."

"On August 21?"

"Whenever we're there, yeah, don't you think that's right?"

R.D.'s voice rumbled out of some deep place: "That'd be nice, that would be nice."

Suddenly I understood the sense of possibility in this attitude and agreed that it was a good idea.

"That would be nice, ummhuuh," R.D. repeated, like a refrain.

"What do you think, Doris?" I asked.

"Well," she answered, "he'll know what we're doing."

Nuthel broke in, "And he will see."

"Money is not an object to that man that's got it. Look, you start here at that fence," Doris said, outlining the cemetery and the fence with pencil on a piece of paper, "and just put yourself a wall around that cemetery and we could go in and out as we choose to. And they still would have that high fence for the elk and everything."

"That's true," R.D. said.

Doris went on, "You know they haven't really thought about this."

"No," R.D. agreed

In this way, Doris attributed the lockout to a simple lack of good sense on the part of the landowners. "Here you got nearly two acres with dead folks in there. People need to go in there to clean off the graves, to talk to their dead if that's what they want to do." Moreover, she saw no excuse for cutting down trees on those two acres.

"That's what they did, though," said R.D.

I told them that I'd been researching the state codes. "There are about three different offenses," I said. "One is a misdemeanor, which is not so serious, and another is—"

Doris interrupted, "That's just a slap."

"—a third-degree felony, for desecrating a cemetery if the person acts without proper legal authority. And you all," I say, looking up from my notes, "—the Love Colored Burial Association—are the only proper legal authority."

Nuthel chuckled, "And nobody checked with us."

"That's right," Doris said.

I went on. "The law is very clear that as long as there are markers up, as long as it's clear that it hasn't been abandoned, and it is known as a cemetery—even if it's overgrown and hasn't been taken care of—it's protected."

I showed them the small plat map I had found at the title office, which had Love Cemetery marked as a rectangle with a cross in it, the designation for a known cemetery. Nuthel asked to see it. I handed it to her, and after studying it for a moment, she said, "This is history."

Then R.D., who had been silent for a while, said to me firmly, "History. That's what I say. You have to write about it."

Write about it. Writing about all this was becoming increasingly difficult, committed as I was to the story. I was running into my own irrational fears of white authority, of family disapproval—even though my own family was actively helping with the cleanup. I was breaking a taboo, a least within myself. When

I told them these fears of mine, which really all boiled down to the possibility that I would somehow be prevented from writing this story, R.D. said deliberately, drawing out his words with great authority, "Not as long as Love Cemetery officials says it's okay. And that's us. We give you the go-ahead. Ain't nobody else can do that. We're trying to get that cemetery fixed up and keep it up. Those who are in charge of trying to build it up give you permission to do whatever you want."

I felt a surge of strength hearing this. "Thank you," I said.

"As long as it's for the upbuilding of the cemetery—and that's what you looking out for—ain't nobody else say nothin' 'cause they ain't got nothing to do with it. We're the ones who have Ancestors back there. If you put out all your hard work trying to get Love Cemetery situated back like it used to be forty years ago, people going in, on a certain time of the year, cleaning up, fixing up the cemetery, law says, ain't nothing they can do. You ain't stealin', you ain't robbin', you with the group, and the group said they would like to have this history wrote up, for our children to come along and read about us and our foreparents who was there. They can get that book. They can say: 'I see where my Aunt Doris, she was in this deal.'"

Doris laughed. R.D. was on a roll. "I see Uncle R.D.'s in there too. And Miz Britton's in there...."

I sped down the highway from Doris's that evening, humming the melody of "Guide Me Over, Great Jehovah," a hymn that R.D. had sung, thinking about the Ancestors that Nuthel and R.D. often spoke of. Doris didn't talk about them as much, but she clearly understood what her brother and Nuthel meant. I could tell that, to them, these were living presences. I knew that a belief in the Ancestors was common to many religions, not only African ones, but it had never been talked about in the Christianity I'd grown up with. Still, it didn't take much of a leap to connect my friends' beliefs about the spiritual power of the Ancestors to those at the heart of the African religions that most enslaved people had been forced to abandon. African American theologians have done pioneering research that shows that these beliefs and practices have never gone anywhere; they float just under the surface of the Christianity imposed upon them.[40] For myself, raised as a Catholic, the Ancestors didn't seem that far removed from the world of saints, blessed souls who'd gone before who could be petitioned for help, protection, and guidance.

As these thoughts of the Ancestors went through my mind, I found myself driving through the piney woods on the same two-lane road where my great-grandmother had been killed by a drunk driver when I was seven. I wondered how we could make room for her and my own ancestors, not only for the descendants of Love. If there is a Realm of the Ancestors, as the African traditions say there is, mine were in it too. How we could honor all the Ancestors as we continued to restore Love? The cleanups themselves were a start. But I was nagged by the thought that there was something more to be done.

Back at my cousins', I turned off the air conditioner that had been left on to cool my room, opened the windows to the night air and the sound of crickets, and climbed into bed. But I lay awake and fretted. In spite of the spontaneous authorization, the empowerment I'd received from R.D. that night, I still wondered what business a white woman like me had getting involved in all this. I thought again of my own ancestors, the ones who had built this home that sheltered me that night. One of the reasons I'd kept returning to East Texas was for the gift of continuity in my life that this "ancestral" home provided. The palpability of their former existence continued to shape my life. On one visit I found my great-uncle George's recipe for grafting wax for the nursery plants. His handwritten note, carefully penned in blue ink, lay inside the leaf of one of the several botanical texts I'd found. It was in a box in the closet of the room I was staying in. The windup clock in the breakfast room, I was told, had always been wound once a week by my great-grandfather. Wound by cousins now, its tick has a resonance like few others. I never met my great-grandfather, but his presence in this old family home steadied me as I lay there. I began to relax as I thought of him, his wife, their children. I remembered that I had never intended to write this story. I thought I was only piecing together fragments of my own family's history when I encountered first Lydia, then Nuthel, these elders who took me out and showed me these burial grounds.

Simone Weil once said that "to be rooted is perhaps the most important and least recognized need of the soul." To know where we come from is to be restored to place. To be rooted. I turned over in bed to plump up my pillow and face the window. I remembered the first time Nuthel, Doris, and I went into Love Cemetery. It was a beautiful, wild, and lost place; but when Nuthel told me that those leafless vines were wisteria and that some of the people buried there had worked for my family and that this wisteria was from their nursery, I realized that I didn't really have a choice about this story. Like the wisteria and the graves, my ancestors, and Philip's, Doris's, and Nuthel's, were entangled. I could endlessly question my role or I could let go, and go deeper. I could follow this sense of being led and step into the mystery of this place called Love Cemetery or not. The choice was mine. The sound of tree frogs in the courtyard wove itself into my reverie. The familiar wail of a freight train in the distance cocooned me. I could feel myself breathe more deeply. In the quiet, I noticed how different I felt when I questioned myself than I did when I chose instead to be here in the bed of my life, with the sounds and the soft summer air in my great-grandparents' house. I could feel myself getting drowsy. The story of Love Cemetery had come for me.

The next morning I was back on the road to Love Cemetery. Sitting beside me in my rented car was David Guvernator, one of the younger scouts, slightly built, five feet tall, with freckles and brown hair. We bounced along the road, following my cousin Philip. His old navy blue pickup had a bumper sticker that read "Water is Life." Full of tools, equipment, and more scouts, the truck had belonged to his father, my favorite older cousin Jack, who had died in 2001. Philip was also towing Jack's fifty-year-old John Deere tractor on a trailer behind the truck.

My passenger, David, loved history. That was a big part of why he liked to come with us. He also loved the outdoors, was a very good student, and was hard at work on becoming an Eagle Scout.

"I don't know what the big deal with girls is," he said without preamble. At twelve years old, he wasn't yet distracted by the adolescent drama that was right around the corner. Having raised two sons and a daughter, I couldn't help laughing. "Friday nights," he went on, "I'd rather be camping out than on a date." He let me know, masking his confusion with disdain, that some of his friends had started to make different choices. I was struck by his innocence. It was the innocence of boys, which so often in our culture goes unsupported and unnoticed.

"That's great," I assured him. "You'll have plenty of time later on for dates." Get in those campouts while you can, I thought. You have no idea how soon this time will be gone.

We passed two clear-cuts, which David pronounced "ugly." I nodded in agreement and started to talk about "sustainability" and the rate of timber harvest in the South versus the rate of planting, but he brushed off that line of thinking and asserted that nature could take care of itself. As he put it, "The woods can handle."

I reminded myself that this twelve-year-old boy was giving up his Saturday to help us clean up Love Cemetery. This was not the moment to try to convince David that the natural world was severely threatened. First, let him fall in love with it, then he would want the knowledge that would surely follow as the natural world continues to unravel around us.

We got to the gate right on time. Nuthel, Doris, and R.D. were waiting in R. D.'s brown and cream pickup truck. Other descendants joined us too, including Willie Mae Brown's brother James Brown. Philip suggested that I take Nuthel—"Miz Britton," as he called her out of respect—in my car and continue following him. David hopped out and into the back. Mrs. Britton got up in front, and shortly thereafter we reached the second gate, the one to the cemetery. As soon as we drove in, David, who was sitting behind us, asked us what those voices were. Nuthel and I looked at each other and smiled. Voices?

"Well," said Nuthel, chuckling good-naturedly, "my hearing is not what it used to be, uh-uh."

"Are there ghosts here?" David asked, sliding down ever so slightly in the backseat, suddenly looking concerned.

"I don't believe so," Nuthel said in all seriousness.

"I don't hear anything," I told David.

"Well, I still hear them," he insisted, looking around through the rear window into the woods on either side of us. Then I remembered. When I got in the car that morning, I inserted a CD—Palestrina's *Missa Nigra Sum,* a sixteenth-century plainchant—into the car's player. When David got in the car, I had turned the CD down so low I'd forgotten that it was still on. I turned it up.

"Was this what you were hearing, David?" I asked. It was. He grinned in a mixture of relief and embarrassment.

As soon as Philip and Doug pulled up alongside the cemetery, the scouts hopped out of their pickups, grabbed their tools, and raced off into the brush so fast there was hardly a moment to gather together to give thanks and briefly pray. We were in a cemetery. We would do it at the end, Philip suggested, rather

David Guvernator

than try to gather them back together now. Most of them had already spread out and disappeared.

Nuthel took a pair of red-handled clippers and made a beeline over to the northwest corner of the cemetery, to one of the overgrown railroad ties her sons had put in to mark the corners. It took her a while, half the morning, to clear around the creosote-covered wood, but then she called me over to see her success—she was so proud of herself.

Doris and I worked together on one of graves we first encountered when we walked into the cemetery, clearing the paths around it. Doris trimmed on one side, I worked on the other. Only ten in the morning, and God it was hot. What had it been like to pick cotton all day, day after day, in heat like this, I thought to myself. It would have been mind-numbing to work "from see to can't"—the old expression that meant working in the fields from the earliest light to full darkness—up to sixteen hours and more in the summer. Had Doris worked like that when she picked cotton as a young girl? I didn't have the courage to ask. But I took that heat to heart.

This cleanup we had brought a chair for Nuthel. When she'd had enough work, she could sit in the shade and direct the others, if she wanted. As an elder and the Keeper of Love, she deserved that.

Doris and I began to clear some vines, a two-person job. To pull them off a big tree, I had to lean back with all my weight, shoulder to shoulder with Doris, then hold the tension while Doris chopped the vines with her machete. Doris did it in two cuts. Doug pushed his cowboy-style straw hat back on his head for a minute and watched. His face was pink from the heat, his t-shirt soaked. After watching for a few minutes, he said, "Watch out! That woman knows how to wield a machete." He said it with good humor, but he was definitely impressed.

Later, on Doug's next break, he told me that he felt this was an important project for the scouts. He said, "We have to remember our ancestors or our kids won't know who we are. And you know another thing, China," he added, "the thing we've lost in this country is respect for workers. You don't have to have a Ph.D. to work. The strength of the people around here is like that brush hog behind Philip's tractor, it just plows right on through a big mess."

That was a pretty good description of what people were doing. Everyone seemed to work well together, from what I could see from the south side of the cemetery. Philip, Doug, and R.D. roamed around, keeping the scouts in line, giving them direction. At one point, two of the scouts had trouble cutting down a vine-wrapped tree. They were after both the tree and the vines only made the tree-chopping harder. I walked over to see the goings-on. R.D. stood there patiently watching, wiping his wet face with a kerchief until finally it was clear the boys needed help. Then he said in his booming voice, "You boys don't know how to work. Give me that tool, I'll show you. You got to start chopping at the bottom, like this," he said, bending over to give the wisteria vines braided around the tree a *thwack*. "No wonder. You got to sharpen your tools too. Where's your file?" They didn't have one with them, no sir, they did not.

"Come on over to my truck. I got one. You got to sharpen up this ax," he told Gavin, a lanky fifteen-year-old scout with glasses.

"Ummh, yes sir, Mr. R.D." said Gavin, as he followed R.D.'s directions. "Looka here," R.D. said as he sat down on the

Henderson headstone and proceeded to show Gavin how to sharpen a tool and keep it that way.

Once Doris and I got those vines down, I took off by myself with some hand clippers to the northern part of the cemetery, where Nuthel's grandmother was buried. It was too hot for Nuthel to make it out that far. Lizzie Sparks, her grandmother, was on the opposite side of the cemetery from where we were.

As I went up the side of the cemetery from the pond toward the Sparks section, I ran into Clauddie Mae Webb. She'd finished cleaning the five graves that belonged to her family, the Webbs, and had moved on to pulling and hacking away at the overgrowth around the grave of Daniel Sparks, Lizzie Sparks's son and Nuthel's uncle.

Clauddie showed me how under the wisteria and ironwood she'd found a small wire fence that used to go all the way around Daniel Sparks' grave. The small open wire fence was low to the ground, maybe ten inches high, gracefully scalloped, bent and wrapped like a trellis with vines.

Clauddie told me that when she was a little girl she'd known Lizzie Sparks. "I remember her, she was Indian. Yes, I do, oh yes," she said. "She was mean! Ain't no man ever seen her backside, no man!"

"What do you mean, Clauddie Mae?" assuming that I had misunderstood her deep southern accent. "Backside?"

"I mean Lizzie Sparks throwed 'em," she went on, "That woman throwed 'em down. She was a wrassler! No man ever beat her. She'd get to them first, wrassle 'em down. They couldn't get to her, no, she was strong!" she told me, through her gap-tooth smile, laughing hard at this recollection.

Clauddie and I pulled and pulled on that wisteria, pulling up sometimes more than ten feet of vine before we found a chopping off place close to the root. It was the first time I'd worked with Clauddie. I didn't know her that well, so I asked her if she knew how to sing "Oh Susannah"—everybody knows that song. "Oh yes," she said with a grin, and we set to singing together as we worked, laughing as we'd fill in the words. Neither one of us could remember all the verses. I was wildly happy in this moment, laughing and singing with Clauddie Mae under a clear blue sky, in the hot summer sun, with the whine of Doug's chain saw mixing with the chorus of cicadas and Philip's tractor rumbling in the background. We were taking back Love and nothing could stop us.

The energy that had started to build the night at Doris's house and had gained momentum on that third cleanup day carried us through our full committee meeting a few nights later at Gail and Greg Beil's place, a handsome three-story blue Victorian with white trim. The house had been given a Texas State Historic Marker and was the former home of the Weismans, a leading Jewish family in the nineteenth and early twentieth centuries in Marshall.

Gail had invited two friends to join our growing burial ground committee: Julia Williams and Annye Fisher, both accomplished, prominent women who were deeply committed to history and were African American themselves. Julia had served on the Texas State Historical Commission Board out of Austin, and Annye was on the Landmark Commission for Harrison County. I had invited Fr. Denzil Vinthanage, the new pastor at St. Joseph's Catholic Church, who had replaced Father Diegel. Until he spoke, revealing a lilting Anglo-Indian accent, people might assume he was African American and not from Sri Lanka.

"Father D.," as he was called, had wanted to join us because he saw—new as he was to the area—a great need to "bind up" the community. He told us that after living through the horrors of ethnic violence that continue to tear Sri Lanka apart, he had decided to follow the example of the priests and nuns he had seen there who, no matter how polarized the situation became, had maintained their devotion to healing and serving everyone, regardless of which side of the conflict they were on. Father Denzil had seen firsthand what race-fueled war and politics could do. St. Joseph's was fortunate to have a priest with his grasp of global realities and understanding.

That night, Doris, Nuthel, and I shared our enthusiasm for the important gathering we would have the following month. Spread out comfortably in Gail's high-ceilinged living room, the rest of the committee enthusiastically approved and elaborated on our plans to get the word out to all those who had family members buried at Love.

Excited as I was, something from the cleanup day still troubled me. As the meeting broke up, I asked Father D. if I could come to see him in his rectory later in the week.

Heavy beige drapes and air conditioning kept his sitting room pleasantly cool. Dressed in a short-sleeved black shirt and Roman collar, Father Denzil seemed calm behind gold-rimmed glasses, his dark eyes endlessly deep, as if there were nothing they could not hold.

I told him that the innocent, unconscious irreverence of many of us who didn't have ancestors at Love Cemetery, including me, was beginning to bother me. During the cleanups I found myself walking on graves, sitting on headstones. I hadn't even noticed this at first, but the more we cleared, the more the situation changed. Love became less of a wild tangle, a jungle of wisteria, and more of an actual cemetery. Not that we needed to be solemn or joyless when we were out there, those of us who were not related, I just sensed that we needed to do something differently. What I was reaching for was more along the lines of what Doris, R.D., Nuthel, and the other elders showed when they prayed and sang over the graves—a kind of practical reverence. Oh, they'd sit on a headstone if it was all that was handy; they'd walk across graves, which at first was unavoidable with all the overgrowth. But it was their families who were buried there. They had a different situation. These were their people, this was their cemetery. I was uncomfortable with those of us who were not related, I told Father Denzil. Sometimes the playful, young-male energy of the scouts seemed inappropriate. For Philip and Doug, handling the machines and getting the work done were paramount, which was also true. But I was concerned that the sacred nature of a burial ground wasn't being honored. How could we also acknowledge that?

Father D. quietly considered what I had said. After a silence, he said, "Perhaps the cemetery needs to be reconsecrated."

As he continued, I sensed he was right.

"When a cemetery hasn't been used in such a long while, it is very appropriate to reconsecrate it. That's what we do in the church."

This is what I had been reaching for without knowing it: a ceremony, a public acknowledgment that we were walking on holy ground—ground made holy by the struggles of the people whose bodies had been given to this land. For many, regardless of background, a burial ground was a liminal space, a place between worlds in which we take time apart not only to honor but to communicate with our ancestors, to feed the family spirits, to receive guidance, to pour out our heart to the ground that receives all. Staying connected to one's ancestors is a way of feeding one's own soul and balancing the world. But then I realized that it might not be so simple.

"Father, that might be wonderful," I told him. "But the people buried there—their descendants—they're Baptists, not Catholics."

Father D. waited patiently for more of an explanation. I told him that, historically in the South there had often been animosity between Baptists and Catholics. Maybe that wouldn't come up. In the short time Father D. had been here, he had already developed a devoted following. As I spoke, it came to me that not only would Doris and Nuthel and R.D. have to approve of a ceremony of reconsecration, but the Baptist minister from Shiloh would also need to participate. Could it be an interfaith ceremony?

"Of course," he said without hesitation. I asked him if he was willing to let the Baptist minister lead the service, since at least some of the Love descendants were part of his congregation. "Of course," he repeated. "Jesus is all about love. He turned the pyramid of power upside down. Our Lord gives us the model. He was the father of living in community and sharing with others. He was a servant-leader. He taught us that we should come to serve the community, not for the community to serve us. Let me know what Doris and everyone decide. I will be happy to help if they want."

I thanked Father Denzil and whatever good fortune had assigned him to Marshall.

I called Doris right away and asked her what she thought about Father Denzil's idea. She was open too. She liked the idea of a ceremony. It felt right to her. When I asked her about her pastor at Shiloh, she gave me his phone number and said to ask him. I did call, but not without some nervousness. Growing up Catholic in the South, I did not know many Baptist preachers. However, he was just as willing as the others to have an inter-faith service of reconsecration at the cemetery. He was glad to lead it, and he would be happy to work with Father Denzil as well, he assured me, though they'd never met.

I woke up a little late the next morning. It was Sunday in Scottsville and I could hear Philip's youngest sister, my cousin Joanie, outside in the garden. She had driven over from Marshall to help their mother, Agnes, pick vegetables and weed before it got too hot. Chloe, Philip and Carolyn's three-year-old grand-daughter, ran in and out of the rows of beans, tomatoes, and cu-cumbers, while Joanie pulled up weeds. Philip had already fed the horse and cows and was trying to round up Chloe to get her dressed for morning Mass. I had gone to evening Mass the night before, so I decided to go to Doris and R.D.'s church, Shiloh Missionary Baptist, where Pastor McCain would be preaching. I had gone to their church a few times before.

I walked into church and took my increasingly familiar place in the third row, behind Doris and the other deaconesses, in the row in front of Willie Mae Brown. Mrs. Ernestine Mattox, tall and slender in a pretty salmon suit, sat on one side of me and Mrs. King on the other. I remembered that we'd found a King marker at the cemetery the day before; I would have to ask her about it after church. R.D. was in a dark gray suit and tie up in front on the right side with the other deacons.

This morning the pastor introduced four young women "praise dancers." "You're out there dancing with the devil, you got to come in here and dance for God," he said enthusiastically. These young women were to be commended, not criticized, for dancing for God. They each wore white gloves and gold lamé tops over black blouses and pants. Recorded music played as they glorified God with their bodily praise, gracefully bending as if blown by the wind, then turning and reaching their hands to the heavens. When they finished, the choir's full thirty voices rose in song while a young man played the drum kit and a precocious ten-year-old tore into the upright piano on the side of the church where I was sitting. The young pianist was a tornado of energy. But suddenly he was jumping up and down at the piano crying out "Jesus! JESUS! JESUS!" louder and louder. Adults quickly came up and surrounded him. He'd been "slain in the spirit"— overcome in an ecstatic union with God. One of the men got behind him, clasping his arms around him to keep him from falling against the corner of the piano, and slowly guided him into the back through the door to the community room. The young man shouted for Jesus over and over, as they gently moved him out of the sanctuary. I could still hear him as they went down the hall. The door closed behind them, and his cries of "Jesus!" grew fainter and fainter. Another young man stepped up to the organ and took up the pianist's part. The service continued. No one looked around or whispered. This was just what happened on a Sunday, I gathered.

After a while the pastor called for announcements. To my surprise, R. D. stood up and started talking about our work at Love Cemetery. He swept his arm in my direction and told the whole congregation that I was making a movie about Love for television. I stared at the floor, dumbfounded by his announcement. Even though I'd gotten various people to shoot video for me during the past year to document what we were doing, all I really had was a pile of unedited video tapes in a box on the floor of my closet. Before I could even begin to do anything more with that raw footage, I would have to finish writing the story, and it changed with each visit I made. How would I ever be able to match the expectations that had just been set into motion?

Then R.D.'s voice cut through my thoughts of failure. He said to the gathered congregation, "She's one of us."

I looked up and had to smile. I was humbled by what I took as a great compliment, being called "one of us." I was amazed at the warmth extended to me. All I'd done was show up respectfully as a visitor, something anyone was free to do.

August 21, 2004, was the first anniversary of our work together at Love Cemetery, and we were gathering for the interfaith ceremony to reconsecrate the burial ground. At eight in the morning, we started assembling under the pines in the Scottsville Community Center parking lot. The air was still, and the temperature had already shot up to ninety-eight degrees. The day we'd been working toward had arrived. Despite invitations to join us for the potluck, neither the owner nor the timber manager attended. They were on vacation.

My son, Ben, in his early thirties, had come from out of town to shoot video of the ceremony. It wasn't his first visit to our group in East Texas. He had already shot several hours of previous committee meetings and interviews. I wanted a video record primarily for archival purposes, but since there was a chance—as R.D. had already announced in church—remote as it was, that we might someday be able to edit a documentary from the footage, I'd been getting people to sign the kind of generic liability release that filmmakers use.

My daughter, Madelon, had also come, making her first visit here since a canoe trip we made together on Caddo Lake years ago, when she was seventeen and we first met Kizzie Mae Hicks. Since then, she had become an artist. Standing here with her in the growing heat, it seemed as if Madelon and I had just stepped out of our canoe. Like Ben, she wanted to participate. She was never comfortable being a bystander. I asked her to help me collect releases from everyone as they arrived.

Eighty-year-old Walter Edwards, "Coach," was already there, waiting in his pickup, when we got to the center. For years he had been the coach at Galilee High School, just down the road from Marshall, where he had trained Olympic gold medalist Fred Newhouse. Like others who had joined with us to save the cemetery, Coach had no family members buried at Love. Nonetheless, here he was, eager to get to work. Even at eighty, he could work a younger man into the ground and never break a sweat or stop smiling.

Willie Mae drove in with her brother, James Brown, who'd moved back to Scottsville after thirty years working in the auto industry in Detroit. She had also picked up Clauddie Mae and her sister Joyce. Then some of the scouts arrived—Geronimo and his father, David Guvenator and his parents, and Gavin McKinley with his. We were going to have a good turnout.

A train whistle blew. It was coming out of Marshall, seven miles down the line. Philip arrived, his trailer clanking and groaning under the fifty-year-old John Deere. Doug was down at the Grub Sack, the combination gas station and convenience store down the road. He was getting extra gas for the chain saws and the tractors. The railroad crossing lights flashed, warning bells went off, the train whistle blew again, louder and closer. I turned to watch the show until the caboose passed with crewmen waving.

R.D. drove up with his older brother Albert and his daughter, Sondra, both of whom had driven over from Ft. Worth. They had started out at three in the morning to get here in time for the gathering.

Mourning doves called from the pines, a cardinal sang out on a pasture fence line, and jays squawked at people carrying food into the community center for the afternoon's potluck. A scissor-tail flicked off the phone line and flew to the quieter lake across the road. A steady stream of baked goods, casseroles, salads, and main dishes made their way into the community center's refrigerator. Carolyn would meet us after the cleanup with her famous coleslaw salad. One of my uncles in Dallas sent half a ham, and a friend contributed a pecan pie.

Gail and Greg Beil arrived with a freshly baked chocolate cake and berries from their garden. Annye Fisher and Julia Williams drove over from Marshall, each with a platter of food,

Gail Beil, Greg Beil, and Walter Edwards

work gloves in hand, and sun hats on their heads. Like Coach, Annye and Julia had no family buried at Love, but they valued history immensely and they wanted to help.

Then Father Denzil drove up. We were now a gathering of at least twenty excited people, and there were still more coming. Nuthel called to let me know she was coming late. She was waiting for her daughter, Wanda Gale Britton Jackson, a high-school teacher, who was driving up from Houston. "Left at six o'clock this morning in a big thunderstorm," Nuthel's voice sounded distant through my cell phone. "Lightning too." I told her not to worry. She and her daughter could meet us out at Love.

The scouts were eager to get going. Thunderheads piled high in the distance. It had poured a couple of inches the day before, but Philip assured me that things had been so dry that this little bit of rain only settled the dust. He wasn't worried about mud on the unpaved road getting into Love. Doug carried a set of chains in the back of his pickup anyway.

Madelon introduced herself to people as she collected the release forms. Several people had already signed releases, but different people had come to each cleanup and I had not been able to locate a number of them in my office before leaving for this trip. The easiest thing was to just get a fresh one from everyone and be done with it.

Ben loaded his equipment into Philip's pickup and kept the scouts enthralled with tales of surfing the wild waters of Northern California.

Today's reconsecration and celebration—along with all our work so far—were the fulfillment of the promise I'd made that balmy night a year before when Nuthel had driven off without her lights on. "I want to see Love restored and everybody come back for grave cleaning day before I die," she had said. I had told her that I would do whatever I could to help, but to myself I swore I would move heaven and earth to make this happen. It was the least I could do. Now here we were. But as I checked off new arrivals and showed people where to put the food, a question nagged at me: where was Doris? She was always on time. No matter how long a day she might have had at the Shreveport Veterans Hospital, she always found new energy for Love.

Finally I saw her drive up in her red Toyota as I was introducing Madelon to Clauddie Mae and Joyce. Doris walked briskly into the center to put her food away. When she came back out, I greeted her. "Doris, can you believe this?" I said, making a sweeping gesture with my arm to include everyone in the lot. I was nervous about the day and a little breathless. Without waiting for her response, I told her I needed her to sign a release as well and handed her the clipboard.

She did not take it. "I'm not signing nothing," she said.

Ben gave me a hand signal: "Leaving in five minutes. Rolling." I nodded and turned back to Doris. "What?"

"I tell you, China, this whole thing is just making me uncomfortable." I had no idea what she was talking about.

"After all this time, why are you bringing up signing some kind of paper now. I was an extra in a movie here once and we didn't have to sign nothing. I don't like this. When you called and left that message on my machine last Tuesday, it just churned my stomach."

I had left a long message on her answering machine asking her to help me get the releases signed this morning. I had been dividing up tasks, concerned that having to organize food, equipment, and people and get thirty or more signatures on my own would hold us up. I had the sensation of ground giving way beneath me.

"We've talked about all this before, Doris," I reminded her. "We've been shooting video for over a year." She had participated enthusiastically in a video interview, had participated in cleanups that Ben or a local videographer had shot.

She stood there shaking her head at me; she was clearly angry, but she said nothing. I felt dizzy: Doris was my friend, an increasingly close one, I thought. Truck doors were slamming, people were getting ready to leave for the cemetery.

"I showed you and R.D. the sample video tape that Ben put together. You said you loved it. What happened?"

Philip called out, "We need to get going, everybody, it's going to be hot!"

I could hear R.D. gunning his engine. Doris said in a flat voice, "You know, Nuthel's son had got a lot done before you showed up. He got us an easement, he figured out how to find the man from the timber company. We should have just waited for him to get home from Iraq."

I opened my mouth to speak but could think of nothing more to say. Doris went on, "We didn't need you." She turned away and headed toward her car.

R.D., his brother, and his daughter pulled out of the lot and took off down the road to the cemetery. Doug climbed in his two-tone blue pickup and slammed the door. Madelon waved impatiently from across the parking lot, "Come on, Mom, we have to go!" Ben was in the back of Philip's truck with his gear and a couple of scouts. For a moment I just stood there, stunned by this sudden breach with Doris. What abyss had I fallen into?

SIX

The Reconsecration of Love Cemetery

One summer we found the past in ruins.
— Steve Orlen,
"Abandoned Places"

I rode out to the cemetery with Father Denzil, and I asked him to pray for Doris and me, saying only that we'd had a misunderstanding. "Our Lord, help your servants China and Doris....," the lilt of his Sri Lankan accent was comforting, but no prayer seemed to dissolve the heaviness I felt.

Philip and Doug began to hand out work gloves and tools as soon as we got there. Willie Mae had brought her own long-handled clippers, and Geronimo proudly showed off his father's machete from Mexico, which he had been allowed to bring. He wore it slung over his shoulder in a rawhide case his father had made for him. Coach and R.D. helped Philip unchain his tractor and back it off the trailer. The scouts scattered like quail into the brush, but Philip and Doug called them back so that we could all circle up for the ceremony we had planned with Father D. and the others.

While we waited for everyone to gather, I walked over to a shady place where Albert, Doris and R.D.'s brother, was standing. He was even taller than R.D. His open face was framed by close-cropped white hair and sideburns. After I introduced myself, Albert told me how glad he was to be back here. It was his first visit since 1943, when he had come for the funeral of Melvinie Brown, one of the many Browns to whom the Johnsons were related.

"I was here alright, that was the last time I was here," he said. "Everything was clean and beautiful."

Gail and Greg Beil strolled over with Julia and Annye.

"People here were farming and sharecropping, people lived around here, everywhere," he said. We all drew closer.

"A lot of African Americans used to own their own land out here, didn't they, Mr. Johnson?" Gail asked.

"Oh yes," Albert said. "Ohio Taylor, his son—my grand-daddy, Richard Taylor—lots of 'em."

"And they were farmers, right?"

"Sure they were," Albert agreed.

"See," said Gail, "they weren't only sharecroppers. African Americans—those who could—bought land after Emancipation."

"That's what I'm sayin'," Albert Johnson agreed.

"But when the Depression hit," Gail added, explaining to the white folks who were listening, "people started leaving their farms. Then there was World War II. They started taking defense plant jobs, at places like Longhorn Munitions up at Caddo Lake."

I wanted to hear more about Melvinie's 1943 funeral, but the scouts were back, everyone was milling around chatting, and we had to get started. A welcome cloud cover and the relatively early hour made the sun tolerable.

R.D. positioned himself next to Ohio Taylor's headstone, leaning on it to include Ohio—and by extension, all the Ancestors—in the circle we were forming. The scouts piped down and people grew quiet. I looked across the circle at Doris. Her head was down. No one said anything. I realized that it was up to me to welcome everyone. I thanked our volunteers. I announced that Pastor McCain from Shiloh Baptist Church had to send his regrets because of an unscheduled funeral that would keep him away. Then, I formally acknowledged Nuthel and Doris— "Mrs. Britton and Mrs. Vittatoe"—for their roles as instigators and prime movers in this restoration. "Mrs. Britton will be here as soon as she can," I said. "She's waiting for her daughter to drive up from Houston." I heard murmurs of understanding from the gathering. Having dispensed with the logistics, I wasn't sure what to say next. How could anything that I had prepared last night be relevant this morning, now that everything had changed between Doris and me? I told everyone how honored I'd been when Mrs. Britton had asked me to help. Working on this cemetery, I said, was teaching me a lot about love. People listened politely, Doris nodded a little and kept staring at the ground.

"There's a special debt owed to African Americans," I said, "a people who were forced to be here, who did not come to America by choice." I was on automatic. I heard myself say something about Native Americans. I was drifting. If I kept going in this vein, I would soon be talking about white people needing to make amends and reparations to African Americans. Fortunately, I realized that I was indirectly speaking to Doris, trying to apologize for my part in the misunderstanding. But, now, everyone was staring at the ground. I made another try: "Cleaning up this cemetery together creates a larger sense of community...."

I stopped and turned to Doris and asked her to tell the story of what we were doing here. With new family members and first-time volunteers from Marshall with us, there needed to be a brief history of Love Cemetery and our efforts to reclaim it.

Doris spoke easily: "When we first came out here, a year and a half ago, I was elated to be here that first day. We found some cousins, my great-grandfather Ohio Taylor here, but I'm still trying to find my grandparents, Richard and Irene Taylor. I know they're here. Thank you all for coming today."

I wanted her to go on. She had a natural ability to speak simply and succinctly. But once she finished, everyone seemed to wait in silence for something else to happen. Instead of simply introducing R.D., who was stepping in for their pastor and, we had agreed, would lead the first prayer, I fell back on an outline I'd written the week before and launched into an eighteenth-century Hasidic tale from Eastern Europe about how the legendary Ba'al Shem Tov saved his community from catastrophe.

The longer I spoke, the more out of place I felt. But, unless I told it all, the story would make no sense whatsoever. I forgot to make the connection I'd planned between the loss of the forest in the legend and the clear-cuts of the East Texas woods that we had driven past on the way out here.

R.D. kept leaning on the plinth of his great-grandfather's grave marker, waiting patiently for me to finish. One of the scouts seemed to be looking for bugs on the ground. Everyone seemed to be avoiding eye contact with me. Only Father Denzil, next to me, his gold-rimmed glasses sparkling in the sun, seemed to be listening. Mercifully, the story reached its end, and I could stop trying to tell it.

When I stopped, R.D. didn't miss a beat. He spoke up and got us back on track with his own words of welcome and thanks to all. Then he started singing and I could breathe again.

"Oh, there's a cross for everyone and there's a cross for me ...," he sang in his sonorous voice, a hymn the African American descendant community knew well and echoed back: "Ohhh, go down ..." Doris, standing next to her brother Albert, may have been singing softly under her breath, but I couldn't hear her.

"Yes there is a cross for me...." R.D. sang a few more verses, then the song broke into a spontaneous, syncopated spoken prayer of call and response. "Our Father in heaven, here we are again, assembled ourselves together once more."

Yes, sir, Albert says softly under his breath on just the right beat.

"Father, we come today in the name of Jesus," R.D. half-spoke, half sang. "We give thanks for the friends and family that have come from far and near. Bind us together, Father, in one family of Christian love.

"Father, you said there's no chain stronger than its weakest link...."

Yes, sir.

"We are weak, our Father, but we know you're strong...."

Yes, sir.

"Father, we pray that you will come in our midst today."

Yes, yes.

"Build us up and tone us down."

Oh yes.

"Father, I pray that you bless every home that is represented here today. Give us that eternal love, Father, that runs from heart to heart and breast to breast."

Umm, oh yes.

"Then we pray, our Father, for the less fortunate. Let us pray, our Father, for those who had a desire to be here this morning and were unable to come."

Yes, Lord.

"Then, Father, bless those that could come and that were too mean to come," I was surprised to hear him say. "Father, we pray that you *continue* to lead us and guide whichever way we go."

Oh yes.

"When this old world can't 'ford us a home no longer ..."

Yes, yes.

"Father, when we come down to the end of our journey, we ask you to come so close."

"Amen, amen," we all answered.

Still leaning on Ohio's plinth atop the two columns on his headstone, R. D. pointed to Father Denzil, indicating that it was his turn now to pray. Father D. stepped forward a little and opened the slender black book of Prayers for the Departed.

"Dear friends," he began, first explaining a little about the Catholic view of a burial site. "This is hallowed ground. We come together this morning because we believe in the power of life, we believe in the power of love. We believe in the resurrection of the body...." As he spoke, Father Denzil opened a tiny box of salt and sprinkled it on the earth, and then made the sign of the cross over the site where it fell and pronounced the ground reconsecrated. And so Love Cemetery became again—officially, formally, between R.D. and Father D. by communal agreement, witness, and participation—holy ground.

Father Denzil ended by asking us all to pray the "Our Father" together. Then, carried away by the moment, he turned to Psalm 8 in his book and spontaneously burst into song, "We praise you, O Lord, how great is your name." R.D. and the descendant community came in humming underneath Father Denzil's hymn as though they knew the song he was singing and accepted his offering.

With the prayers and reconsecration finally done, it was Philip's turn to talk about what he hoped to accomplish by bringing the tractor that day, where he wanted to start in the cemetery. "What do you think?" he said to R.D., who'd been wanting to get a tractor out here since the first cleanup. R.D. was fine with the plan. It was going to take a lot of people working with R.D., Coach, Doug, and Philip to do it right. A brush hog can kill you if you don't work it right or watch where you are when it's spinning. Some of the scouts would go ahead with Ben, helping him by diving down underneath the wisteria to check for tree stumps, markers, and headstones.

While Philip and Doug got that effort organized and the tractor started up with a small roar, Coach just picked up a hoe and started cleaning around Melvinie Brown's grave, scraping dirt off the concrete slab and using the corner of his hoe to dig up weeds around her cracked white headstone.

Father Denzil had put on a blue baseball cap. He walked over to me while I was watching Coach quietly at work. Father D. had to leave to do a baptism back in Marshall.

"Before I leave, China," he said, "I wanted to tell you that I'm completely fascinated with this name, Love Cemetery. You know that even Mary Magdalene ran to the tomb of our Lord because of love. Love is everything!"

"Yes Father," I said, unable to meet his excitement.

"Thank you for including me," he said. "This is wonderful! The Lord will take care of your misunderstanding with Doris." I could only hope for as much.

Nuthel finally arrived with her daughter. Wanda Gale was a tall, handsome, big-boned woman in her late thirties, about the same age as my daughter Madelon. Wanda Gale joined in, laughing and talking with Madelon and Sondra, R.D.'s daughter, as they cut and pulled wisteria from around an elderberry bush. Greg Beil, down on all fours trimming, had discovered a funeral-wreath holder when he cut back some undergrowth. "Now look at this," he said in his soft-spoken way, wiping the perspiration from his heat-flushed face. Gale, Madelon, and Sondra gathered round to help.

Nuthel and another elder sat in folding chairs among a cluster of graves out of the sun.

Nuthel Britton

The air was filled with a shrill cacophony of Doug's whining gas-powered weed-whacker and Philip's roaring older tractor pulling the brush hog close to the ground, chewing up and spitting out vines, branches, small trees, rocks, and whatever Philip pulled it over. R.D. and Coach guided Philip along. Ben and the scouts were diving into the undergrowth to get below the wisteria and check for headstones or grave markers. Ben popped up, his face drenched, raised both his arms above the shoulder-high wisteria, pulled off his cap, and waved, whistling and shouting to make himself heard by R.D. and Philip, "Clear to here!" That meant that Philip could run the brush hog up to where he stood, that they'd found no markers.

Doris was working off in another part of the cemetery. I didn't try to approach her. I'd gotten myself into this—whatever it was—and I had to just be with it. I swore and cursed for a moment, but I'd never been able to take much satisfaction from that kind of behavior. I tried to pray, but I was too furious with the weather, with Doris, but most of all with myself. Then I remembered, with chagrin, the can of peanuts and the small but expensive bottle of rum waiting in my day pack.

In preparation for the reconsecration, I had tried to learn something about traditional African beliefs regarding the Ancestors. My curiosity had grown deeper on that song-filled night at Doris's house, which now felt so very far away. Back in California, I had an African American friend who had studied the Dagara tradition from Burkina Faso, with Malidoma Somé. Malidoma, born and raised in Africa, had been educated as a Westerner by the Jesuits. He attended the Sorbonne and earned a Ph.D. in the States, from Brown University. Then he had to go back to Africa. He realized that he was a black African who knew only white ways. He went back to his village and over time was initiated into his own Dagara tradition. He returned from Africa to the United States, and now teaches the wisdom of the indigenous Dagara ways to Westerners. My friend told me he knew exactly whom to talk to: Reda Rackley. She was one of the few students his teacher, Malidoma, had sent back to his own village in Burkina Faso for an initiation by the tribal elders. She worked specifically with the Ancestors. He gave me her phone number and said to call her right away. I did.

During that first phone call, I discovered that Reda was a white southerner like me. I felt tricked. How could she help? Another white southerner? She and I were part of the problem. But her voice—even over the phone—was compelling. I listened to her story.

Reda was a descendant of Georgia slaveholders on both sides of her family. After years of study with Malidoma, blonde, blue-eyed Reda had indeed been sent to Africa for an initiation. Her specific task had been to learn how to receive guidance from the Ancestors, known as Kantomble. Two weeks of initiation by the tribe's elder diviner turned her world upside down. The elder did a divination for Reda and told her that she had a role to play in bringing the wisdom of the Ancestors back into a world that has come unmoored from its foundation—the world of the spirits. That experience, which felt like a homecoming to Reda, prompted her to dedicate her life to racial reconciliation, reparation, and healing.

Calling Reda, and later spending time with her, gave me a new sense of both the limits and the possibilities of my upbringing, my own mixed European heritage. Though my mother's family hadn't come down from Chicago until 1900 and had never enslaved people, that didn't mean they hadn't taken advantage of a system that exploited and disenfranchised African Americans. Reda's example offered an alternative to the extremes of denial, guilt, and anger that had too often been my response to the racism I bumped against in my background and in myself. But I would never have suspected that these unlikely ways of connecting to the Ancestors could have any bearing on my search.

The simple instructions that Reda had given me to pray and purify my heart before this trip felt very close to what I would do anyway. I knew long ago that I had to "water my roots," to return to Texas regularly. When in Dallas I always visit Turtle Creek and stand on the limestone bed of its tributaries to give thanks to the spirit of the waters. Though the language Reda used was different, the spirit felt much the same.

Reda's instructions to bring peanuts and rum to make an offering at the burial ground I took at face value and simply followed them, unfamiliar as they were. The important thing was to approach this other world on its terms, not mine. I did this to show respect, like I did when I was in another country and visited someone else's temple. Why not here? I reasoned.

Belief in the world of Ancestors is common to indigenous cultures the world over. From the indigenous perspective, the unseen world where the Ancestors reside, a world that defies measurement, is as "real" as the world of materiality, of things, of all that we can measure. Reality is also made up of what is nonvisible and nonmaterial.

Though physicists and shamans describe the path and the contents of their nonvisible worlds quite differently, they seem to agree on two points: we cannot see it, and it is powerful beyond our most extravagant imaginings. No wonder South

American Indians teach that to become human, one must make room in oneself for the immensities of the universe.

How close this idea of the Ancestors is to the story that Einstein told, in response to repeated requests to explain what he was seeking: "I want to know how the Old One thinks. The rest is a detail."[41] The Old One. The Ancestors.

Reda supported my sense that the world of this historic black cemetery was very different from mine, no matter how ordinary it looked, and that I should approach it with respect. I didn't have to understand the world of the Ancestors to make offerings to them. Though I might not be able to translate the language of which the offerings were parts of speech, the Ancestors could, and Reda's suggestions had helped me approach this day of re-consecration with a sense of wonder. I would bow to that mystery, to all I did not know. Humility was essential.

While looking around for a good location to make my offering, I came upon a low spot in the ground near where I had been working. It looked as though the earth had collapsed above a coffin. I could find no marker of any kind around. I decided that this sunken ground was the place, so I knelt down on the warm earth and dug a small hole for the offerings. I unzipped my day pack, pulled out the blue can with Mr. Peanuts on it and the unfamiliar small bottle of Puerto Rican rum. Under my breath, I called on the Ancestors of Love to please be with us that day and to please understand and accept my offering, humble and culturally garbled as it might be.

I worked furtively. I was especially afraid of being seen by my devout African American Baptist friends and being asked what I was doing. I didn't want to have to explain that this was a fragment of an African ritual I'd been told to do in honor of *their*

Ancestors. It was enough that Doris was upset with me. I took a quick look around to be sure that no was looking, shook the can of peanuts and poured it out into the ground and followed it with the rum. I looked up again. The coast was clear. I covered up the hole, zipped the empty peanut can and bottle back into my pack, took a deep breath. No one had seen me or asked what I was doing. I could relax.

We made a lot of progress that day and left well after noon to get back to the community center for our potluck. Carolyn was there putting out coleslaw, bowls of potato salad people had brought, cold bean salad, a tray of deviled eggs and raw vegetables, ham, beans, chicken, and of course Gail's cake. There was watermelon and iced tea, and the air conditioner had been working to cool the space since Carolyn arrived earlier. We had a place to wash up, cool off, and eat—you couldn't ask for much more. At first there was so much to do, I forgot about the hard place I was in with Doris. Nuthel's daughter Wanda Gale dived right in to help, while Nuthel sat at a table inside, where it was cool. I sat down with Nuthel for a minute. She said it was good, really good, that we finally got this to happen; she was happy, even if we did have a ways to go.

While we worked on putting the food out, and the napkins, paper plates, and utensils, the scouts were horsing around outside, hungry and ready to eat. There were too many people in the kitchen, so I went outside to see what was going on there. Off a little ways from the building, out in the field, Ben was interviewing Geronimo on camera, asking him why he took his Saturdays off to help us. I went over to listen.

Geronimo, a growing fourteen-year-old, about five feet ten, told Ben about how, on both parents' sides, his family visits their families' burial grounds and takes care of the graves regularly. He didn't think it was right that these descendants of Love had been locked out. He seemed offended by the idea that people had died and been buried and their gravesites had been lost. He said that he couldn't imagine going to where his family is buried and not being able to find his relatives—his great-grandmother, his aunts, his uncles, any one of them. Geronimo's father was from Mexico, and his mother came from Chicago. He never met his grandfather, and yet he has visited his grave several times and talked to him. He would have loved to have known him, and he tells him so on his periodic visits.

"Here there are family members we're helping who've been looking all over the place for their relatives," he said. "It takes a long time to cut down that wisteria to where you can even see the ground. We have been trying our best to find their relatives. It's hard, real hard, but it makes me feel good to try."

Finally it was time to eat. Julia, Gail, and Nuthel circulated outside, inviting people to come inside. We stood and said a quick blessing, giving thanks for all the hard work, the food, and the cooking. People then filled their plates and took seats at the four rows of tables. As the places filled, my heart sank. I watched the group divide itself almost exclusively into black and white. One table was all African American but for one white woman; the other table was exclusively white. After all this time working together with seemingly little sense of separation, here it was. I tried to tell myself that it was natural, folks wanted to be with family members. But I felt a pall in the air. Whatever misunderstanding I had with Doris seemed to have grown and spread beyond just us. I sat down at a table with Nuthel and Wanda Gale. They seemed untouched by whatever was happening, I was relieved to find.

Potluck supper (left to right): Albert Johnson, Doris Vittatoe, James Brown, China Galland, Wanda Gale Britton Jackson (at the head of the table), Nuthel Britton, Willie Mae Brown, Mary Wallace, and Walter Edwards.

As the afternoon wore on, I felt increasingly uncomfortable with R.D. and Albert, with whom I had enjoyed such warmth. I didn't know whether it was real or my own imaginings, brought on by sadness and discomfort with Doris.

When we got back to Philip's house in the late afternoon, I went upstairs to shower and realized that behind my sadness and confusion, I was furious. I had a headache and I was exhausted. I had poison ivy. I felt like Doris had closed her heart, shut me out, and I didn't know why.

I wanted to forget about Love Cemetery. I wanted to give up, pack my bags, and leave that night. Forget about race and reconciliation—it was all too complicated. If, as Doris had said, she didn't need me, what was I knocking myself out for? I sat on the edge of the bed, then got up and paced. I had my own family.

I wanted to go home.

I picked up the phone and called to tell my husband, Corey, that I was coming. He listened patiently as I told him what had happened and then said, "You can't just walk away from this, not when you're so upset." He could hear my exhaustion. His gentle voice cut through my agitation. "You know this. You need some sleep. Sleep on it, China, and listen—" he paused, "remember Sam Adkins? Remember what he told Mabel when she was furious?" This was why I loved this man, why I had called him. "You've got to choose love when there's reason to hate, right?" Corey said.

"Choose love, China. I don't know what that looks like in this situation. I can't tell you what to do. Just don't do anything tonight." How could I? His voice was already lulling me to sleep. I could hardly keep my eyes open. "Think about Mabel and Sam," he said, "and go to sleep. You'll know what to do in the morning."

———— • ◆ • ————

SEVEN

"You Got to Stay on Board"

"To be rooted is perhaps the most important and least recognized need of the human soul."
—Simone Weil

When I woke up, Sam Adkins's words were with me still: "You got to choose love." Perhaps they had never left me. In order to "choose love" that morning, I would have to go to Shiloh Baptist Church and try to speak with Doris after the service. I needed to pray with community, not turn away from them.

I went downstairs to the big front porch and found Madelon sitting in the old brown rocking chair with the cracked and faded red leather cushions. She sat with her legs tucked underneath her, while Ben leaned back, a little precariously, in a tubular aluminum chair. In the background, an aged floor fan whirred noisily and stirred the air. Creamy gardenia blossoms heavy with sweetness weighed down the branches of a bush off to one side.

I'd already told Ben and Madelon that we were not going to film the service at Shiloh this morning. Even though the minister had given us permission, I needed to show up by myself, unburdened with cameras and recorders. They were relieved to not have to load gear and set up in a new location. We had a quick breakfast together of toast and cantaloupe, then I took off for Shiloh alone.

The organ had just started up as I slipped through the swinging back doors from the vestibule into the church. Doris was sitting up front in her usual spot in the front row, dressed in a white suit with long fringe falling from the shoulders. She turned around and nodded when she saw me. Willie Mae Brown was in the row behind me with a few other women whom I'd seen before at services. I relaxed, glad to be there after all.

After the service, I immediately went up to Doris and asked if she had time to speak with me. She stood still for a moment and then said, "Well, I suppose we could do that, alright." She warned me that I would have to wait for twenty to thirty minutes. As an officer of the church and the secretary of the congregation, she had a series of responsibilities to discharge first. I told her I'd be glad to wait.

The service had been conducted by a visiting preacher who seemed to be waiting around for someone himself. I went up to thank him for his remarks about the passage "Without a vision, the people perish," and somehow we ended up in a wide-ranging theological discussion. He eventually changed the subject.

"Are you waiting for Doris Vittatoe?" he asked.

I told him I was.

"You know," he said, "I heard that somebody asked her to get everyone to sign over their rights to Love Cemetery."

I felt the blood leaving my face. I could hardly believe the level of misunderstanding that this had escalated into within twenty-four hours. He went on. "You hear anything about that?"

No, I told him, I hadn't heard that. It made no sense to me. There must be a misunderstanding, I said. I thanked him for visiting with me and left the vestibule.

I went outside to wait in the 101-degree heat. I found a towel in the trunk of my rental car and spread it out under a sweet gum tree on the church's newly mowed lawn. I was rattled by the minister's comments. Had he been testing me, knowing that I was the alleged culprit in the rumor? Or was he genuinely unaware that I was involved with Love Cemetery? I couldn't tell. I didn't know how to read the signs. What I did grasp immediately was that this small black church community had a swift and efficient way to get the word out when one of the their members was troubled or felt threatened.

There was an undeniable value to this reaction. The genius of the black church lay in its response to the lives of its people. It had grown beyond itself to become a way of life that carried people through enslavement, through Emancipation and Reconstruction, and through the decades of upheaval, migration, lynchings, injustice, and discrimination that followed. The African American church was the alchemical vessel in which elements of the old African spiritual culture transformed the Christianity imposed from slave days into something life-sustaining and unique. The church was the place where the community was "built up," as R.D. would say.

That morning it had been announced in church that the son of a congregation member had just graduated from the University of Texas law school, passed his bar exam, and taken his first job with a law firm in Austin. Everyone burst into applause. Good news was celebrated; sorrow was contained.

But I was startled and disturbed by the rumor's speed, power, and inaccuracy. It had already passed right by the actual event and taken on a life of its own. It let me know that the misunderstanding between Doris and me was even more complicated than I had imagined.

Doris finally came through the doors of the church and joined me on the grass, spreading out a towel to sit on too. She seemed as puzzled as I was. We started out with small talk: "How are you doing?" "How are you doing?" As soon as I felt it appropriate, I repeated my apology from the day before for whatever I might have done to offend her. I was willing to be instructed. Would she please tell me what happened from her perspective?

For the next half-hour, Doris and I spoke cordially. But no matter how hard she tried to tell me what had happened from her side, I couldn't understand. Nor, I knew, could she understand what I was saying. We both were trying to speak truthfully and clearly, but neither one had the words to articulate why we each felt so wounded and confused. We were two people trying to speak to each other under water. Everything was garbled.

It became clear the more we struggled to talk that a phone message I'd left on her machine a week earlier asking her to help me get people's signatures on the releases had touched a raw nerve. Doris had fallen back on her one experience as a movie extra. She had not been asked to sign anything back then, so why now? I countered by talking about the changing nature of the media today and the litigious bent of our society. The stately sweet gum tree was our only witness as we rehashed our positions. When I spoke, Doris listened carefully, nodding her head, and when she spoke, I did my best to hear her without resistance or reaction. But something essential was missing.

"I understand that friends have misunderstandings," Doris said finally. "People make mistakes," she added softly, "they misinterpret each other." She seemed to accept the fact that I had meant no harm.

I heaved a sigh of relief. It seemed that she at least understood that nothing I had done was intentional. And yet, I sensed that we were in the magnetic pull of something so much larger than the two of us that we could not possibly make out its shape.

Doris and I walked to our cars. She got in hers and was about to turn the key in the ignition when I knocked on her driver's window. She rolled it down.

My words tumbled out. "Doris, please understand. I don't care about the release," I said. "It's beside the point now. Forget it. The whole documentary idea was just a dream anyway. I got ahead of myself. I'm a writer, not a filmmaker." I paused for breath. "The most important thing to me is our friendship. Can you understand that?"

She nodded, but I couldn't read her face.

I was over half an hour late for an interview with R.D. back at my cousins' house. I couldn't have left Doris any sooner. Madelon and Ben would have set up the camera and microphone by now. I checked my voice mail as I drove away from the church. There was an impatient message from Ben wondering where I was.

I flew through a tunnel of tall East Texas piney woods, then past a new clear-cut, a red dirt cutout on my right, then bore down on the old Motley cemetery (black), then the woods again, a field of locust trees, a house. I rolled down a gentle hillside and crossed over Harrison Bayou as it ran out to Caddo Lake.

Cleared pastures whooshed by on both sides; I passed my great-uncle Peter Fax's farm in a heartbeat. I glimpsed the rusted-out, honeysuckle-entwined gate to Verhalen Lake. Rock Springs Cemetery (black) loomed on the other side of the fence from the Scott cemetery (white). I caught a flash of marble angel wings, and then the springs for which people settled here flowing under a wisteria-covered pagoda. I crested the hill, where I had to slow down and turn left. This hill was the highest point in Harrison County, and hence determined which way the waters would drain. East, all the waters ran into Harrison Bayou and Caddo Lake. West, they drained into the Sabine River in adjacent Panola County. On the right, wisteria grew thirty feet high and more, climbed the telephone pole, wrapped itself on the line, and spread over the fifty-foot pines. On the left were the homes of two more of my Verhalen cousins. I felt the rumble of tires running over loose railroad ties and braked hard as I crossed the tracks, coming up on the Scottsville Community Center and the old Verhalen Nursery barn still falling in on itself, waiting to be cleared away. The nursery closed in 1976. I glided by a tranquil marsh, a small, still lake with two white egrets flying low over their own reflections. Tall cumulus clouds rested on its surface. I sped past the two-fire-truck barn and down between a mile of white-fenced pasture on the right and a fringe of woods on the left, thinned so you could see the pastures just on the other side of what used to be my family's flower fields—fields of jonquils, King Alfred daffodils, narcissus, roses, wisteria, balled stock, Cedars of Lebanon, Voorhees Cedar, privet, American hollies, nandina—I didn't know the names of all they grew. Only that I still hurt inside. Only that I still didn't understand what had happened with Doris.

As I turned into the drive and pulled up to the house, I could see Ben filming a conversation between R.D. and Philip. They were sitting comfortably in the shade of the long front porch. Madelon held the boom-mounted microphone between them, out of camera range. The crunch of my tires on gravel interrupted their recording. Ben looked as if he'd relaxed since he left the voice mail on my cell phone. A warm wave of pleasure washed over me. My family, R.D., everyone seemed happy and engaged. I parked under some Spanish oaks where a mockingbird was singing.

R.D. seemed glad to see me. I detected none of the caution I'd sensed from Doris, but I didn't know R.D. as well. I apologized for being late and added that I'd had a little misunderstanding with Doris and had stayed at church to speak with her since I would leaving town tomorrow.

R.D. leaned back a little in the brown rocking chair and smiled. I thought what I said had gone by him and was relieved that he made nothing of it. He and Philip went back to their conversation as I pulled up a chair and sat down with them. Ben signaled to Madelon that he was recording again, and she unobtrusively raised the mike. R.D. turned to me.

"Look, I'm not responsible, China, how you treat me. But I am responsible for how I treat you. The only thing we really have to do is trust."

I recognized from R.D.'s cadence that he had started in on a spontaneous, personal sermon.

"You have to have faith. Faith is the substance of things unseen," he continued. "I don't see it but I just have a feeling. That's faith. And that's where he wants all of his children to be, in faith. And if we keep the faith in Jesus Christ, we'll be able to weather the storm.

"If you remember the story when Paul was in that shipwreck, they got out on the ocean and ran into a storm that tore up that ship, and Paul got a word from God tellin' him, 'Paul, tell your passengers to stay on board. If they stay on board, no one will be lost. Although the ship is tore up, you got to stay on board.' All them in the water, everyone had his hand on a piece of that boat, holdin' on. Now what you think about that? They were a-cryin' and a-sobbin' … sure they were goin' to drown, but they stayed on board!"

I was aware of nothing but R.D.'s voice resonating between the arches of the porch, giving me something to hold on to.

"That's the only thing you got to do—'stay on board'—put your faith and trust in him, and he will see you through. It may seem hopeless, you may not see your way out, but all you got to do is trust in him. He said, 'I'm the way maker, I make ways out of no way. When you can't see your way, that's what my eyes are for. I got eyes that never shut.'"

There was nothing I could say but "thank you, R.D., I needed that." I was amazed by how thoroughly he seemed to understand that I was struggling, though I had said nothing to him about anything. He was telling me through his own language of parable that giving up was not an option. That I didn't need to figure everything out. I didn't need to understand why he was telling me these things, whether his sermonizing was a coincidence, or if it was just the way he spoke to everyone, or if he knew something that I didn't. It didn't matter, it was a gift to me in that moment. I just needed to "stay on board."

By late afternoon, a thunderstorm was moving into the area, and there were severe-weather warnings posted. Thunder rumbled, a light rain fell, then stopped close to six in the evening. At the last minute, Philip's sister, our cousin Mary Lou, called up with an offer Ben and Madelon and I could not resist, exhausted though we all were. She and her husband, Charlie Reeves, an avid bass fisherman in his late fifties, would take us out on Caddo Lake in their boat. Then we could have catfish at Johnson's Landing, overlooking the bayou. Could we meet them in half an hour at the boat landing for a run? We could.

We were out on the water by seven in the evening, when the light was glowing pink and gold. Charlie was up front, Mary Lou in a seat behind him, next were Madelon and me with Ben just behind us, in the last seat, his arms around us both, his head touching Madelon's. A green, violet, rose, blue, and gold rainbow shone over Mary Lou's head.

Madelon and I hadn't been to the lake together since we went canoeing here twenty years earlier, the summer before she left for college. The dark-haired woman in her mid-thirties sitting next to me was such a different person from the quiet seventeen-year-old who had drunk in the wild beauty of Caddo Lake twenty years ago. She had crossed so many waters since then. I wondered if she was also remembering our last time together on this lake.

I remembered how all those years ago we had started out before dawn. Just as we paddled out of a bald cypress grove into open water, the sun rose, pulsing and blinding us with a light so fierce that, for a moment, we could see nothing and had to stop. Then the sun caught the early mist and burned it off in a blaze of mauves, salmons, and pinks—fire on the water.

As the sun rose, the birds started up, first only one or two but soon a chorus that seemed to wake up the frogs and set the insects buzzing. We started paddling again, moving slowly into the revelation that surrounded us. Rising still, the sun scattered its light into a million tiny mirrors rippling into reflections on the steely green surface, reflecting so much brightness that my eyes could barely take it in. Our guide disappeared from view in the labyrinthine bayous. I asked Madelon, in the bow, to stop paddling. I was blinded. I closed my eyes and rested my paddle across my knees. The canoe rocked gently from side to side as we sat together quietly, breathing, feeling the warm honeyed light pour over us, a benediction, until the boat was still. By the time I opened my eyes, the dark greens and reds of cypress were paling fast, the gray-green of mosses fading. The world was changing every second, turning and turning, no way to stop it.

I felt the landscape breathe—the birds sailed off on its exhalation, then settled back down on the branches, its inhalation. We were part of this great breathing out over the waters of creation. For a moment it was easy to understand that everything continued, nothing was ever over.

"Mom, look!" Madelon cried, bringing my attention into the boat. "Something's moving, in the duckweed, there." She asked if I could see the tiny brilliant yellow beads that had appeared on the surface. I could see tiny movements all over the mantle of duckweed, making it ripple and come alive. "Watch," Madelon said. "Frogs, Mom, there's hundreds of them. It's their eyes we're seeing. Just their eyes, moving."

We started paddling again. I had to shade my eyes to read the water, the light was still so blinding. I thought we'd lost our guide altogether, he'd surged so far ahead, until I noticed that there was a ribbon of darkness moving across the surface, a hundred or so feet ahead. It was opening and closing, opening and closing. I whispered to Madelon. She saw it too. It was the wake of our guide's canoe folding back in on itself, showing us the way back. That's what we followed—that darkening of the water, its stirring. It was all we could see, but it was enough. A line from the old hymn "God's Gonna Trouble the Waters" came back to me.

All these years later, Caddo still enchanted me. Whatever had been unsettled in me back on land was washed away in the spray of the turns Charlie took us through. We motored between two islands, approaching the favorite bass fishing spot he wanted to show Ben. Charlie cut the motor and pulled out fishing poles for himself and Ben. Suddenly we were bathed in the lake's quiet—and the sounds of frogs. Mary Lou was quiet also. Madelon smiled. We drifted slowly past pale yellow lotus blossoms. The lake's current was all that moved us now, and we were free to marvel at the way water beaded on the two-foot-wide lily pads. Refracted in those drops of water we could see our boat with Madelon leaning over the side to marvel at their jewel-like clarity, and me, behind her, worlds within worlds.

The next day, Ben and Madelon went back to Dallas to visit their grandmother, my mother, Ruth Verhalen Langdon. I stayed over in Scottsville to finish up my research as best I could and pick up the pieces of the story. I still felt storm-tossed, but I saw a way to "stay on board:" go back to the early history of Love Cemetery. The obligation I felt I had to the Ancestors themselves didn't stop with the restoration of the cemetery. I also needed to piece together the untold story of this place, its secret history. I wanted to understand how I fit into it—if, indeed, I had a place at all or if, as Doris had blurted out, I was not needed.

I planned to drive to Dallas that evening. With one day left in East Texas, I quickly packed and drove a few miles to Marshall,

the county seat. The courthouse had become a familiar haunt
from the many hours I'd spent researching the history of Kizzie's
grandfather's land. That day, as I walked down the white-walled,
beige-wainscoted hall, I could see, through the double glass
doors, that the county clerk's office was unusually busy.

When I walked in, the room was packed with fifty or sixty
people. Rollers squealed and made tiny screeches as people
pulled out volumes of records that weighed ten to fifteen pounds
each. They were so heavy they had to be stored horizontally.
Three copy machines whined and clicked steadily in the background. People were standing in lines to use them. The room
was a beehive.

When I got to a table with the volume I needed, I asked the
woman next to me why it was so crowded. She told me that she
was a landwoman—almost everyone in the office that morning was a landman or woman—and that she was researching oil
and gas leases and mineral rights. The man on the other side of
me was from California. From what she said, I gathered that
these folks were tracing the sometimes impossibly tangled
threads of land ownership in East Texas in hopes that they could
discover leases that were still available or overlooked mineral
rights that might be purchased. This was all part of a general
frenzy to reexamine existing domestic supplies of oil and natural
gas and to find new ones. The price of crude had taken off with
the invasion of Iraq. With new technology, there was hope of getting more oil and gas out of old wells, and the funds were available to make it a priority. The landpeople were either freelancers
or employees of any number of oil companies, land speculators,
investment groups—anyone, really, who recognized the skyrock-
eting value of domestic properties that had any potential of

yielding up more oil or natural gas. I thanked her for the lesson and got to work.

The landman from California showed me how to handle the heavy volumes and remove the pages I needed. I did manage to turn up a deed record for Della Love's father, Wilson Love: a purchase of 225 acres northeast of Marshall with three partners, and a second deed as well, of a 56½-acre purchase. I looked up the original deed to the cemetery again. It was as I had recalled: a "burial plot," dated August 9, 1904, when Della deeded the land to the Love Colored Burial Association. But where did Della get the land she deeded Love? Had her father willed her some of his property? She was born the year he died. Had she bought it herself, like Lizzie Sparks, Nuthel's grandmother, was said to have done with her farm nearby?

I asked the landman from California how one went about getting a photocopy of a record under the circumstances.

"We're on the honor system here," he explained, "it's so crowded. You make your own copies and just keep track of how many. Put the pages back where you got them."

The honor system? Fortunes could be made and destroyed here, depending on these records. What was to prevent an attractive record from simply disappearing?

While I waited in line, first to make the photocopy, then to pay for it, I ran through the story as I had pieced it together so far.

Wilson Love, Della's father, was reportedly a free black man, born in 1829. I had learned from materials in the County Historical Society that his father was Robert Love, an Irishman who owned a plantation in the western part of Harrison County. His mother, whose name is lost, was one of Robert Love's enslaved African women, a "house slave."

As the son of a white plantation owner, Wilson might have been brought up outside of slavery altogether as a free black man or been given his freedom at some later point. Before the Civil War, free black men were rare. Texas had outlawed their entry, perceiving them as dangerous and liable to give enslaved people "ideas." The settlers were already having problems with their labor force running away to Mexico, where slavery had been outlawed in 1821, as I'd discovered earlier.

In the only photograph of Wilson Love that I could find, he gazes forcefully at the camera. He has high, sculpted cheekbones and a carefully trimmed goatee. His brother, Nathaniel or Nat Love, was the famous black cowboy "Deadwood Dick," who rode throughout the West and was befriended by the likes of Wyatt Earp. By now, little about the Loves could surprise me. For example, I discovered that Wilson's first wife was named Phoebe Love before Wilson married her. She had apparently once belonged to a different family of white slaveholding Loves. Might they already have been related?

Sometime in the 1870s, after fathering several children with her, Wilson left Phoebe and married Sarah Williams. By then, he and his partners had purchased nearly three hundred acres in the northeast part of the county. Still, one cannot conclude that this is the area where Love Cemetery is found. There are thousands of acres in the northeast part of the county, and there were Loves up around Caddo Lake, also northeast of Marshall, both black and white families. The Love I tracked down claimed no relation to Della and her father's line.

I wanted to assume that the area around Love belonged to Della's father and that it was passed on to her when he died.

I was unable to find out if Love Cemetery corresponds with

land that was owned by Wilson Love and his partners in the 1870s. It's reasonable to assume that there's some connection; however, there may be no connection, no matter how reasonable the assumption might seem. Tracing land ownership in East Texas was famously frustrating, with all its dead ends, loopholes, missing pieces of information, and missing records, to say nothing of the number of nineteenth-century courthouses that burned down. In one fire, only records of black land ownership burned.

The nineteenth-century maps that I found years ago showed a lot of "invalid" surveys. It was explained that an "invalid" survey was a nice way of saying that the question of ownership had come to blows, generally in a gunfight. In some cases, the name on the "valid" survey was actually a record of who was the best shot, not who had the legitimate claim. The gentleman who explained these things refused to be quoted or named, since clearing titles was such a loaded subject still.

Years ago, one of the former owners of a local title company in Marshall told me that a lot of black land ownership was put together in the 1870s and the 1880s by former slaveholders who had fathered black children. They wanted to help their offspring once they saw how difficult it was for African Americans to establish themselves.[42]

Some African Americans (like Deacon Hagerty) spoke of white friends and white relatives who helped their ancestors get their own land. Yet many African Americans acquired land with no help from white people, only by dint of phenomenally hard work, not only farming but hauling, clearing, sewing, cleaning—almost any manual labor. One African American family showed me a deed carefully handed down in their family that showed that they had bought and paid for their land with bales of cotton.

In 1883, Wilson and Sarah Williams Love had twin girls, Della and Stella. Wilson died at the age of fifty-one that same year. I'd already found out that he had been declared mentally incompetent by the Harrison County courts in 1882, but I hadn't been able to find out anything about the nature of Wilson's breakdown. Was it really mental illness, or might it have been a device used by family members to gain control of his estate? The two wives fought to be appointed administrator of his estate. A court battle ensued, with an administrator finally appointed in 1890. Though I looked it up again that morning, I could still find no record of the disposition of Wilson Love's estate. I could not confirm whether Della had, in fact, inherited Wilson's land. Yet she clearly must have owned enough land by 1904 to bequeath the small parcel to the Love Colored Burial Association. Della, according to a family account, married Lee Walker and moved to Oklahoma, where they had five children and lived on a Native American reservation in Chickasaw County. According to the family history, Della died in 1920 from poisoning.

By now I'd made the photocopies of the deed records I had pulled and had returned the originals and put the oversized volume back in its place at the county clerk's office. The room was gradually emptying, as people headed out for lunch. There were still a few people ahead of me in the line to pay for the copies, though. I stood there wondering whether this flurry of research on Della Love was necessary that morning or whether it was a distraction from thinking about what had happened with

Doris. I asked myself what I hoped to find embedded in these pages covered with the tight, formal, extraordinarily curvilinear nineteenth-century handwriting.

I wanted confirmation of the hidden story that existed among the shards and fragments we had been discovering at the cemetery, among the memories of the elders and in the scraps of records here in the courthouse. I wanted to know more about the secret history of what seemed to have been a thriving black farm community that had existed in eastern Harrison County from sometime after the Civil War until sometime in the 1950s or 1960s—the community that Doris's great-grandfather, Ohio Taylor, and Nuthel's grandmother, Lizzie Sparks, were part of.

Sabine Farms, Marshall, Texas, 1930s

Sabine Farms of the 1930s—the ten-thousand-acre resettlement project for black farmers—we knew about, but the area known as Love seemed to have left no written trace.[43]

But I was beginning to understand that I was looking in the wrong place. There was an inherent problem in trying to coax the story of the black experience from these records. Here the story would be told by the silences, the omissions, the gaps in the records, what was missing. The records did not say whether a title was obtained ethically. They didn't indicate whether a transaction was proper or if it was an egregious theft. The records, I realized, were the victor's story. They were elaborate lists of who ended up with the title, not whether they had gained the title legally or ethically. That information was not recorded.

Finally it was my turn at the counter. Since there was no one in the line behind me, I had a moment to chat with the clerk, a woman about my age. I told her about Della Love and the difficulty I'd had finding a record of her ownership of the parcel from which she had deeded the acreage to Love Cemetery. She had no suggestions other than visiting the Historical Society, which was my next stop anyway. I commented on how packed with land-people the office had been just moments ago. That was the way things were lately, she allowed. Then, in a quiet voice, she told me that there was a troubling side to all this activity. The land-people at work here were scouting for a number of large corporations that were intensely interested in oil leases and mineral rights. The clerk—who asked me not to use her name when I wrote about this—was aware of cases of elderly people, especially black elders, who had accepted offers to sell the mineral rights to land they were living on, only to discover that because of some loophole, they had sold the land itself and suddenly had nowhere to live. The kind of land theft that had haunted me in the years since I heard Kizzie's story was still taking place.

Later, I would speak with Spencer Wood, a professor who is a nationally recognized expert on black farmers and black land ownership.[44] Spencer confirmed that while it might not be possible to verify stories like the one the clerk told me that day in Marshall or the one that Kizzie had shared with me earlier, both of them were, as he put it, "completely in keeping with a pattern of deceit and depredation that has led to a lot of black people losing their land."[45] In the end, the name on the deed is all that counts, not how it got there.

The pattern Spencer spoke of was as old as Reconstruction. Like segregation, disenfranchisement, and lynching, land theft had grown and thrived in the long shadow that slavery still cast—in spite of its abolition. In fact, all of these horrors could be seen as responses to the new possibilities that had opened to African Americans after Emancipation, even as forms of revenge for daring to even begin to claim the rights of education, the vote, ownership of property, employment, freedom of movement, and equal opportunity.

I left the courthouse sick at heart. At a moment like this, racism seemed so deeply rooted in—what? Society? The System? These were abstractions. If racism lived anywhere, it was inside each of us, sometimes consciously, often unconsciously. With racism rooted inside us and cultivated over centuries, we have institutionalized our prejudice and built white bias and privilege so thoroughly into the structures of our society that we mistake it for normalcy. Like the wisteria at the cemetery, perhaps we'll never be rid of it. Our only hope might be to keep attending to it, trimming it here, uprooting it there, cutting it back, cutting it back, and contending with it.

From the county clerk's office, I went a few blocks north to the train station and the old Ginocchio Hotel, which housed the Harrison County Historical Society Library and Museum. The volunteer librarian, white-haired Edna Sorber, with her bright blue eyes, was a trained librarian by profession. It was Edna who had helped me find everything I'd gathered about the Love family. She introduced me to their library.

Edna had nothing new to tell me but suggested I talk to Jimmy Oliphant before I left town. Jimmy was a retired military man whose ancestors on both sides had owned slaves. Like Edna, he volunteered at the Historical Society. When she told me about the unusual task he had taken on, the way another person might go on pilgrimage or join the Peace Corps, I was impressed. Jimmy had decided to find, record, and index the name of every single person who had been enslaved in Harrison County. Edna thought maybe he'd come across someone in the Love family, or something about Robert Love's plantation.

Jimmy was sitting in an old-fashioned wooden library chair near the corner of a long library table, wearing a gray shirt the color of his hair, and jeans and boots. He unfolded his tall frame and stood up to greet me, asking after my family. I sat down across from him, where the mid-afternoon light streamed through the long casement windows.

Jimmy used deeds, wills, bills of sale—anything that listed slaves—as a source for names. Until the census of 1870, enslaved people did not have last names, so Jimmy was compiling an index of first names. As a volunteer at the Historical Society, he had taken it upon himself to answer every query that came in from African Americans wanting to trace their ancestry. He showed me what he was working on that day.

"I got someone writing me who's looking for a 'Henry Cook,'" he said in a gravelly voice with a southern drawl. "They know he was born in 1855." He pointed to a stack of paper. "So I got my list out and I went lookin' at the Henrys. There's about a dozen Henrys on there, but only one of them was born in 1855." He grinned, deepening the creases in his well-worn face. But the grin faded as he went on. "I found him in some property records dated 1859. He was four years old and belonged to the William J. Blocker estate."

The 1870 census, which listed black peoples' full names, was first census after the Civil War. Newly freed people made up names, took names of their heroes, of occupations, sometimes of former owners if they'd been halfway decent. After finding him in the 1859 property record, Jimmy then found Henry's last name in the 1870 census by looking for his mother, Hannah, matching ages. Hannah Cook was listed with Henry's name under hers. Maybe Hannah had been a cook on the Blocker estate. Hannah and Henry, rescued from oblivion.

Jimmy grew silent. His already deep-set blue eyes receded further under his brow as he scanned one of the photocopied lists. After a moment he said, "It's hard to look at these. Just a name with a price after it, like 'Sarah, 13, $900,' or 'John, blacksmith, $1,800,' and 'Elizabeth, 50, $400.' And turn the page, now look at this one: 'Sarah, very old, $5.' Or how about this: 'Sterling, 5 weeks, $100.'"

List of enslaved people of Mimosa Hall plantation,
Harrison County, Texas. Original text from a planter's journal: "Inventory and
Appraisement of the Property of
the Estate of John Webster."

He drew in his breath with a sniff: "And sometimes you'd see horses and cows and pigs on the same page. They just lumped people in with livestock and traded 'em. Slaves were livestock—property—and that's kind of hard to comprehend." He cleared his throat. Then, he said "oh," as if he had remembered something. "I ran across a strange one here," he said, "doing my Hilliard research."

I knew that Jeremy Hilliard was Jimmy's great-great-grandfather and that he'd been a well-off planter. Jimmy explained that Hilliard had a stepdaughter who married a man named James Sims.

"Now, look here," he pulled another photocopy from a manila envelope. "James Sims owned a slave named Henry Sims." He paused to make sure I was following. "James Sims. Henry Sims. Henry was James's half-brother." His bushy gray eyebrows rose, then he shrugged his shoulders and turned up his open palms.

"A person could own his brother." He chuckled softly as though he didn't know what else to do about this disturbing discovery but to make light of it.

I felt awkward too, and changed the subject to Della Love, but Jimmy told me he hadn't run across any Loves yet.

I thanked both Jimmy and Edna for keeping the Historical Society Library—this rich resource—open. They promised to let me know if anything about the Loves showed up in their research.

I made a quick stop by Nuthel's home to say goodbye. I found her outside collecting the mail, wearing a brown straw hat from her large collection. She invited me in for iced tea, but I knew that if I accepted, any chance for a timely departure to Dallas would be wiped out by Nuthel's generous hospitality. Besides, I enjoyed visiting with her. I begged off and we stayed outside, catching up.

She was happy we'd made so much progress on Saturday. She asked me again if I'd liked the beans that she had picked from her own garden and cooked for the potluck. I told her I had, though I did not tell her that, in truth, I had been too taken up with Doris's anger and my own to notice what I was eating that day.

"You know," she said, "I am real happy that Coach, R.D., and Philip—and we'll see who else—are going back out there in September with their tractors. Now that's gonna be something, to finish it off from like it is."

The September cleanup would be the first one to happen without me. That's good, I thought. It's healthy for the group to rotate the leadership, for someone else to take over. Yet I couldn't help letting Doris's words about not needing me color my feelings about the day. I said nothing to Nuthel about any of this, just gave her a long goodbye hug and resisted telling her I'd changed my mind and would come in for tea after all. I would miss her.

I backed out of her driveway and headed away. I could see Nuthel waving in my rearview mirror until the road curved, and then she was out of sight. The three-hour drive between Marshall and Dallas would be good. Three hours to begin to digest all that had happened in the last few days: the complexities of human relationships; the intricacies of slavery, with relatives "owning" each other and the mixed blood; the hidden history of land theft, and the land theft still going on.

Even a few minutes with Nuthel had been a balm. She lived with a kind of healthy distance from the world, in a place that was informed by the perspectives of age, education, and travel. Above all, she was, as she'd said many times, a farmer. She was grounded in the land itself.

That deep connection to the land was shared by almost all the people who had been drawn into the communal effort at Love. I was convinced of the connection between our treatment of the land

and our relations with our fellow humans. The racial wound, so deep that it was making itself felt between Doris and me despite our best efforts, had its origins in the same worldview that had led to the cruel and thoughtless exploitation of the earth. It seemed no accident that East Texas, historically considered one of the most racist parts of the state, should also be home to one of the worst toxic "superfund" sites in the country, Longhorn Munitions.[46]

I did not want to be alone with these thoughts. I had one friend, besides Philip, who might share this bubbling stew of historical, environmental, sociological, and human concern. Born and raised in the area, my friend was one of the engineers brought in to analyze the hazardous materials at the Longhorn, the eight-thousand-acre "superfund" site adjoining Caddo Lake and its rare and fragile wetlands. Caddo Lake is also the community water supply for the area. My friend had explained how the plant manufactured rocket fuel during the Cold War, and then years later, when hitherto unknown toxins were discovered at the site, the scientists were called in. It turned out that the plant had also been charged with experimenting with explosives. In doing so, toxic compounds were created that never existed before or since. Detoxifying the most dangerous parts of this site was complicated beyond imagining. Nonetheless the site was being designated a National Wildlife Refuge.

I was able to stop and visit with my friend on my way back to Dallas. She was glad to hear from me and eager to hear the latest developments at Love Cemetery. I filled her in on the progress we'd made and how invaluable the generous sense of community of my cousin, Philip, whom she knew, had been.

I quickly got to the part about Doris and me. When I told her about Doris's reaction to the releases I had asked people to sign, the first thing she said was, "Of course Doris would be upset by a white person coming in and saying 'just sign here.'" Her father, who'd grown up in that area, had told her that during the Depression, one of the local storekeepers had offered people cash to "help them through the hard times." The "store system" again. All they had to do was sign a piece of paper. At that time, out in the country many of the African American people he dealt with were illiterate and not by choice. The forces arrayed against their becoming literate were legion, including the infamous Jim Crow laws, which were a holdover from slavery. They didn't understand the severe terms of the "loan" he gave them, described in papers they couldn't read, and which they had to sign with Xs or else not be able to put in the season's crops or feed and clothe their families. Many lost the deeds to their land. The storekeeper ended up being one of the biggest landowners in the area. "It caused a huge amount of bitterness among black folks," she explained, "and deepened mistrust of whites."

Though the storekeeper in her father's story was infamous, I now understood all too well how pervasive was the practice of taking deeds to African Americans' land in exchange for cash or flour, sugar, cloth, or seed. This was how the plantation system of bondage reasserted itself, how whites attempted to regain control over a black work force they could no longer call their own. Whether it was called "the store system" or was actually debt peonage, which is a crime, each time I encountered an iteration of this system, I developed a clearer sense of the deep, ingrown resistance to the very idea of black land ownership that was embedded in white history.

Now I began to understand that I had unwittingly stepped into an archetypal role. I had become the white-person-with-a-piece-of-paper for the black person to sign. If this was true, how could Doris not feel suspicious? Whatever had come between us was larger than the two of us, too large for us to be able to talk about. Even language itself was part of the problem, full of unconscious associations. Our interchange had taken place within a context in which African Americans had suffered devastating economic consequences anytime they signed the white man's paper.

I drove into Dallas close to dusk. I wanted to get off the freeway as soon as possible. I needed to slow down. I needed to collect myself before walking into my mother's for a late dinner. Though we had not yet spoken of what I was doing in much detail, my mother, Ruth, among all the family and friends I had in Dallas, seemed to grasp what I was trying to accomplish at Love Cemetery.

I turned off at Lemmon Avenue, an older, crosstown street that would take me to Turtle Creek, a graceful, curving street that followed the path of the creek. As I sat at a long red light at Lemmon, I realized that directly across the intersection, at the corner of Lemmon and Central, was the Dallas Freedman's Cemetery. That's where I needed to stop. I turned off when the light changed, parked my car, and got out.

The Dallas Freedman's Cemetery and Memorial Park was a long way from the remoteness of Love Cemetery. The Freedman's Cemetery is the largest reburial project to date in the United States, with 1,157 remains reinterred in 1994. The Freedman's Cemetery project was even larger than the African Burial Ground Project in New York, which is now a National Monument.[47]

On either side of the marble entry arch were two larger than life-size dark cast bronze sculptures by David Newman. On the

left was a powerful, calm, broad-shouldered African warrior
holding a large sword with its tip to the ground between his feet,
a cemetery guardian who looked directly at anyone approaching
the entry. On the right side was a serene, regal woman, draped
in a graceful robe, turbaned, and holding a lyre. This figure too
gazed directly at me as I walked closer. Both had the faintest
hint of a smile. The woman depicted was the "griote," the keeper
of communal memory. Both the warrior and the griote had an
uncanny presence, a command of their worlds. The sculptures
were simple and stunning. I peered through the iron bars of the
locked entry gate between them and saw a walkway with an incised marble slab in the center. Off to the right was a well-
tended grove of post oaks surrounded by recently cut grass. No
one was in sight. The peacefulness of the place, the mystery,
beckoned.

I walked the perimeter looking for another way in but could
find nothing. Across the street was Greenwood Cemetery, one of
the oldest in Dallas, and across from that, Calvary Cemetery. It
was a quiet neighborhood of cemeteries on two sides and high-
speed traffic on the other two. Why this park had been locked
every time I had driven by on my way to and from East Texas
was beyond me. I'd been wanting to see it from the inside for
over a year. It was a well-kept place, inviting and clearly meant
to be used.

After pacing back and forth, I finally found a way in that no
one seemed to have noticed. I kept looking around, unable to
understand why this memorial was locked up when all the surrounding cemeteries had their gates open. They had elaborate
marble carvings and headstones, carefully incised granite markers, tiny streets within name "Hope," and "Faith," whereas the

Freedmen's Memorial had no individual markers, only a quiet grove of oak trees. Still, there was no one around, only speeding cars and the dead. I slipped in and quickly found myself standing on the site of Freedman's Town, once a remarkably vibrant, self-sustaining black community.

A vagrancy ordinance passed in 1865 in Dallas on the heels of Emancipation imposed fines and a six-month prison term on blacks for walking on Dallas streets. This draconian legislation directed against African Americans, along with other discriminatory conditions that persisted well into the twentieth century—prohibitions against black participation in civic life, lack of schools, churches, medical care, housing, transportation, jobs, economic opportunities, banks, public bathrooms, social clubs, swimming pools, athletics, and voting rights, to begin with—led to the growth of Freedman's Town, which, in those early days, stood outside the Dallas city limits. It had been established just after Emancipation as African Americans tried to reconnect with family and find employment.

During its heyday, which seems to have lasted into the 1930s and 1940s, Freedman's Town housed four black churches, which had each started grade schools and a high school. The *Dallas Express,* the African American community newspaper, was established in 1892. There were women's associations—the Ladies Reading Circle was started in 1891, to mention one of dozens. The first local black Masonic Lodge was organized in 1876 in Freedman's Town. There was a center for music and concerts where local black jazz and blues musicians like Blind Lemmon Jefferson and bands from New Orleans often stopped to play on their tours of the country. There was a swimming pool, a YWCA, and a branch of the public library. Freedman's Town had its own medical clinics staffed by black doctors, dentists, and nurses, its own funeral home, bank, insurance companies, art clubs, movie theater, and cemetery. Freedman's Town became the center of black intellectual, social, educational, religious, and cultural life for a good part of the city.

As Dallas grew, it lost the name Freedman's Town; the area became North Dallas and was incorporated into the city. Burials in the Freedman's Cemetery reportedly continued into the 1920s, when the City of Dallas Sanitation Department forced its closure, supposedly because of overcrowding, a claim later proven to be false. The cemetery itself, where I sat that evening, was turned into a park for children.

Part of the cemetery was desecrated and paved over in the 1940s. The city bulldozed the tombstones, ground them up for road fill for the big freeway, and opened Central Expressway with enormous fanfare in 1949—a shining example of civic growth and progress.

Finally, in the 1980s, when the city wanted to widen Central Expressway again, the African American community of Dallas, especially Dr. Robert Prince, a physician in Dallas who had family buried there, and Black Dallas Remembers, under the leadership of educator Mamie McKnight, organized and joined forces with the city preservationists. The City of Dallas, the Texas Department of Transportation, Black Dallas Remembers, the Dallas Historical Commission, the African American Museum of Dallas, and hundreds of volunteers arrived at a compromise: the creation of the Freedman's Cemetery and Memorial Park, in which I sat that night. It took twelve years to negotiate, design, and create the memorial. More land was added to the cemetery to replace what the city had taken and would need for the expansion. Then more than 1,100 burials were reinterred. The city agreed to permanent maintenance of the memorial. The book *Facing the Rising Sun: Freedman's Cemetery* was published and a documentary made for national television.[48] A solemn celebration took place for the opening,

From inside the memorial I could see the figures that had drawn me in. The warrior and griote that guarded the cemetery on the outside appeared again, but inside the memorial they are in chains. Stripped of their power—the sword and the lyre—stripped of their clothing but for the barest covering, they were caught by the sculptor in the moment when they had been thrown off their feet and chained in the hold of a slave ship. Overpowered, broken, and crushed, they lay on either side of the entry arch, on the opposite side of the wall from their former, powerful selves. The warrior now had heavy chains on his left arm, which was thrown back over his eyes. His face turned away from the gaze of the onlooker. The woman, bareheaded now, held her face in her manacled hands. She covered her breasts with her crossed arms. They were frozen forever in this ship's hold, making their way on the hellish Middle Passage from Africa across the Atlantic.

We will never know the exact numbers of Africans kidnapped from their homelands by Muslim traders and warring African tribes. Europeans joined in and fueled the plunder, escalating the number well into the millions. Roughly 20 million people were kidnapped, "disappeared," and an estimated half of those captives, in wooden collars and chains, died on the forced march from the interior of Africa to the coasts. Those who survived were sold to the highest bidder and put aboard ship. Of the more than 11 million sold on the African coast, 9 million survived the horrors of the passage.[49]

The degradation and helplessness of being enslaved was captured more eloquently in each statue's gesture than in the thousands of pages I've read on the history of slavery. I stood in front of first one bronze sculpture, then the other, taking in the images for a long time. I marveled at this simple and magnificently understated memorial to the suffering of America's African ancestors who arrived here in chains. The cruelty of the Middle Passage is emblematic of the brutal history of slavery.

One slave ship captain candidly noted in his journal: "Women were taken aboard trembling and terrified. The prey is divided up on the spot.... Resistance or refusal [to be raped] would be utterly in vain." Once sold, slaves were branded on board with the initials of the ship's owners. Death ravaged the holds below deck before the ships even got started. The author of the hymn "Amazing Grace," John Newton, for many years the captain of a slaving ship, mentions sixty-two people out of two hundred captives dying before his ship could leave shore. Deaths were so common that reportedly sharks circled the ships at anchor, then followed them out to sea. The voyage lasted months, and death dogged them at every turn. Captives rebelled: there were three hundred known uprisings shipboard and countless numbers never recorded. If freed from their shackles, some people jumped overboard rather than remain enslaved. Others refused to eat. Captains and crews administered lashes, they used thumbscrews, they used a metal instrument to force feedings. People rebelled in every way they could. One ship was commandeered by a group of enslaved women, who were able to turn the boat around to Africa but were unable to sail it back by themselves.

We know from the rare journals of former slaves, like Olaudah Equiano, that life in the ship's hold was pure hell. The stench below deck—the combined odors of sweat, urine, feces, and vomit—was suffocating, he reported from firsthand experience. There was little room to move or turn over amid the hundreds of slaves crammed into the holds. The cries of the sick, the groaning, and the calls of the dying gave rise to the moans still heard in African American spirituals.

As I sat in front of these two sculptures, I wondered if it was even possible to imagine the terror of the Middle Passage. Of course I could not, and yet these sculptures gave the unimaginable a face, a sorrow, and a vulnerability so human that they invited me to try. I'd been drawn in by their beauty and power on the outside. Could I now take in their sorrow, their defeat, their cries? If I had any hope of understanding what had happened to my friendship with Doris, I had to try. There was so much pain between us, at least on my side.

I imagined. I imagined that I was living in a village in Africa, that I was out working in a field. There are other women in the field too. I don't know how it happened, but suddenly I am being ripped from the pulsing center of my own life by thick, rough hands; ripped out of my mother's, husband's, children's, father's, sister's, brother's, lover's arms; ripped away and bound, wrist to ankle, forced to march away from everything I've ever known—my native tongue, the shape of my lips as I spoke it, the place in my throat it comes from, the familiar smell of the land after rain, the color of the winter light, the way light beats down in summer, the shapes of the harvest, the smell of my land's wood burning, the shape of the flowers, their smells, their color, the sounds, the tinkle of bells, young children laughing, a wedding song. Little to cover myself with but scraps I've held on to.

Where would I be today, or where would my family be, if 150 years or so ago, only five or six generations back, one of my ancestors had been the one captured and enslaved?

I tried to imagine being crammed into a crowded room with strangers, with no one who speaks my language, waiting, waiting, fighting for scraps, dying for water. For the first time in my life, I am in a place where no one knows my name or the names of my ancestors or the names of my gods. And I begin to forget all these things myself.

Forced to eat strange food that makes me sick, nothing of my home remains except the memories I cling to—that is all I have left, memory, but even my memory is torn, gnawed by the curse of hunger and burning thirst. I stand in my own filth. Soon I will lie in it.

Those hands that stole me now chain me to the floor of the ship's hold. The boat is rocking, rocking me, like my grandmother used to do, but where are her arms? The stench, the wailing, the cacophony of cries—suddenly the person next to me gasps and screams close to my ear. Then she is silent. She has died. The hatch closes. They take away the light. There is barely any air. Consciousness, once a gift, is now the cruelest burden of all. I want nothing so much as to die, but we sail on like this. We speak different languages, yet our moans translate our differences into song. We barely live through this hell. Many don't and are thrown overboard, sometimes dead, sometimes alive. I live.

After this I am put up on the auction block and sold to my "owner." Then there is the journey that follows. I am in chains, whether they show or not. I learn to sing into the cracks, into holes in the ground, into wash pots. I learn to keep my being a secret in order to stay alive.[50]

As I sat in the Dallas memorial at dusk and allowed myself to imagine the life depicted in these bronzes, I began to understand the complexity of this history, its agony, and the devastation of being stripped of family, language, religion, even one's name. I began to understand that healing my relationship with Doris wasn't simple or easy, not at the depth I knew was required. I would have to earn my part of it. In order to even dream that our work at Love Cemetery could succeed, I had to be willing to sit inside the pain of Doris's reaction to my behavior. The fact that much of it was unconscious on my part didn't matter. Something very deep had surfaced. A shadow had fallen across my relationship with Doris. Was it my own racism? Did I assume that good intentions could override my unconscious actions, like the way I documented everything, photographed it, videoed, took notes, and recorded it? Some of this desire came out of the sheer excitement of being entrusted with this story and recognizing its depth. Some of my documenting came out of my own shyness and insecurity, my need to learn experientially, and my need to mask my discomfort first of all from myself.

Was my documentary instinct my craft, or was it my way of avoiding being present? Was it my way of defending myself? I knew what it was like to have people deny my experience. Was I documenting events, or was I buttressing my experience of them in order to control the narrative? I was getting a look at my unconscious white presumption about the white way being "the way things are done." Looking for records in the Harrison County Courthouse had shown me how white people made the rules, kept the records, and wrote the history. There was power in being someone who knew how to use that system. I could see that. Now I was beginning to see the lens of whiteness that I was wearing, beginning to feel the glasses on my own nose, becoming aware of this distortion. I had a long way to go, and I had Doris to thank for piercing the shell of my whiteness, forcing me to see it more.

I sat there alone in the early evening light, still stunned by the breach with Doris, the Scottsville story of land theft my friend told me, and the awareness that driving on Central Expressway meant driving over ground-up tombstones from the Freedman's Cemetery. I sat there, haunted by the knowledge of the community that had once lived, thrived, cared for their dead here, as once the community around Love Cemetery had. The community at Love had arisen out of the same hard times as the Dallas Freedman's Town and had been able to claim the land and work it and prosper, for a time. I knew that I would not be able to write this story if I remained untouched. I had to learn these lessons, no matter how much they hurt. And I had to see that even having my feelings hurt came out of the privilege of being white. I could let this pain take over or I could say thank you for this lesson and be willing to sit and let it drive me deeper, let it broaden me to include more of what I'd been taught was other. It was teaching me that the other was also myself and that we are not separate.

And I knew that whether Doris still felt that I was needed or not, I needed to see this situation through. I may not have known why, but some instinct told me that the real story unfolding around Love Cemetery demanded that I—a white woman—and Doris, an African American woman, find a way through this together.

EIGHT

—◆—

Shiloh

"America is a great nation," he shouted out, but if America doesn't deal with its racism, "I'm convinced that God will bring down the curtains on this nation, the curtains of doom.

"You know," he said, "there are times that you reap what you sow in history." He pounded his big King James Bible on the pulpit. "I believe it! Be not deceived. God is not mocked. Whatsoever a man soweth, that he shall also reap. America must resolve this race problem, or this race problem will doom America."

—Martin Luther King Jr.,
sermon, July 1967, in
To the Mountaintop by Stewart
Burns

By eleven o'clock on this Sunday morning in May 2005, the weather in Scottsville is clear, hot, and humid. I drive over to Shiloh Missionary Baptist Church for services and make my way inside to the cool, dark foyer to sign the guest book. I hear the organ playing, the choir softly singing, and Pastor McCain beginning the service, as I open the double swinging doors and slip in quietly. I find a seat next to tall, slender Mrs. Ernestine Mattox, whom I'd often seen in church, and just in front of Willie

Mae Brown, who gives me a nod of welcome. Willie Mae is dressed in a sharp matching skirt and jacket of vertical black and white stripes, with a matching black hat and veil. R.D. is in front with the deacons, dressed in a dark suit, white shirt, and tie, a white handkerchief folded neatly in his breast pocket. He gives me a small nod when he sees me come in. But where is Doris? She's not in her usual place in the front row with the other deaconesses. Despite the number of familiar faces I see, without Doris I feel awkward. Somehow, without our ever having spoken of it, I realize that I've been relying on Doris as my guide into this spirit-filled world of the rural black Baptist church.

Suddenly I see her, and I'm relieved. She's at the end of the row in front of me. When she turns around and sees me, she smiles and my spirits are buoyed up. That smile, along with Willie Mae's nod and R.D.'s acknowledgement, makes me want to stay despite the headache I feel coming on. Two teenage boys provide the accompaniment for the choir this morning, and their music is painfully loud. A clean-cut sixteen-year-old dressed in a sport jacket, white shirt, and tie keeps up a heavy, happy, percussive beat on the drum kit, while a precocious fourteen year-old, just as neatly dressed, wails on the electric organ. The melody is drowned out by the volume of sound that sets my head pounding.

The choir director turns to the congregation and invites us to stand and join the chorus. I gather my energy. The wooden pews creak and clothes rustle as people pull themselves up. I pull myself up too, determined to find the beat. I need to get with it or get out, I tell myself, that's the way to treat the headache. I begin to move, to relax with the waves of energy that wash over and swirl around me. I shift back and forth on my feet, let myself sway and clap, try my best to sing along.

"He is able," the choir shouts, "Jesus can fix it!"

The choir director raises her arms, palms up and open, then turns back to the twenty-member choir facing us from the back of the altar. They are rocking in place, swaying and clapping, beaming, full of conviction. They're contagious, hollering, "He is able, yes, yes! He can fix it."

The choir director turns back to the congregation and signals for us all to be seated.

Pastor McCain steps up to the pulpit, an attractive, broad-shouldered man in his forties. The choir hums softly in the background, the organ plays lightly, the drums almost stop. Rev. McCain stands there smiling and nodding, looking around the room through tinted, light-sensitive glasses, greeting everyone from his pulpit. His hair is trimmed neatly into a dark flattop squared off at the corners, like his small moustache. Turning to the choir director, he signals that he is ready to speak. Today is Pentecost Sunday according to the Christian calendar, in the days after Christ's resurrection and ascension, the day on which Christians believe the Holy Spirit descended and anointed his disciples who were gathered together awaiting a sign. Suddenly, as they sat in the upper room, a whirling wind blew through, disturbing them, disrupting them, and out of the wind came tongues of flames, which hovered over each disciple's head, filling them with the Spirit, giving them each the ability to speak in tongues, and letting them know that despite Christ's departure, he had fulfilled his promise to send an Advocate, the Holy Spirit. That Spirit was with them still, whirling in the wind, hidden in the flames.

Pastor McCain signals the choir for quiet and calls up a young woman who is sitting next to his wife on the front row. She is a stout and earthy woman, tall, dressed simply in black, her hair marcelled and waved, pulled back smoothly from her long oval face. She is the guest preacher this morning.

The electric organ comes up softly under her and floats in the air. She steps in front of the pulpit, turns to us, and begins to pray, softly at first.

"Father God, I ask that you anoint my mouth as I stand behind your word, Father God.... Father God, everything I say from my mouth, let it be directly from your throne." She continues, as her voice grows louder, "Father God, Lord, right now I ask that you *saturate* me, Father God." I start warming to this unlikely preacher, to her hefty, commanding presence.

"Father God, let me step *bold* to proclaim your Word, Father God," she shouts. "Lord, I ask right now," she says on a syncopated beat, "Father God, that you allow your anointing to *saturate* this place."

"Yes, yes," people shout in response, "yes."

Bold, she says when *boldly* would have been more usual. But "step *bold*" is arresting, stops me, makes me sit up and notice. It won't fly past me; I have to think about it.

"In the mighty name of Jesus, Father God ..." she calls out more loudly.

"Yes, yes!" everyone shouts. "Alright now, alright!" The energy builds, the call and response, one feeding upon the other, building the intensity.

"Lord, decrease my flesh. Father God, I ask that your Spirit dwell *richly* within me, Father God, in the mighty name of Jesus, I pray. Amen."

"Amen, amen."

"Those who can and are able, please stand and give reverence to the Lord."

"Hmmm, hmmm," the congregation says under its breath.

"Today's reading is from "2 Kings, chapter 5, verses 8–14," she announces with authority.

Everyone pulls out the Bibles they carry with them for church. I pull a small red and gold brocade bag out of my purse and fish out my marked up, dog-eared, yellow and red, Post-it-flagged, miniature copy of the New Testament.

"I don't have the Old Testament," I whisper to Mrs. Mattox, sitting next to me. She sees that I've at least got part of the Bible, smiles, puts her Bible where I can read along in the Old Testament with her, and points out the verse we're on.

The fiery young preacher continues; she chews up her verses, she devours them, spits them back out at us, and showers us with her powerful voice, with her rhythmic, angry bellows. I feel like I'm being attacked with scripture, it's being hurled at us, forcefully, and it works. It gets through, at least to me. I begin to crack open. The congregation punctuates her talk with their call and response. They seem to be, we seem to be, egging her on to say more, to be bolder, wilder, and she is, thundering now, "And it reads that when the king of Israel ... learned of the warrior Namaan's request that he be healed of leprosy, the king despaired and tore his clothes.

"He thought that Naaman's king, Aram, had sent Naaman to him as a trick in order to start a quarrel.

"'Am I a god to give life and death?' the king of Israel exclaimed when he read Aran's letter. The prophet Elisha heard of the distress of the king of Israel, and he got word to the king and said, 'Let him come to me and he will find a prophet in Israel.'

"Naaman came with his horses and his chariots and stood at the door of the house of Elisha. Elisha did not come out. Elisha sent a messenger unto him, saying go and wash in Jordan seven times ... then Naaman would be healed.

"Naaman says, 'I thought surely Elisha would come out to me and stand and call upon the name of the Lord, his god, and stretch his hand over the place and heal my leprosy.' The River Jordan is known to be muddy, Naaman says, so why can't he wash 'in the rivers of Damascus? They are clean, can I not wash in them?' he tells Elisha's messenger with indignance. The Bible tells us 'he turned around and went off in a rage' that Elisha had not personally come out to heal him.

"When Naaman storms off, his servants approach him and remind him that if Elisha had told him to do something difficult, he would have done it. They reason with him. If he would have done something hard, why will he not follow Elisha's simple instruction to dip in the Jordan seven times? Naaman heeds their counsel and turns back. He goes down to the Jordan and immerses himself seven times, 'according to the saying of the man of God, and his flesh came unto him again, like the flesh of a little child.'"

"Amen, amen, I say, let us give praise and thanks, you may be seated now," she said.

"Pastor McCain, and all my brothers and sisters in Christ, I want to let you know that great is my boldness of speech to you today. I have word directly from the Throne."

Directly from the Throne? I ask myself, caught off guard by such an outlandish claim. In another moment I realize that I have rarely ever heard a woman of *any* color make this kind of claim to power. It's refreshing. She goes on.

"The subject for the day: *anybody been dipped?*" she says loudly and knowingly.

"*Whooooooo!*" a woman shouts. "*Come on, come on,*" a man calls out.

"To *dip* means to immerse," she says.

"*Come on, come on, baby,*" the man's voice again.

"It means to *re*-pent," she says slowly.

"*Come on,*" a woman says.

"It means to turn away."

"*Yes.*"

"Naaman had a problem with leprosy on this body."

"*I got it.*"

"Leprosy is considered an un-clean disease," she says drawing out the *un-clean*.

"*Yes, yes.*"

"His skin was contagious."

"*All right.*"

"When people came around Naaman, they might not want to be in his presence, but leprosy was not the only problem Naaman had. No, he had the problem that most of us church folks have right now today: it's *pride*."

That's right, I say to myself, as a woman's voice calls out insistently, "*Come on now, come on!*" I'm right there with her.

"It's pride. Naaman had a *big* problem with pride. He felt like because he was a great man of valor and he had won many battles, he deserved special treatment. He felt like Elisha the prophet should come out to *him* and just speak a word and call on his God, and heal him."

"Come on, come on," another man encourages in caressing tones, as if his words could kiss her, arouse her further.

"But Elisha just sent a *word*. When you are a true man or woman of God, you ought to be able to just speak a *word*. Speak a word! You don't have to go out and proclaim and lay hands on nobody, you ought to be able to just speak a word and that situation ought to be healed."

"Yes, yes, come on now!" Some women are starting to fan themselves; it's getting hot.

"There's a lot of lepers in the house of the Lord right now! A lot of church folks right now in the house of the Lord. We got contagious diseases in this house! Here you sit on your pew, Sunday after Sunday, you piled up and you puffed up, you can't get up and you can't worship the Lord—you've got an unclean disease," she shouts on a roll, in rhythm, her voice rising higher.

People start clapping.

"You got to be like Naaman, you need to turn back, you got to go back down, go to the Jordan, to the muddy Jordan."

"Yes," claps, and *"yeah!"*

"You got to dip seven times in that water—seven times in that water means completion. I am sick and tired of church folks coming to church: 'I'm dressed, I'm looking clean, Sunday after Sunday, I've got on my best-looking dress, amen, I've got on my best pair of shoes, amen.' But you pumped up and puffed up, you sitting on your pew every Sunday, wrapped up in your pride, and ..."

Voices rise louder, shouting starts, and I can barely make out her words, people are clapping, then more shouts, men and women together, she's getting hot.

"Come on, come on ..." a man calls out insistently; he demands of her.

"... you got a contagious disease, you need to go back down in the Jordan, you need to ask the Lord, 'Cleanse me,' go down, ask the Lord if there's anything in me that's not clean...."

"Yes, yes!"

"I need to purge, Lord, I need you to purge it out of me, Lord, right now! You sit on the pew, Sunday after Sunday, without forgiveness in your heart! Just looking clean, but your heart is dirty!"

"Whoooo!" She's uncovering it. *"Come on now, come on ..."*

"Clothes ain't going to take you to heaven, baby. If my heart is right with the Lord, that's all that matters."

"Tell it, tell it."

"Because I been dipped! God taught me you got to *love* when it hurt!"

Here it is, here it is: love even when it hurts, don't run away now, that's what love is, holding the ground, staying on board—the message I need today.

"We need a little hu-mil-ity, we need a little more compassion, I am saying that word today, com-passion. You got to love people even when they hurt you so bad...."

This is my struggle, she's right on it, exhorting us, encouraging me, all of us, to keep choosing love, to keep being willing to be uncomfortable. I have to give up my pride, I have to not know how Love Cemetery will turn out, I have to keep choosing a vision of reconciliation and healing, even though I have no idea how to bring this about, even though I, as one individual, have utterly no power to bring this about, people have to want it. Is this just some crazy idea of mine? Let go, let go—I have to keep choosing my friendship with Doris, even if I don't know what's ahead.

"You got to *love!*" the preacher thunders now, raining down the memory of Sam Adkins on me. Brought up in slavery, Sam Adkins who said, "You got to choose love when there's reason to hate, Mabel, choose love. *Choose* love."

Love despite pain. It's easy to love people who like us, who treat us kindly, but the great transformation happens when we love our enemies, love those who despise us, love those who are difficult.

A month before this day at Shiloh, I had led a retreat for fifty people in Charleston, South Carolina. There were two African American and forty-eight white participants.[52] Feeling myself carried by the call and response in Shiloh Baptist Church, the ebb and flow of rhythmic voices, I let myself remember how boldly those two African American women had spoken *that* April Sunday morning, the last day of our gathering, how they described the pain of being black in a white-dominated society. Elayna Shakur was a painter, an African American woman from Charleston who had three daughters. Elayna, a tall and elegant woman in her mid-sixties with short silver hair, large brown eyes, a high forehead, and warm brown skin, explained to us that she had been hugely invested in cross-cultural dialogue and racial understanding.

"Forty years ago, I helped start a group called the Panel of American Women, made up of black, white, Catholic, and Jewish women. We met weekly for ten years and spoke publicly as a panel in the North Shore and Chicago communities about our personal experiences with prejudice. I've always been passionately committed to racial reconciliation. Thirty years have passed now since I left that work," she said, looking around the room at the almost all-white faces, "and I see that in many ways we're as separate as ever."

After all these years, including starting another short-lived group in South Carolina when she moved there, Elayna felt close to despair. The state of affairs between races in our country is still bad. "No matter what the appearance, there's a level at which white people not only don't understand racism—they don't care."

"They just don't get it," she said, and then corrected herself, "You don't." She was no longer protecting us from her sorrow and anger. "I almost didn't come back to our group today. I felt like I needed to retreat into the black community. There is just too much whiteness here for me at this retreat, so I went for a walk just now, that's why I was late. I'd found that beautiful black wrought-iron gate by Phillip Simmons, the famous Charleston black artisan, that's near here and I just stood there holding on to it, holding on to that beautiful blackness."

Silence. The room was hushed; no one moved; we were—I was—completely transfixed.

Then Cookie Washington spoke up. Cookie was a fabric artist, a quilter, and a seamstress, a diminutive African American woman with her hair covered by a colorful turban. She began to weep the moment she opened her mouth. "I feel that most of my white 'sisters'' commitment to racial healing stops at their bedroom door. I feel like you are sleeping with the enemy, and you would not extend yourself to help me or any other black person if it threatened your relationship with white men.

"I feel so sad when white women still say to me, 'You speak so well.' Why are they surprised? Have you people never *met* an educated black woman? Sometimes I feel like a token black friend. I don't feel seen as a mother, an artist, as a friend."

I was stunned by Cookie and Elayna's honesty. I had never had an African American woman friend open to me in this way before, much less in a group of people. Tears welled up, which embarrassed me: *they* were the ones hurt—why was I in tears? But as I looked around I could see that almost everyone else in the room was moved to tears too. People were talking softly among themselves. One of the other participants, Sheila Hill, was relieved that we were finally talking about race, that elephant in the American living room; she'd felt it here.

Finally my friend Bonnie O'Neill began to speak, her blue eyes glistening with moisture. She turned to Cookie and Elayna and said to them both directly, "I am sorry for the racism in our country. I am so sorry. It's terrible, I know it, you know it, we all know it in one way or another," and then she paused. "I am so sorry for any way in which I have participated in racism, consciously or unconsciously. Please forgive me. I am truly sorry."

At that, Elayna, ever composed herself, began to let the tears roll down her cheeks. Cookie cried too, even harder, we all did—tears of connection, tears of release. We were no longer trying to act as if this pain was not between us, as if we did not intimately feel the corrosive touch of a past that is still so much with us. It's the pain of our stitched-together American democracy, torn and unraveling.

People began to approach Cookie and Elayna one by one, off to the side, to offer their own apologies, to ask for their forgiveness. I asked everyone to stop right where they were. This was an extraordinary moment, and it shouldn't be happening on the periphery. I asked Cookie and Elayna if they would be willing to let us form a circle around them, if they were willing to be in the center. Would they be willing to hear our apologies? "Yes," they both said.

"This is a rare opportunity for us as white women to apologize directly for racism and to be forgiven by African American women," I said to the others, "a true gift" for those who feel so moved.

A small, blonde, blue-eyed woman came up to Elayna and Cookie, a woman whom I had dismissed in my own mind as a well-to-do housewife with nothing to do. She began to tell them how she had spent eleven years working full-time with young African American men in prison, and how it had torn her up, how she had seen their pain and all the obstacles in front of them, how our criminal justice system destroyed them, ate them alive—how it killed their hope and hers too. She apologized as Elayna and Cookie nodded, listening, taking in everything, the three of them now in tears. I was startled by the depth of feeling of this participant and brought up short by the shallowness of my own assumption about her.

Another woman apologized because she said that her grandparents brought her up to believe that black people didn't have souls. They told her she didn't have to pray for them or worry. She was so sorry she'd ever listened. She knew it wasn't true even as a child. Over and over I heard, "I am sorry, please forgive me," spoken by each person there in her own words. So this is what it means to speak in tongues.

This Sunday, a month later in East Texas, was Pentecost Sunday. But for me Pentecost had already come the month before in Charleston. The biblical story says a "whirling wind" entered the room in which the apostles waited on Pentecost. It blew open the windows and doors, this wind, this spirit. It appeared as a dove, then as flames that did not burn but ignited their speech, giving them tongues of fire.

The spirit had been with us that morning in South Carolina, and it was with us here at Shiloh Baptist. I am standing up with the congregation; the preacher is close to ending.

"We got to go back to that muddy Jordan," she is saying.

The choir is singing—everybody's singing full out—I'm on my feet too, singing and swaying, clapping and praying.

One singer takes a solo and is then taken over himself by the Spirit. A woman shrieks and cries out, "Jesus, Jesus, Jesus, Jesus!" She screams louder and louder, now, steps into the center aisle, starts up to the front; her arms uplifted, waving, her eyes closed, she stumbles forward. Two young women immediately step in, get close around her, slip their arms around her waist, hold her up, protect her, and begin to fan her. Sweating and crying, "Jesus, Jesus!" She is gone, gone into another world. Her cries get louder, more insistent, "Jesus, my Lord, JESUS. JESUS. JESUS."

People make sure that this woman's taken care of—and she is—and just keep on singing. I've seen this happen before in a service here, several times. This is being slain in the spirit, filled with God. I know this place, I know this depth of feeling, and in a flash I see the genius of the black church, the key it gives to survival of the human spirit—to say nothing of God.

There is no embarrassment, no hurrying out of this woman, no telling her to stop, to be quiet, that she's interrupting the service. No, the singing flows on around her, incorporates her cries. She is accepted exactly for where she is with whatever is going on, supported, held up, attended to in a deeply human way that I've rarely seen in my own white America. I can't imagine this in the church in which I grew up. This person would be hurried out, told to get a hold of herself. But not here.[53]

Another woman in the back of the church on the left cries out from her pew. The organ soars, the choir's voice rises higher, the drum beats faster, as the intensity grows and goes right through me.

Then a young woman steps into the aisle with a mighty shout and goes down, falling like a tree. Half a dozen other young women rush to catch her. They have her now and lift her up and carry her to an empty pew in the back of the church. They lay her out carefully and hover over her, fanning her and watching over her as her shouts and cries continue, her calling out to God.

The heat in the room grows. The woman up front who went into a trance is weeping now, calling out more softly, sobbing, "In the name of Jesus." Doris leaves the front of the church now and goes to the back to check the young woman. She takes her pulse. Doris is calm, her years of experience as an LPN at the Veterans Hospital emanate assurance. Each person is safe in the other's hands, each is cared for and attended in ways that are natural, spontaneous, and deeply human. They are witnessed.

The room is "covered," as the Quakers say about a meeting, meaning that there is a palpable sense of the spirit being with us; there is a quickening in the room, a benevolence that surrounds us. These women are cocooned in profound acceptance. They are safe in this moment within this community.

The choir's voices grow fainter; the pastor steps back into the pulpit and begins to pray softly.

"The church is open, does anyone have something to say?"

My hand shoots up, I can't stop myself. Pastor McCain doesn't see me. I drop my hand to my lap, then in a moment edge it up—I need to speak. Mrs. Mattox on my left sees me, gets his attention, signals him. Finally he nods and invites me to stand up and speak. I get to my feet, unsure of what I have to say. As soon as I open my mouth I feel the heat rise up, a wave of feeling sweeps over me, washes away my words, strips me of my defenses, and leaves me standing there speechless and bare. I let go of my pride. I may not have another opportunity.

I want to tell everyone about our gathering in Charleston, but as soon as I try, I feel the heat leave me. I try to tell them what I've been doing, about Blossom Hall and the unmarked burial ground, about Love Cemetery. I want them to know that African Americans have been part of every story I've written, but that's not what I need to say either. I want to speak so badly, but the words aren't coming out, not words that will release me, only words that take me further and further away from the heat of what I have to say.

I stop mid-sentence, cut myself off, and say, "Here's the point." My voice thickens with emotion, I feel the heat coming back, my voice cracks, I'm still struggling. Tears well up and start to slide down my face. A man steps forward to help, comes up beside me in the pew and offers me a microphone. I shake my head and tell him, "I'll speak up." He puts the mike in my hand anyway; I take it, barely aware of my surroundings. I'm burning now and my palms are wet. My voice breaks again, only this time I breathe and push through that crack and speak.

"I know that we live in a racist society. I know that there's racism of all kinds, white against black, black against white, black against black."

"Yes, yes! All right!"

"White against brown, against red, against yellow, black against brown, brown against black, on and on—it is endless. Racism is wrong." This is so easy now, so simple. "I am sorry for my part. I am so sorry for anything racist I have done consciously or unconsciously to hurt you and your people."

Suddenly, I'm aware that Doris has come up behind me now, her open left palm is warm and strong against the small of my back. I feel her support flow into me. I am so grateful not to be standing there alone any longer.

"I apologize. Please forgive me."

I take the tissue Doris offers and thank her. I look around at this room full of faces, some familiar and friendly, many unfamiliar, many inscrutable. Doris continues to stand there next to me. She leans over and says warmly, "It's all right, China," under her breath. "Yes," I say. Our rift is mended in that moment. I can feel it now and I know that it is true.

After the service a few people come up to me, shake my hand, and greet me for the first time. No one makes a fuss or says much except for R.D., who comes up to shake my hand and gives me a big smile and says approvingly, "That was beautiful, baby, beautiful!" and goes on about his day. Then a young girl, maybe six years old, with clear bright dark eyes and a fresh young face, comes up to me in her ice-blue dress and simply gives me a hug. I lean down, take her hand and say, "Thank you. My name is China, like the country. What's yours?"

She tells me that her name is "Russia, like the country." Then she adds, "It's spelled R-U-S-S-Y-A, Russia!"

NINE

Underneath the Surface

"Now I am laying a stone in Zion, a chosen, precious cornerstone and no one who relies on this will be brought to disgrace."

—I Peter 2:6

"The stone which the builders rejected has become the cornerstone."

—Psalm 118: 22

Back in Dallas in February 2006, I was getting ready to drive to East Texas, and I had a moment to reflect on the progress we had made at Love Cemetery in the months prior. By the fall of 2005, we'd gotten most of the wisteria and overgrowth finally down to the ground. We had found thirty-seven markers by the end of that last work day, but the elders assured us that there were many more graves out there. The cemetery had been opened up: we could see from one side to the other. With the burial ground as clear as we'd gotten it, the archaeologist and director of the Texas Historical Commission's Archaeological Division, Jim Bruseth, had agreed to drive up from Austin with his assistant, Bill Pierson, and go with us to the cemetery to assess it. He was bringing the state's grave-finding machine, a cesium magnetometer. Though Jim couldn't guarantee how well the machine would perform—it could be affected by soil composition—he hoped it would give us some indication of where more burials lay.

Bruseth was going to assess whether Love Cemetery should be given a Texas State Historical Marker. That would give it additional protection, so that there could be no mistake about its existence and its historical importance. Black cemeteries were especially at risk of being lost, making them a special concern of the Texas Historical Commission and their archaeologists.

The markers we had found so far ranged from Ohio Taylor's handsome landmark, to a rusted rifle barrel, glass jars set into the ground, a filigreed Singer sewing machine leg, a piece of ironstone, and pieces of blank white marble lying broken on the ground. With the vegetation now cut to the ground, we also found long depressions in the earth where we could only assume that the ground had caved in over a coffin. Philip found one with a rusted funeral marker, but the name was gone without a trace.

Unknown markers in Love Cemetery

Philip Verhalen at Love Cemetery, caved-in grave.

Though there were granite and marble headstones dating from the turn of the twentieth century to the 1960s too, small rusted funeral home markers, and a body-length concrete slab, there were no markers after 1964, which supported the story of the community lockout forty years prior.

This February cleanup would also be an opportunity to weave in what had been a missing piece for me, a way to acknowledge the Native Americans who had lived in this area for centuries, especially the Caddo, the earliest inhabitants. Their main tribe, the Kadohadacho, had been esteemed as peacemakers to whom others turned for mediation of differences and help with treaties. Might the Caddo have something to teach us now? The repeated mention of Nuthel's grandmother Lizzie Sparks as being both Indian and black made us realize that we needed to invite a member of the Native American community to join us. I turned to a member of the Caddo Nation in Oklahoma, Richard Subia, whose great-great-great-grandfather was the last traditional Caddo chief, Show-e-Tat, also known as George Washington. Show-e-Tat was born in 1816, in the vicinity of Caddo Lake.

Richard too had agreed to join us for our February workday, and had driven four hundred miles from Oklahoma. He had already worked in the area with the Jeffersonian Institute in

Chief Show-e-Tat, the last traditional Caddo chief,
also known as George Washington.
Born in 1816, in the vicinity of Caddo Lake.

nearby Jefferson, Texas, to preserve the last home of the Caddo, Timber Hill, on a bayou north of Caddo Lake. Jim, the state archaeologist, had been involved in that effort too. Given the import of the day, I turned back to Reda, the student of the Dagara tradition, and asked her what guidance the Ancestors might have to offer.

Reda got back to me just as I was packing up my car to leave Dallas. She said that the Ancestors were very happy that Richard would be joining us. We were walking over the Rainbow Bridge, bringing people back together through Love Cemetery. I needed to bring a handwoven cloth from Africa as a gift for Richard.

I had no idea where I was going to find such a cloth in Dallas, yet everything that Reda had suggested I do to honor the Ancestors at Love had proved important in ways I could not have predicted. I opened the Yellow Pages and started looking for "Africa." Luckily I found a listing for the African Experience, a shop in downtown Dallas not far from the interstate. They were open late, and they had a handwoven neck scarf from Mali.

When I arrived, the clerk handed me a beige and dark brown, four-foot-long, narrow scarf with large geometric symbols on it. He apologized for not being able to tell me what the symbols meant, and I hadn't even thought to ask, I was in such a hurry. I was just grateful to have something handwoven from Africa. We laid the scarf out on the counter and examined the cloth together. To someone from Mali, he pointed out, each straight-edged splash of dark brown and each circle would have meant something specific. To the two of us standing there in downtown Dallas, looking at the cloth as I held it up to the light, the patterns were ghosts, ciphers of a forgotten past.

"I'm sure they mean 'good luck' for the wearer," he told me. "Maybe even some kind of protection," he said with a winning, innocent smile. I thanked him and carefully wrapped the scarf in the tissue he'd given me and left for Marshall.

In 2004, when my relationship with Doris had fallen apart before the reconsecration of the cemetery, I had said nothing about the offerings I'd brought for the Ancestors. It was all I could do to keep clearing a corner of the burial ground and find a place to make the offerings on my own, hoping that no one noticed.

By the following year, 2005, we'd had more work parties at the cemetery, and in October, R.D. and Doug Gardiner had glued Ohio Taylor's reassembled headstone back together with a special glue for stone. It no longer stood precariously, in danger of toppling. That same year, I'd had that deeper awakening in South Carolina about how sharp, constant, and intense the pain of racism still is today. I'd made my open apology to the congregation at Shiloh. All the while, Doris and I continued to be faithful to our work at the cemetery. We'd kept after the wisteria, working side by side in the heat, uprooting it where we could, cutting it back where we couldn't, and cleaning the graves. We had kept at it in spite of the awkwardness that was sometimes still between us. Our friendship was slowly mending.

At our August cleanup that year, 2005, I took a risk and told Doris about Reda's work to repair the damage done by the slave-holding ancestors she had on both sides of her family. Doris was interested. I told her about Reda being sent to a Dagara village in Burkina Faso by her African teacher and how she had been initiated into the Dagara form of divination with the Ancestors.

I had no idea what Doris's reaction would be to this information. Here I was, a white woman telling her about an African tradition. My discomfort was compounded by my self-conscious awareness that I was sharing instructions that had been given to me by another white woman, a white woman who had been initiated into an African spiritual tradition. Everything seemed backward; nonetheless, there we were, and I was stuck with the truth.

I was afraid to tell Doris initially because she was a Baptist. Still, a lot of ground between Doris and me had been cleared. The courage to open my mouth had come in a flash, when I saw in my mind's eye the painted plate of Jesus, pointing to his heart, on the breakfast room wall in my great-grandmother's house. I'd dismissed that painting with the Catholic trappings of my childhood, but there it was, saying, "Follow the heart."

I told Doris that for me the point of making offerings was to honor the Ancestors of Love Cemetery with something from their motherland, from Africa. I assured her that though I knew little about traditional African culture, I trusted the power of love and healing—the realm of the Ancestors. I was counting on them to see through my ignorance and accept my humble offering. Would she like to join me?

"Well, I believe I will," she said, to my surprise. She walked over to the grave of her great-grandfather, Ohio Taylor, near where she and I had been working. I pulled the blue pouch of loose tobacco out of my pocket, cut it open with my pocketknife, and offered it to her. She put two or three fingers full in the cup on his headstone, and I followed her lead. Together we walked around the headstone, sprinkling loose tobacco, circling it in silence.

I then pulled two miniature bottles of rum out of my day pack and handed one to Doris, explaining that we were to offer this too by pouring rum onto the ground. As with the tobacco, Doris first poured some into the cup on Ohio's grave. We circled his headstone again, sprinkling the rum on the ground. Doris prayed aloud in the simple, calm, powerful way she had, asking both God and the Ancestors to accept these offerings we had made, and then we laughed, happy to share this secret. That was in August 2005.

When we gathered six months later, early on a brisk, chilly, sunny February day in 2006, to go to the cemetery, I had no idea how a nameless ceremony with a member of the Caddo Nation, an evaluation by the state archeologist, and a cleanup with the scouts and the community was going to come together. Richard Subia arrived from Oklahoma at our appointed meeting place on time. The scouts were there, the archaeologists, Philip and me and Doug, Doris's brother Albert from Ft. Worth, and the rest of the community, twenty of us in all. But where was Nuthel, who had started all this? Her daughter, Wanda Gale, was driving up from Houston to pick up her mother and join us. After waiting as long as we could, we had to leave for the cemetery without them, assuming they would join us there later, as once before.

As soon as we got to the cemetery, Jim Bruseth, a tall and rangy man with lank, sandy hair that lay flat on his head, and Bill Pierson—medium build, with silver hair and beard— wheeled the cesium magnetometer out of their van, a silver metal–tubed wagon on which the machine sat. To the untrained eye, the small machine, about the size of a wheelbarrow, with large, thin wheels from a wheelchair, looked like an invention made in an eccentric neighbor's basement, not the sophisticated piece of technological equipment it was.

But before anything else could happen we had to form a circle at Ohio Taylor's grave. Gathering around Ohio's grave had become our ritual for pulling together as a group. It allowed us a moment to express gratitude for our members and for the day, and to remember the Ancestors. For some of the scouts, the excitement came from the prospect of using axes and machetes to chop down trees and clear vines; for others it was the possibility of finding pieces of history, the mystery of never knowing what might turn up, like the rusted gun barrel we had found last time. Because of what R.D. and Nuthel had told us about grave markers, and because of Doug's knowledge of shotguns and hunting rifles, we knew that shotgun barrel wasn't a piece of junk tossed in a field seventy-five years ago—it was a grave marker. As we had with the Singer sewing machine leg Philip had found and the broken marble slab, we left the shotgun in its place, but we stood it up again in the soil—planted it, so that once again it marked a grave.

While we waited for everyone to join the circle, Albert Johnson, Doris's older brother who had driven over from Fort Worth, made his way over the uneven ground to touch Ohio's headstone and stand by it. Doris followed Albert, then I joined them at the headstone. Albert's grizzled gray hair was visible under a smart dark wool cap. His smile was like the sunrise, fresh and bright, warming, wide with unexpected sweetness. As everyone gathered, Mr. Johnson told us that he remembered funerals here too, back when he was still a very young man and the family came in "the old way" by mule-drawn wagons. He remembered that in 1943 they were still using wagons, but that the dead—Melvinie Jackson in this case—"was brought in by a big black hearse from the funeral home, the kind that had the bump on the back. I was young, the hearse scared me." He added, "Doris was probably too young to remember; she'd been fourth in the family, I was the first." Melvinie was related to Doris, R.D., and him, as well as Willie Mae and her brother Jim Brown. She was their grandmother. They were part of interlocking families.

Philip called out to the scouts as he walked over to Ohio's grave, "Circle up, guys, come on." Doug Gardiner punctuated Philip's order with a short, loud whistle, and the scouts reappeared quickly. As they joined us, I noticed that for once Doug was without his cowboy hat; even Bill Pierson, Jim's assistant, had taken his hat off. I took Richard Subia's hand with my left and Jim Bruseth's with my right, aware that their presence meant that we were taking a step out into the world beyond the cemetery. We had asked for their help and they had said yes; they too thought Love was important, and I was grateful. Doris seemed happy about it too, and she beamed as we gathered. Julia Williams, Annye Fisher, and Walter "Coach" Edwards were there with us too, generous volunteers who understood the value of black history, even though they had no one buried there. Both Julia and Annye served on historical and landmark commissions, Annye at the county level and Julia at the state. Walter Edwards was a man of service, lending a hand to help whenever and whomever he could.

On the other side of our twenty-member circle, Doris reached out and took Philip's hand, as everyone linked up with the people next to them. Ohio Taylor was part of our circle again, another member, unseen but present and felt, his stone standing between his great-grandchildren, Doris and Albert. Doris took charge and began to pray in a strong, clear voice.

"Thank you, precious Father, we bow our heads on your heart. Thank you, heavenly Father, for allowing us to meet here at Love Cemetery today. Thank the people who came from far and near to help us, bless each and every one individually and collectively, my Father, bless us as we go on the dangerous highways back to our various homes. We ask you to strengthen us where we're weak, Father, and build us up where we're torn down. And heavenly Father, we thank the individuals who have helped us from the beginning of when we started cleaning up this cemetery, China, Philip, and Doug, and the scouts. We thank you for everyone who has come to help, and Father, we ask you to bless each and every one. Heavenly Father, teach us how to love one another and to show our love to each and every one, as you would have us do. Lord, we ask this in the name of thy son, Jesus. Amen."

"Amen!" we all answered, and broke out laughing.

As people started talking quietly among themselves, I quickly walked over to Doris, took her aside, and gave her the African cloth I'd brought from Dallas. I felt that she should be the one to give it to Richard. "It's was the Ancestors' idea, Reda's suggestion," I explained, and she understood. "I brought tobacco and rum too, for the offering, if we want to do that."

"All right," she said, with a big smile. "I'll take care of it."

By then the voices were louder, and everyone was talking at once. The scouts were itching to start pulling things up or cut them down, and they started to drift off. I raised my voice: "Hey guys, stay in the circle, Mrs. Villatoe has something else to say, listen up."

Once everyone was quiet again, Doris began. "We'd like to thank Richard Subia for coming," she said, stepping into the circle and pulling the cloth out of the tissue. "We have a little gift of welcome for you to thank you for coming."

"Thank you," he said. A substantial, well-built man with black hair and deep-set dark eyes, he stepped out to meet her as she held out the cloth out for him.

"This is a little token for you from our African American community here," she said, smiling as she handed the cloth to Richard. Doris's suit was dark rose, her voice was warm. Then she announced that we were going to do a special ceremony today, African style, and asked me to tell them about the tobacco and the rum. Doris said, "This tradition lets our ancestors know how much we appreciate them. We make a tribute to them, using this vase that's on Ohio Taylor's grave. China?"

"In remembrance of our Ancestors, and the Ancestors who are buried here and who have brought us back together," I said, as I slit the tobacco pouch open and offered it to Doris. Doris took a big pinch, held it up, and explained, "We can put some in the bowl here on Ohio Taylor's grave, a pinch or so, and then scatter the rest of it on the ground around his grave." She rubbed her fingers together, dropped some loose tobacco into the bowl, and then scattered the rest on the ground in front of the stone and behind it. Albert took some next, then handed the pouch to the person next to him to go around the circle.

What had started out as a private, self-conscious gesture on my part, an attempt to connect with something authentic in a tradition different than my own, was in that moment being transformed by Doris's intuition and wise response. Doris understood that Love Cemetery needed new traditions as well as the old ones. She accepted what had been offered and gave it new energy by incorporating it into the life of this place.

I brought Doris the bottles of rum, and following her example, I poured a few drops of rum on top of the tobacco, then sprinkled some on the ground. I gave my bottle to Richard. Doris started singing "Amazing Grace," and we all joined in, as each person came up to Ohio's grave, one by one, to make their offering. We sang "Amazing Grace" over and over until we had finished. The Ancestors had been acknowledged; our work had begun.

Now it was time to move back across the cemetery to where we'd left the magnetometer. Jim and Bill would explain how the machine worked. They needed to keep us moving, as there was a lot of ground for the machine to cover, literally, and they had only this one day to map out the cemetery.

The scouts sat on the ground around the machine, their interest finally fully engaged. Others shared a tree stump, and the rest of us just stood as we got our first science lesson together. Drifting tall white cumulus clouds sailed across the blue sky. A storm had been predicted, some rain had fallen, but as Philip said, yesterday's rain only settled the dust and today was clear. Once again, our luck held.

Jim explained that the magnetometer operated by using cesium. Once they turned the machine on, we had to keep a certain distance from it, not because the cesium was dangerous, contained as it was, but because it was so sensitive to magnetic metals that it could pick up a nail in the ground, twenty feet under, or a belt buckle, and signal the computer to mark the place. Jim hoped they would get indications of old coffin nails, temporary metal grave markers, anything metal on a coffin, or a metal coffin itself. By getting too close, we could throw the machine off and generate false positives. But before they even turned the machine on, Jim explained that he and Bill had to finish walking off the ground and marking it every four feet with fluorescent orange powder to create a grid.

Philip, a college chemistry teacher, took over the role of lecturer, explaining in layman's terms that cesium atoms bounce around indiscriminately until they encounter a magnetic field. Once they pick up metal, they line up instantly, pulled together by "the energy of alignment." That alignment signals the computer to mark the grid and would hopefully, by the time we were done, show us where to look for more graves.

When Philip finished, everyone got up and started off in the direction of the Sparks section, talking among themselves. Jim rejoined us briefly when I explained that we were going to hear Richard talk about the Caddos and their beliefs about burial, telling a few of us—me, Julia, Annye, and others—about his commitment to and responsibility for protecting archaeological sites across the entire state. He was passionate about Native American burial sites.

"In Texas, people dig up Indian graves for a Sunday afternoon activity with their family. They think it's a wholesome family activity. I think it's horrific," he explained. "Digging up Indian graves is illegal in every single state that surrounds us—Louisiana, Oklahoma, New Mexico. Indian sites are protected on private land in those states, not just public lands.[55] Not in Texas. Grave-digging, grave-robbing—what does this teach children? Texas is a very strong private-property rights state," he explained, "and private ownership trumps everything in Texas.

"We've been trying for over twenty years down there in Austin to change it, but the property rights lobby has beaten us back every time but once. We got a bill to protect Native burial sites through the legislature once, we actually got it passed, but the governor vetoed it. It's an outrage, the way these graves are robbed." Jim shook his head. "See, the Caddos were very skilled potters and they buried valuables with tribal members," he said, then paused. "I better not get started. I've got to get back over with Bill so we can get through making the grid and get the machine turned on."

Doris and Richard had already walked over to Lizzie Sparks's grave. When the rest of us got there, Doris was showing Richard the round clear glass lip of a quart canning jar that marked Lizzie's grave. It was level with the soil, open, with no top, and it was filled with leaves.

"When we first started coming over here, that glass was whole, didn't have a chip out of it, but it does now," she explained, bending over to show him. "Mrs. Sparks was buried in 1964. See, it's written here on her marker, '100 yrs. old,'" Doris said, getting down to point out the rusty blue temporary marker for Lizzie Sparks that we'd found a couple of feet from the jar.

Where were Nuthel and her daughter, Wanda Gale? It was getting late in the morning, so late I'd begun to conclude that, sadly, they weren't coming. Either something had happened on Gale's drive up from Houston or Nuthel wasn't up to it. I knew if there was any possible way for her to be here, she would have been, especially today, when we were talking about her grandmother.

We gathered around Richard now, to hear what he had to tell us about the Caddo people and their beliefs. He started by introducing himself and telling us a little about himself and his family, going back to his great-great-grandfather, the last traditional Caddo Indian chief, also known as Show-e-Tat, George Washington.

"This part of Texas was a real melting pot in the early nineteenth century," he began, and went on to explain that waves of settlers came in, driving tribes from across the Southeast before them as they advanced—tribes like the Cherokee, Creek, and Choctaw, to mention a few.

One of the scouts piped up, "I'm part Cherokee!" He was the third member of the troop to claim Native American heritage. "That's good," Richard said, "you know your ancestry." He then explained that by the time immigrants started pouring in, in the 1830s, part of the Caddo Confederacy had already withdrawn to the Brazos River area, closer to central Texas.

The Kadohadacho, the lead tribe, had already been driven down from southwest Arkansas and upriver from northwestern Louisiana to Caddo Lake. That happened around 1800. When hostile tribes who had been driven off their lands to the east and north came down, the Kadohadacho were pushed south into what became their last settlement, above Caddo Lake at Timber Hill.[56] Jim Bruseth and the state helped with excavating and restoring that site. Richard had been coming down to this area for years and was already working with the Jeffersonian Institute in Jefferson, Texas, to restore Timber Hill. He often brought young Caddos down from Oklahoma to learn about their ancestral heritage.

"There is no doubt in my mind about the link between the Caddo and the African American community in this area," Richard explained. "Mrs. Sparks here might have been part Caddo, might have been part Cherokee." He knew several African American families around the lake who said they were also

Caddo descendants; he had gotten to know some of them. They had some of the same recipes that had been passed down in his family. No matter which tribe Lizzie was part of, he found the jar interesting because Caddos traditionally brought pots and dishes to be buried with the dead. It was believed that the deceased needed a meal on their journey to the realm of the Ancestors.

"We believe that the soul stays around for seven days to say goodbye to their loved ones and friends here. I know for myself," Richard confided, "I can feel the person is actually visiting with me during that time. I like to be alone then. My mother said she always knew where to find me at those times, because I'd go off into the trees."

Richard looked down at the African cloth in his hands. Unfolding it, he added, "This cloth that Mrs. Vittatoe has just given me is very special to me, and I'll tell you why. I recently accepted a position at Southwestern Oklahoma State University, where I'm heading up a new department that focuses on 'underrepresented students.' This cloth will go in my office display case with a little history about Love Cemetery and how this was given to me. When I'm working with the black students on campus, I'll share with them about your community here."

Richard's comments highlighted a point I encountered increasingly in my research: not only were whites and blacks much more mixed in blood than most people realized, but African American and Native American communities are also intermingled. The deeper I looked, the more it became apparent that "race" was a construct, the fictions that make it up more obvious.[57] It had become increasingly clear as we reclaimed the cemetery not only that African Americans and Native Americans have been devastated and nearly destroyed by "whites," but also that white people have been deeply harmed by these false dichotomies. Racism is a soul-sickness with terrible consequences, no matter what your color.

After Richard's talk, the cleanup started in earnest, and we worked hard until Jim and Bill finally signaled it was time to go. From the cemetery, we would go back to the community center for a potluck, at which time Jim would give us a report and a printout of what the magnetometer had found and take questions.

As we were packing up the trucks to leave the cemetery, Jim told us that someday we should replace the temporary wooden stakes he and Bill had placed in the ground for taking measurements. That way we could always go back and take a reading off his archaeological survey. We could then use the graph to locate places where metal had shown up, where it was most likely that we would find a marker.

Jim didn't know our group or understand that "someday" wasn't part of Doug, Philip, or Coach's vocabulary. Before he had finished talking, Philip produced some rebar from his truck, Doug returned with four pieces of pipe from the back of his, and Coach produced a sledgehammer. I had to laugh at the archaeologists' surprise. In no time, Doug had the rebar in and Philip and Coach had set to work pounding in pipe around them so the rebar wouldn't be run over by one of their tractors. James Brown, Geronimo, and a couple more scouts stepped up to help. "Someday" was over and done in twenty minutes.

When we got back to the Scottsville Community Center that afternoon around two, Nuthel and Gale were sitting there waiting for us. They'd been waiting for hours. Gale was late getting up from Houston, and by the time they tried to join us at the cemetery, the gate was locked. Still Nuthel would not give up. I was so happy to see them—after all, we'd paid special honor to Lizzie Sparks that day, and Richard had come down from Oklahoma because of Lizzie's grave. Now we were together again, and we could proceed with the potluck and the archaeologists' report. Nuthel had brought homemade beans. I brought Richard over to meet her and went off to help get the food set up. Carolyn arrived with minestrone, Doris got hot dogs boiling for the scouts, Julia pulled a big plate of deviled eggs and stuffed celery and crudités out of the refrigerator, Annye laid out her contribution, and I uncovered the sliced ham I'd brought from Dallas. The potluck was on.

While we put the food together, Jim and Bill were busy downloading the magnetometer's findings to a laptop computer, so they could leave us with a printout. After we gave thanks for the food and the day, Jim gave us his report and interpreted the graph.

First, he said, Love Cemetery was probably much older than we thought it was. Though the deed was dated 1904, it was likely that Love surrounded or was built on top of a slave cemetery that dated back to the 1830s, if not earlier. It was indeed an important site, one very much worth preserving. The Texas Historical Commission would work with us to erect a historical marker. That would keep the surrounding landowners apprised of its existence and the permanent right of way that the community had. All questions of access would be dealt with.

Second, he said pointedly, we needed legal counsel right away. With the Western world's seemingly unquenchable thirst for fossil fuels pumping up prices, the pressure to drill or to open up existing wells was fierce, and oil and gas leases in this area were changing hands right and left. This wasn't going to stop; it would only intensify. There were active leases in the area. I had showed Jim the Tobin map, which was updated and used by the oil and gas industry. Many deeded cemeteries show up on it, but Love Cemetery didn't. Jim encouraged me to contact the map company and insist that they put Love on their maps, and to contact the oil and gas companies working in the area and put them on notice about the cemetery. I sank lower in my chair. I thought we were wrapping up the work on the cemetery, but now I was hearing that a whole new level of activity and advocacy was needed if we really wanted to protect it. After three years, it was hard to think of Love being drilled into by some oil company. Doris and I looked at each other. I looked at Philip and Doug. I shook my head and laughed. What were we going to do? There seemed to be no end to Love. Jim was telling us to get it on the map? Looked like we'd better see to it.

Then Jim pulled up the graph that the magnetometer had spit out, showing us what he got with the reading. He projected it on a screen from his computer. It looked like the landscape of Mars, with a lot of blank gray space and then dimples and craters in the surface. Using a laser pointer, Jim pointed to the bubbles on the surface and explained that those bubbles showed where the machine had picked up magnetic metals. A lot seemed to be clustered on the northern boundary of the cemetery. He said that while the machine indicated where there was metal, it couldn't tell us what it was. From reading the graph, his best guess was that there were more of the temporary metal funeral home markers buried not too far underground. He suggested that the next time we went out, we should dig a little under the surface and see what we found.

He also told us that we needed to tell the preserve owner that the state is now interested in this site and that the burial ground probably runs under the road he built and that he should move his road and give us another 1.5 to 2 acres.

"But, Jim," I tried to say, but he went on with his presentation.

"First of all, you've done the best thing you can do to preserve this cemetery: you've cleaned it up, you've cleared it, you made it obvious that it's a cemetery. No one can mistake it for anything else. Second, you've gotten us involved. We don't like to litigate or go to court, but we can if we have to. You've got a friend in Austin. Don't forget that.

"If I can leave you with anything right now, it's the importance of getting legal counsel and being sure Love Cemetery is protected in the face of this oil and gas drilling.

"I'll take questions now."

Nuthel and the scouts were full of them. My head was spinning with all he told us to do. It was Saturday. I was returning to California on Tuesday. Doris would have to go back to work in Shreveport on Monday. I took that to mean that I had to find a lawyer who would see me pro bono on Monday. Gail Beil would know who to call.

Monday afternoon I was sitting in the office of Rodney Gilstrap, an oil and gas lawyer right downtown on the square— "an honest one," Gail assured me. "Rodney's a good man. Known him for years." Gail's "tell him you're a friend of mine" once again opened the door.

Rodney looked over the 1904 deed and pronounced it worthless. "This won't hold up to a challenge in court, hate to tell you. It's too old. Look, I'm just playing the devil's advocate here.

"You've got to get the cemetery resurveyed before anything else can happen. You get it resurveyed and then come back to me. Then I'll take it down to the courthouse and get it properly reentered in the public record. That's the only way you can protect it. Don't bother trying to chase down who's holding leases out there now. They're changing hands like there's no tomorrow with this energy crisis. They don't matter. What matters is the public record—that's the courthouse."

I told him that the burial association, as far as I knew, had no funds, no way to contract a surveyor and pay those kinds of costs. He said that I could expect a survey to cost between $500 and $1,000 and that we should just pass the hat—take up a collection and see what we've got once all the families out there chip in. Then we should go to a surveyor, tell them what the situation is, tell them what we've got, and see if someone will work with us or do it for the amount we come up with. There was no way to protect Love Cemetery without that. We had to know the boundaries.

I stopped to visit Father Denzil after I left Rodney's office and started "passing the hat" immediately. Would Father Denzil and St. Joseph's participate? In addition to himself, several members of our committee were his parishioners, as were a handful of the scouts. Of course he would help. To whom should he make out a check? I didn't know, I told him. That was the first question to get answered. It had to be someone in the descendant community. At eighty-three, Nuthel was no longer up to such a task, so it had to be Doris.

I could see that this was a turning point for me. My first instinct had been to get cracking on raising the money, doing the math, setting a goal of $500 to start—divide by ten? Twenty?

Father Denzil's generous pledge helped get us off to a good start. I had to stop myself. This was not my job, I didn't live here. Love Cemetery had taken over my life. I had to think this through.

We had worked together for three years, from March 2003 through February 2006. But now Love Cemetery had to stand on its own. The descendant community had to take the lead. These were their ancestors. The vision Nuthel had called into being—the return of the community, the honoring of the ancestors, the meal-sharing, the praying, the singing, the tradition—had to be more than her dream, or mine, or Doris's.

The vision of a community reconciliation ceremony I had years ago at Blossom Grove with Lydia came back. In my mind's eye, whites, African Americans, Latinos, Native Americans—whoever had been deemed "other" in the community—would be present. Together we would put up a marker, and we would tell this buried history, these stories that have been cast aside, kept secret.[58] Like the biblical stone that was rejected only to become "the cornerstone of a new foundation," these outcast histories could tie us together in a new covenant—between black people and white, among all peoples. We could use them to build community.

This was not something I could make happen or carry alone. I had to let go. The descendant community would pull together and protect Love Cemetery or they wouldn't. I told myself I had to turn Love Cemetery loose, let it sink or swim, hard as that might be—the time had come, visions or no.

I had a long talk with Doris and Gail that night about the meeting with Rodney. Doris agreed to organize the fundraising, but she didn't want the responsibility of checks being made out to her personally. We wanted to keep personalities out of the picture. We worked out a plan for people to make out checks to Shiloh Baptist Church, which would hold the funds until we had enough to pay a surveyor and then write the check to the company we chose. The church agreed.

In a week or two, Doris raised about $450 from our committee and friends and took the checks up to Shiloh for them to deposit. To her surprise and confusion, the church declined to hold the funds as agreed. Doris was taken aback. "I was devastated," she told me. She had been the secretary of that church and served the congregation for twenty-five years. There was a misunderstanding.

Doris sent everyone's donations back with a polite note thanking them for contributing and saying only that "it didn't work out." Doris and I talked to Father Denzil, but he couldn't help us without taking the idea to the bishop in Dallas for approval. And since none of the people buried there were Catholic, it made no sense to ask him to take the matter further. There we were. The people in Love had been Baptist, many of them from Shiloh.

Moreover, as months passed and we moved further and further away from February 4, 2006, I realized that the letter from the state acknowledging Jim and Bill's visit, summarizing their findings, and giving their report to us had failed to materialize. Jim had concluded that the cemetery was most likely built around and on top of a slave cemetery. He thought it was actually larger, maybe closer to three acres. He felt strongly that it had to be protected quickly given the oil and gas drilling going on all around it, and that we needed a lawyer to do that. In order to get the formal, legal protection he had convinced us we needed, we needed his findings to confirm Love's importance. Our whole endeavor seemed in jeopardy.

Gail Beil explained that things were so bad in Austin that Texas had actually contemplated selling off state parks and was doing budget cuts across the board. She wasn't at all surprised that I hadn't heard back yet. She knew Jim and assured me that he would respond eventually—which he did.

There wasn't such a simple, impersonal explanation for Doris, though.[59] I was frustrated, but Doris was deeply disappointed. The sadness of it didn't hit me until I received my own contribution back from her. My check fluttered out of her gracious thank-you note. I felt sad and hollow. After all we'd been through to save this cemetery, was this the end, really? I tore up the check and reentered the amount in my register.

As I sat with my sense of emptiness, I remembered that day months before, at Shiloh Baptist Church, when I'd apologized to the congregation for my part in racism and had been so shaken. Doris's silent touch had told me that I had been heard and accepted, that the damage between us had been healed.

All this came back as I looked at Doris's note of apology. I remembered the absence of any hesitation in Doris's response to my need, that day in church, the warmth of her hand, her quiet presence. An answer, now, was welling up inside me.

The vision of the cornerstone came back again as I stood up from my desk, that image of laying a new foundation. A new covenant between black and white people, red and white people, brown, yellow, among us all. A covenant to acknowledge each other, to listen to each other, to respect each other, to value and treasure each other. To love. The cornerstone in the Gospel was the stone that had first been rejected.

It was *relationship* that was the cornerstone of that new covenant. It was the relatedness that brought about healing. And in that moment, it was my relationship with Doris that needed tending. No congregation, no church, no state office or institution could bring about change at the level we as people needed. It was between us, at the level of the human heart, where change was needed. Human organizations could help, they could facilitate, contain, and support, but they could not ignite. That spark comes from the human heart when it says yes, when I say yes. Doris and I had forged our friendship out of grief, misunderstanding, and struggle, out of the sweetness of hard work, laughter, and the Texas summer heat.

In that moment I understood that enormous change happens through tiny pivotal choices. Standing there looking at Doris's note, I realized that I could not leave her alone in this situation. I didn't know what had happened at Shiloh or at the Historical Commission. I didn't need to. No one need be blamed. Reclaiming love and reclaiming Love Cemetery were not projects to wrap up and move away from. The work of Love was ongoing. There was no time limit, no expiration date. Our problems were small in the light of what we had learned through our friendship over the past few years. Friendship now was what remained and I had to be true to that, whatever it would bring.

I picked up the phone and dialed Doris's number.

Funeral Home Records of
Burials in Love Cemetery

—— • ◆ • ——

Floyd (High) Brook, d. 22 February 1937. "Near Roseborough Springs, TX. Age 22 yrs 7 months & 24 days (6-28-1914). Accidental death. Judge Calloway Carronor" (coroner?)

Mr. George Brown, d. 25 December 1940

Mrs. Melvina Brown, d. 25 July 1943

Mr. Albert Henderson, d. 22 May 1939, b. 16 April 1865

Mr. Gus Jenkins, d. 18 August 1954

Mr. Gus Jenkins, d. 3 November 1949 ("cause of death Dr. Perry, Jefferson, TX")

Infant of Lee Estes and Izana Jenkins, d. 27 January 1936 "in Kahn Hospital. Still born. Dr. Granby in charge. Internment in Love Cemetery 27 January 1936."

Sidney Johnson, d. 11 November 1961

Harret Johnson, d. 13 April 1961

Baby Mineweather, d. 31 July 1943. Coffin, $10, paid in full.

Sarah Samuels, d. 17 May 1933, age 65

Mr. Richard Taylor, d. 4 October 1938. Richard Taylor was son of Ohio Taylor (therefore related to Doris, Albert, and R.D.).

Q.T. Webb, d. 27 April 1962

Oscar Webb, d. 26 July 1943 (that date is actually the "Shipped from Ft. Worth" date in record)

Baby May Woodkins, d. 5 March 1940, at 8 months old, "on Verhalen Nursery" (2 ft. coffin cost $8. Funeral paid in full by Wilt Powell)

These records almost all mention the attending doctor who certified the death and stated its cause, but only few mention an actual cause other than for one twenty-two-year-old man whose death was listed as "accidental."[60]

Love Cemetery Burial Map

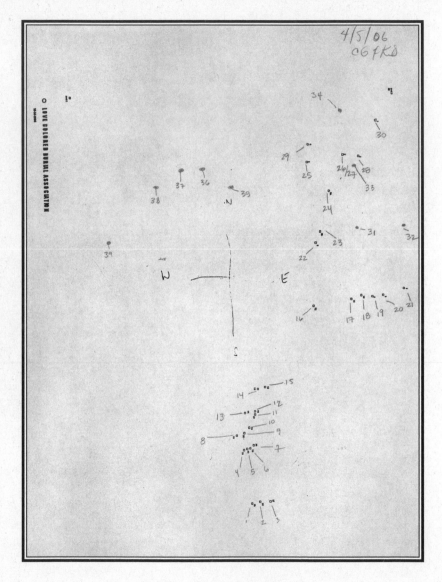

Map of Love Cemetery

Love Cemetery Burial Map List

1. Mattie Henderson
2. Albert Henderson
3. Metal marker, no name
4. Metal marker, no name
5. Metal marker, no name
6. Willie D. Jackson, April 16, 1964
7. Melvina Jackson
8. Sidney Johnson
9. Harret Johnson (spelling according to blue metal marker)
10. A stone footer (may or may not be separate from Ohio Taylor)
11. Father Anthony Taylor
12. Rusted metal marker (located on top of Father Anthony Taylor's marker), no name
13. Ohio Taylor
14. Rusted metal marker, no name
15. Aubrey Brown
16. Bettie Webb, b. 1843, d. 1923
17. Metal marker with glass, b. Aug. 22, 1918, d. Feb. 16, 19—, no name
18. Metal marker with no glass, no name
19. Claude Webb d. 9/26/54
20. Marker, no name
21. Metal marker, no name
22. Agusta Jenkins 1854 (?) (spelling on marker)
23. Andrew King
24. Rusted metal marker (daffodils planted nearby), no name
25. Daniel Sparks
26. Oscar Sparks
27. Daily Sparks
28. Lizzie Sparks (metal marker and glass jar sunk in ground)
29. Metal marker, no name
30. Metal marker with inverted glass jar sunk in ground, no name
31. Rusted metal marker (laying flat), d. June 22, 1941, 100 years, no name
32. Found pottery shard
33. Looks like a footer between graves
34. Nineteenth-century shotgun barrel, rusted (we stood it upright in the ground)
35. Large black iron stone/rock
36. Flat white marble broken up (four to five pieces), no lettering, no name
37. Metal marker (daffodils planted nearby), no name
38. Sewing machine leg
39. Metal marker, no name

Epilogue

There have been essentially two major national narratives
about the meaning and evolution of race and racism that
have been constructed over time in the United States. . . .
[C]an a reconciliation be forged that bridges the racial
chasm of our history to create a new national consciousness,
a new dedication to a democracy that has never truly
existed, but one that could conceivably be made whole?
— Manning Marable,
The Great Wells of Democracy

In the months following the visit of the chief archaeologist for the Texas Historical Commission, Jim Bruseth, Doris and I did as he suggested and stayed focused on protecting the cemetery from the intensive drilling for oil and gas that was going on in Harrison County. Limits for drilling had been changed from one shallow well for every 640 acres to one every 40 acres.[61] It was, in effect, a race to the bottom for oil and gas reserves. Having the cemetery resurveyed became our foremost task.

Jim's archaeological report and the letter we received from Gerron Hite, the head of the cemetery program for the Texas Historical Commission, in support of our work, confirmed the significance of Love. The cemetery was important to Texas state history and not only to the descendant families, our committee, and the communities of Marshall and Scottsville. For Jim and Gerron both, Love represented one of the increasingly rare historic African American cemeteries that were still roughly intact. Based on his experience of sites like this around the state, Jim surmised that Love was probably on top of or surrounding an even older black cemetery that might date as far back as the first days of Anglo American immigration in the 1820s and 1830s, into what was then Mexico. That made the protection of Love even more important and meant that the cemetery might be closer to 185 years old. Then through Lizzie Sparks, Nuthel's grandmother, the Native American tradition was brought in. Nuthel was happy that after all these years she'd been talking about Love Cemetery, now even the state of Texas agreed that it was important.

When we started cleaning the cemetery, we wanted to document it so that word of what we were doing might serve as a model to spark other people's interest in their roots and help draw communities back together. Doris summed it up: "When people hear about what we've been doing at Love Cemetery, they're going to start asking, 'Where are our ancestors? Where are they buried? Can't we do the same for them?'"

The interest in preserving Love Cemetery heightened at the same time as Gail Beil was suggesting more outreach to broaden people's understanding of history, especially young people's. Our ongoing project drew in people not only from Marshall but from other towns, and from out of state. The Vermont painter Janet McKenzie came to paint Mrs. Britton and Doris.[62] Together, Janet and I named her painting "The Keepers of Love." Over time, "the Keepers of Love" also became the name for our project of preserving and tending Love Cemetery. The Keepers of Love project, in turn, established a link for Doris and me with "the Alliance," an umbrella group that emerged under the aegis of the William Winter Institute for Racial Reconciliation at the University of Mississippi. Love Cemetery gave us a new, reconsecrated ground to stand upon and reach out to others. The Alliance for Truth and Racial Reconciliation (ATRR) is an umbrella group of organizations, people, and churches across the South, indeed, across the country, who have been working for years in repairing past harms, restoring justice, remembering, and reconciling.[63]

I continued my talks with Spencer Wood, the professor who studied Sabine Farms in Marshall, about the black farmers movement. As noted, Love Cemetery was a vestige of a black farming community. Why not combine efforts with Sabine Farms, the ten-thousand-acre black farming project of the 1930s in Marshall? We need to preserve the past *and* plant the seeds for the future.

The longer we worked on Love, the more I saw how this cemetery could help us weave together missing pieces of the American narrative—what's been left out, lost, kept secret, buried or repressed, narratives and histories, including the natural histories of any place in the United States.

Love Cemetery also revealed how and why there continue to be missing pieces in the American narrative. A survey was finally to be done of Love Cemetery on March 10, 2007, thanks to Ark-La-Tex Survey Company. On March 9th, Doris received a call at work, informing her that we couldn't go into the cemetery on March 10th for the survey unless we had $1,000,000 worth of liability insurance to protect the owners of the surrounding property while we used their road. There were new locks on the gates, too, so the Love descendant community had no access to their burial ground, despite their valid easement, nor had they been given notice. I was in Marshall when Doris called from Shreveport and asked me to investigate.

Locked out. I called the number Doris gave me. This is where the story of Love Cemetery began—was this where it would end?

By late that afternoon, I was able to see the timber corporation's attorney in person and arrange a stop gap measure for the next thirty days. We went into Love Cemetery as planned on March 10th and got the survey done and filed at the courthouse. What would get worked would come later. The story of Love Cemetery continues.

One final story.

Between 1865 and 1868, a remarkable newspaper was published in New Orleans, a bilingual paper, French and English, called *Tribune de la Nouvelle-Orléans*. In this paper, the intellectuals and poets of the nineteenth-century Creole community of New Orleans, a vibrant group of free people of color, not only hailed the Emancipation of all people, but they believed in the possibilities of good in the era despite the violence of Reconstruction that followed. Many were educated, many studied in Paris. Some were wealthy and privileged, some had held enslaved people themselves, but once the Civil War ended, they all threw their weight behind the newly freed. Many of the Creoles provided financing to newly emancipated men so that they could buy land that they had once been forced to work for others. According to Caroline Senter in "Creole Poets on the Verge of a Nation," the brutal episode in New Orleans was part of a white response to

Emancipation that set off the call for what became known as Federal or Congressional Reconstruction.[64]

"In the summer of 1866, several hundred people—Creoles, white Anglo-Americans, and recently freed black American citizens—gathered at the New Orleans statehouse to reconvene the suspended 1864 state convention that had established equal rights and universal male suffrage. [Women still could not vote, no matter what their color.] Convention members were unarmed as the police and independent, armed whites, with the approval of the Mayor, stormed the hall to break up the convention and stop the proceedings. When this armed mob advanced on the assembly and opened fire, nearby Federal troops took no action. Inside, convention members were trapped in a storm of gunfire. Over three dozen people were killed and dozens more were wounded. The violence of that day came to be known as the Massacre of 1866."

Shortly after, the South was divided up into five military districts and U.S. troops were stationed throughout "to protect the newly freed men, women, and children and to help provide their first taste of equality, marred as it was by the violent reaction of the defeated white community."

The *Tribune de la Nouvelle-Orléans* denounced the massacre in its pages, and then their writers went further and seized that moment to envision the future of the United States, the greatness that this country might still achieve. For the next two years of publication, they sought valiantly "to catalyze a nation devoted to racial equality and [male] suffrage."

Writing as descendents of people who had fought in the Haitian Revolution (1791–1804) and the French Revolution before that (1789), or as educated people who simply knew the history and the fever of those uprisings, these Creole poets, men and women alike, believed deeply in the idea of innate human rights for all people. At the beginning of Reconstruction, these poets were articulating a positive, dynamic dream of what Reconstruction could mean in the best sense for the United States.

Take a moment to remember 1865. At the end of the Civil War, there were four million newly emancipated men, women, and children who overnight were thrown out on their own to survive for the most part without land, shelter, clothing, property, animals, or much food, and with little if any education.[65] The South was in ruins.

In September 1866, after the summer's massacre, the *Tribune* editors warned their readers about the explosive and violent climate that was created by Reconstruction. Presciently, they wrote: "Never in the history of our dear but unfortunate country ... has there been a time whose events and vicissitudes called for greater care and watchfulness, and mutual counsel regarding our civil and political welfare, than the present." The Creole poets went about their business and in the *Tribune* pages boldly laid out their imaginings "of the nation based on the newly declared rights of all humans." Reconstruction was revolutionary, Senter notes, and the poets took it upon themselves to imagine nothing less than "a nation of equality." They knew their work of envisioning was essential "to carry people's spirits through the violence and disappointment that lay ahead."

Reading about this vision of a new United States that emerged out of nineteenth-century Creole culture in New Orleans, I sense that we are at that turning point still, when the very idea of our country being a democracy is itself at stake.

Starting with the literal reconstruction so desperately needed in New Orleans still today, can we join these Louisiana Creole poets in their visionary thinking, and in so doing, reinvigorate our own efforts to be a democracy?

The poets have articulated our task: to become a nation with "a composite citizenry dedicated to liberty, justice and equality for all"; and in so doing, we will bring to life their dream of "an unprecedented United States." Only we need to go further now, to enlarge their vision. We need to create an unprecedented global community. We need to remember that love is not only a feeling, love is a choice—the only one worth making. It is always within our reach.

Acknowledgments

———◆———

Though writing seems to be a solitary act that can be done only by one person, in fact this book would never have come into being but for the large community that has supported it for years. Before I acknowledge individuals and organizations, I want to acknowledge first the earth, so imperiled at this time. May this book be worthy of the natural and human resources that have gone into publication. May it be of benefit to all.

Doug Adams, Ph.D., and President Joan Carter, Ph.D. of C.A.R.E., the Center for the Arts, Religion, and Education at the Graduate Theological Union in Berkeley, have long believed in the work of the Keepers of Love and have sponsored this ongoing work. I am especially grateful to Professor Doug Adams for his constancy and his vision.

The burial grounds in these pages, though confined to Texas, are emblematic of larger histories that have been locked up, denied, trivialized, lost, paved over, or kept secret throughout the United States.

My thanks to the Ancestors of Love Cemetery and their descendants, R.D. Johnson, Sandra Johnson James, Willie Mae Brown, James Brown, Clauddie Mae Webb, Joyce Marie Schufford, Rev. Marion Henderson, and all their relatives who came from far and near, as well as those who couldn't. Special thanks to Nuthel Britton, the Keeper of Love, and her family, including Wanda Gale and Christopher, who despite the obstacles, refused to give up reclaiming Love Cemetery.

Doris Vittatoe became my close friend and partner in our ongoing effort to preserve Love Cemetery and to leave a legacy for future generations. My gratitude to Doris for her patience, her forthrightness, and her courage. Reda Rackely introduced me to the wisdom of the Ancestors in the Dagara tradition of Burkina Faso in West Africa. Reda's generosity and belief in this work was essential to this writing. Sobonfu Somé shared the brilliance of the Dagara tradition too. Wendy Grace brought her experience as a healer to bear and supported me all along. Her generosity was unsurpassed.

Members of Boy Scout Troop 210 in Marshall, Texas, provided the hard labor needed to clear Love Cemetery to the ground. It would have been impossible to reclaim the burial ground without them. Scouts such as Jeronimo Holguin, David Guvernator, Ulysis Bedolla, Tony and Adam Harman, Gavin and Graham McKinley, Luke Girlinghouse, Ehrin and Luke Emerson, Cody Lay, J.R. Griffith, Chris Williams, and all who came to help, including their parents, deserve special thanks. My cousin Philip Verhalen, their troop master, and his assistant scout master, Doug Gardiner, were enormous pillars of support. Philip's patience and calm, coupled with Doug's commitment and constancy, made our work a success. Boundless gratitude to Philip, Doug, and Troop 210.

Walter "Coach" Edwards, Annye Fisher, and Julia Williams helped time and again, even though their own relatives were buried elsewhere. Gail and Greg Beil gave unflagging assistance of all kinds and provided hospitality for years, and deserve thanks far beyond what I write here. Gail generously shared her research for *The Banquet of My Years*, her forthcoming biography of James Farmer, Jr. and James Farmer Sr., his father.

Fr. Denzil Vithanage, pastor of St. Joseph's Catholic Church in Marshall, has been a great supporter of our work. My friend, artist Joe Goodwin of New York, deserves thanks for telling me to go to the spiritual leaders in Marshall first for guidance about getting the unmarked burial ground honored. Special thanks to our early members Fr. Steve Sellers, Fr. Ron Diegel, Rev. Bob Johnson, and Rev. James Webb.

The volunteers at the Harrison County Historical Society Library deserve special thanks, including Edna Sorber, Ruth Briggs, and James Oliphant. Gratitude as well to Garrett Boersma, president of the Harrison County Historical Museum, for his help.

Dwight Shellman, founding director of the Caddo Lake Institute helped me understand the importance Caddo Lake as a Ramsar site, a rare wetland of international significance. Gratitude to Richard Lowerre, the director of the Caddo Lake Institute, Roy Darville, Ph.D., biologist and limnologist at East Texas Baptist University in Marshall. Tom Walker shared his photographs and knowledge of its birds. All contributed to my learning about the Big Cypress Creek watershed and the place of Caddo Lake within it.

Spencer Wood, Ph.D., Kansas State University, was generous with his research on black farming, especially Sabine Farms, in Marshall. Reporters from the Associated Press, like Allen Breed, contributed with background on their investigation of theft of black land. Scott Beasley, the dean of the School of Forestry at Stephen F. Austin College, in Nagodoches, Texas, added greatly to my understanding of contemporary forestry and the issues before it. Gerron Hite of the Texas State Historical Commission and Jim Bruseth, their chief archaeologist, were instrumental in placing Love Cemetery in the broader historical context. Carol Harrell and Gary Endsley helped with Caddo history. Historians Steve Hahn, Randolph Campbell, Adam Hochschild, Stewart Burns, and Manning Marable were reliable, generous sources. Any errors are mine. Gratitude also to Susan Glisson, Gerard Pigeon, and Kevin O'Malley.

Appreciation to my family in Dallas, especially my mother, Ruth Verhalen Langdon. My aunt, Sue Verhalen Padgett, introduced me to the other side of the story. My uncle Robert Verhalen, aunt Dorothy Verhalen, and my brother Scott Walters helped generously too. Thanks also to Margaret Juko. My gratitude to my Ursuline teachers in Dallas—they planted the seeds of dissonance that ripened into this book.

My cousins in East Texas happily made my work there possible. Philip's mother, my cousin Agnes, provided generous hospitality that knew no bounds. Her husband, Jack, was an inspiration to me. His older brother, Steve, like Jack, was unfailing in his help. Thanks also to Philip's wife Carolyn Verhalen for her immense hospitality, and to Frances Verhalen, Joanie Campbell, Martha Roberts, Betty and Gene Verhalen. My cousin David, Fr. Verhalen, a Holy Cross father at Notre Dame, and his colleague Fr. Steve Gibson, of the Holy Cross video ministry, provided enthusiastic support and help.

My appreciation to photographer Jeffrey Braverman who provided the initial photo editing needed. Artist Ruta Bertolis helped with maps. Anthony Fendler, a photograph technologist, helped with some of my digital stills. David Simpson and Ryan Thompson did videography in East Texas. Will Avery contributed sound and backup video too. Alan Pogue, human rights photographer, contributed photos still to be published. Photographer Dan Lent, and Kathleena Gorga, lent their skills as well. My son, Ben Galland, contributed travel, videography, sound recording, and film editing. My daughter, Madelon Galland, traveled to East Texas too, and assisted with recording sound, production, and still photography. Being supported by the professional talents of my adult children was an extraordinary gift.

I am grateful to Lucinda Ewing for her generous spirit and quiet hospitality in New Mexico. Thanks also to Marx Cazenave for his generosity and commitment to this work. Gratitude to Eric Cazenave also. Catlyn and Fred Fendler, Ann Grace McCoy, Joan Kiley, Bonnie O'Neill, Bess Carrick, Genevieve Vaughan, Gwendolyn Grace, Carol Edgar, Meggan Watterson, Rev. Sandy Gess, Betty Simmons, Christy Michaels, Bob Knechtel, and Bill Wilson—all have been generous beyond measure. Helen LaKelly Hunt provided abundant New Mexico hospitality and support and I am grateful for her generosity. Janet McKenzie's support and her painting, "The Keepers of Love," transformed this work and took it deeper. Kathy Barry, Mary Evelyn Tucker, Karen Buckley, Mary Ford, Sarah Crowell, Jane Hirshfield, Lama Palden, Jennifer Welwood, Maria Housden, Susan Shannon, Rev. Melinda McClain, and Rev. Ann Jefferson all have my deep appreciation, as does Pastor Veronica Goines of St. Andrew's, Marin City, California.

Dallas attorney and friend, Vincent Perini, generously helped with Texas Cemetery law. Attorney Franklin Jones Jr. of Marshall provided legal assistance pro-bono and supported this work. Ike Lasiter, fellow Texas and San

Francisco attorney who specializes Non-Violent Communication (NVC) contributed. Rodney Gilstrap, attorney and judge in Marshall, helped too, and I am grateful to them all.

Leslie Keenan, freelance editor, helped me cut away the burden of too much history. Leslie's skillful help came at a critical time. Ed Lempinen, a former editor at the *San Francisco Chronicle, Slate,* and *Newsday* in New York, helped greatly in editing the overall manuscript. Ed immediately understood what I was trying to do and helped me find ways to hone the narrative. His dedication and intelligence benefited *Love Cemetery* greatly. Alexia Paul, freelance editor, helped me find ways to tell parts of the story more efficiently. I am grateful for her skills as well. Kate Danaher provided invaluable assistance throughout. Layla Smith gave excellent help with transcription, copy-editing, and art. Carla Pollard and David Verhalen helped with transcription as well.

My agent, Joy Harris, shepherded this book into life with her rare abilities. I am especially thankful that she found a home for it at HarperOne, initially with Renee Sedliar. My editor Eric Brandt took over, brought a keen intelligence and quiet touch to our work together. His editorial suggestions helped shift the narrative in subtle but powerful ways. His calm presence made him a pleasure to work with. His assistant, Kris Ashley, managed the process and interplay of the elements in this book with warmth, care, and skill. I am especially grateful to Eric and to Kris. Alison Throckmorton, the assistant production editor, performed miracles with grace and intelligence to get this book into print. Special thanks also to Helena Brantley, the director of publicity, who believed in this book early on. My gratitude to the entire staff at HarperOne, including Terri Leonard, Claudia Boutote, Laina Adler, and Sam Barry.

The following people have helped support *Love Cemetery* in numerous ways also. I make no distinction between the kinds of support given, financial, professional, or other. Each was essential and I am grateful: Rachael Adler, Ella Alford, Marion and Alan Hunt Badiner, Joan Baker, Kathleen Barry and Bob Burnett, Mary and Stuart Bartholomaus, Jane Bay, Sera Beak, Melissa Blake, Janine Bonepath, Peggy Brown, Kathleen Burgy, Katy Butler, Hattie Byland, Joy Carol, Pamella Cavana, Paul and Jan Chaffee, Johnnie Chase, Stephanie Clohesy, Louise Todd Cope, Meinrad Craighead, Sally and Joe Cunneen, Kath Delaney, Lynn and Gerard Dempsey, Elizabeth de Veer, Tara Doyle, Ebenezer Lutheran Church, Carol Edgar, Eugenia Anderson Ellis, Hope Farr, Rachel Fitzgerald, Sarah and William Galbraith, Holley Galland, Barbara Getrost, Georgia Goldberg Gwendolyn Grace, Lori Grace, Jacqueline Greedy, Vivian Hahn, Paul Hawken, Emila Heller, Cynthia and Bill Hersey, Barbara Holifield, Carol and David House, Rev. Ann Jefferson, Heather Jelks, Diane Jenette, D'Ann Johnson, Erik Johnson, Franklin Jones Jr., Margarita Jones, Phyllis M. Jones, Dahlia Kamesar, Sophia Keller, Elizabeth Kelley, Carolyn Kellog, Sue Monk Kidd, Nancy Kittle, Robert Knechtel, Anne Lamott, David Ledeboer, Marylou Hillberg Lennox, Barry Lopez, Sumi Loudon, George Lucas, Christina Lundberg, Elizabeth Lloyd Mayer, Dominique Mazeaud, Claire McAuliffe, Janet McKenzie, Christy Michaels, Letitia and Milan Momirov, Mary Moore, Barbara Mumford, Susan Murcott, Yeshi Neuman, Ann Fursman Nix, Brenda Novick, Geoff and Leslie Oelsner, Elizabeth Owen, Dick Pervier, Robert and Joanne Phelps, Antonia Pizzari, Richard Platt, Noel Poncelet, Lisa Rafel, Maja Ramsey, Amelie Ratliff, Emma Farr Rawlings, Maryann Ready, Nina Reznik, Allyson and Ralph Rickard, Cynthia Ries, Geshe Champa Lodro Rinpoche, Carolyn Rivers, Jane Roper, Lydia and Robert Ruyle, Leonard Schlain, David and Jan Semling, Elayna Shakur, Hope Shaw, Betty Simmons, Anna Chavarria Shore, Lani Silver, Diane Solomon, Sophia Institute, Linea Stewart, Audrey Swanson, Linda Tillery, Judith Tripp, Sara Verhalen, Sally Roesch Wagner, Solace Wales, Mary Wallace, Johnny Wallace, Lailja Leila Ware, Cookie Washington, Marion Weber, Anita Weissberg, Noni Welch, Rebecca Westerfield, Akaya Winwood, Irvin and Marilyn Yalom, and Anna Yang.

The following foundations have generously supported this work: the Summerlee Foundation, the Shaman's Fund, the Tara Fund at the Tides Foundation, the Angeles Arrien Foundation/Cross Cultural Education & Research, the Roy A. Hunt Foundation, the Rachel and Ben Vaughan Foundation, and the James Dougherty Foundation.

My husband, Corey Fischer, has been my loving companion through all my books but for the first, yet it is this book in particular that I gladly and rightly dedicate to him. This work has had the benefit of his reading and editing as well as his mature artistry and skill as a writer himself. He pored over this book; he knows everyone in it. He challenged me and made this story the better for its difficulty. His narrative and structural skills from making theater all his life have benefited me greatly.

My three grown children, Matthew, Madelon, and Ben Galland, have enriched my life and work beyond telling. My gratitude to Kelly Galland and Angelica Galland, for the children they've brought into our lives: River, Sebastian, Phoebe Rose, Skylar, and Elijah. May this offering help restore the world for all children.

Notes

———◆———

PROLOGUE

1. My grandparents bought their home in 1916, when Highland Park was largely open fields. I grew up two blocks away from the black neighborhood.

2. Steve Orlen, "Abandoned Places," *Poetry Magazine* 23, no. 6.

3. "Prisoner of Highland Park," *D Magazine* (Nov. 1977).

CHAPTER ONE

4. *Epigraph.* Robert Pinsky, the American poet laureate of the day, spoke of Chief Seattle and Chief Seattle's words about the dead in his commencement address of June 13, 1999, to the graduating class at Stanford University (www.english.uiuc.edu/maps/poets/m_r/pinsky/speech.htm; see also www.chiefseattle.com/history/chiefseattle/chief.htm). Both Pinsky's and Chief Seattle's remarks are so germane to this narrative that I provide key excerpts here.

"Graduation exercises, like this one, embody one of the great secular rituals in our culture.... On some deeper level ... what we see today is the celebration here of the two great obligations or standards, two great tests that apply to every tribe and culture on earth, the two values by which any human society must be judged.... [By this] I mean the two great requirements of the human animal, without which human community is corrupt or useless, namely, caring for the young ones and honoring the wisdom of the old ones, including the ways and wisdom of the dead. The tribe or community or nation that fails at either of these missions brings woe and destruction on itself....

"Maybe the most powerful, even disturbing, statement I know concerning that process of receiving from the old ones to give to the young is the legendary half-mythical speech given by Chief Seattle, the Suquamash Indian leader. In the most authentic of the many versions of Seattle's speech, he recognizes that the white invaders have displaced and conquered his people, reduced now to a remnant who have to rely on the goodwill of the white leaders.... He muses that the white men have said that their god is the god of the Indians as well, but Seattle says he has to doubt that. Why, if the two peoples have this one father, does he treat the one so much better than the other?

'And how can we be brothers,' he says to the triumphant newcomers, 'when we're so different?'

"As his great central example of that difference, Seattle points to how differently the two peoples behave in relation to their dead. He says, 'To us the ashes of our ancestors are sacred and their resting place is hallowed ground. You wander far from the graves of your ancestors and seemingly without regret. Your dead cease to love you and the land of their nativity as soon as they pass the portals of the tomb and wander away beyond the stars. They are soon forgotten and never return.'

"'Our dead never forget this beautiful world that gave them being,' he says, and he explains that they often return to advise and comfort the living.... And then Chief Seattle makes a remarkable statement, a sentence that has rung in my mind since I first read it: 'They are not powerless, the dead.'

"'They are not powerless, the dead.' I believe that these famous remarks of Chief Seattle speak to something deep in the nature of the United States of America, as though Seattle intuited something profound about our possibilities and our risks. I associate his saying that the dead are not powerless with the nature of American memory—our particular national ways of honoring the old ones.

"It's been said that while the United States is beyond doubt a great nation, it remains to be seen if we are a great people, or whether we are perhaps still engaged in the undertaking of becoming a great people. I propose to you that a people is defined and unified not by blood, but by shared memory—a people is held together and identified by what successfully gets passed on from the old ones to be remembered by the young. A people is its memory, its ancestral treasures."

5. The following text is quoted from the *AFRO-American Almanac* Web site (www.toptags.com/aama/events/jtenth.htm) and lightly edited. It begins with the announcement General Granger read on a street in Galveston, Texas, on June 19, 1865, and refers to the Emancipation Proclamation:

"General Order Number 3:

'The people of Texas are informed that in accordance with a Proclamation from the Executive of the United States, all slaves are free. This involves an absolute equality of rights and rights of property between former masters and slaves, and the connection heretofore existing between them becomes that between employer and free laborer.'

"Many attempts have been made to explain the 2½-year delay in the receipt of this important news, but no one really knows for sure why it took so long. For whatever reason, conditions in Texas remained the same well beyond what was statutory. When change finally did arrive in Texas, the reactions to this profound news ranged from pure shock to jubilation. While many lingered to hear about this new employer-to-employee relationship, many left before the offers were completely off the lips of their former masters. Even with nowhere to go, many felt that leaving the plantation would be their first taste of freedom. The North was a logical destination, and for many it represented true freedom, while the desire to find family members in neighboring states drove some into Louisiana, Arkansas, and Oklahoma.

"The celebration of June 19th was coined 'Juneteenth' and grew with more participation from descendants. The Juneteenth celebration was a time for reassuring each other, for praying, and for gathering remaining family members. Juneteenth became highly revered in Texas, and is celebrated throughout the United States.

"The civil rights movement of the 1950s and 1960s yielded both positive and negative results for the Juneteenth celebrations...." In 1968, the Poor People's March on Washington revived interest in Juneteenth. Many attendees started Juneteenth celebrations in areas where the celebration had previously been unknown.

"On January 1, 1980, Juneteenth became an official state holiday in Texas through the efforts of Al Edwards, an African American state legislator. The successful passage of this bill marked Juneteenth as the first Emancipation celebration to be granted official state recognition. Today Juneteenth celebrates African American freedom throughout the United States while encouraging self-development and respect for all cultures throughout the world."

6. Robert George, of the Botanical Research Institute of Texas (BRIT) in Ft. Worth, Texas, clarified that there *is* a variety of wisteria that is native to Texas. "Native" means basically that it was found during the sixteenth century, when European expeditions first came to this area and reported their findings (www. BRIT.org). George explained that there might be a seed of truth in the story, though. The Verhalen Nursery may have introduced a second kind of wisteria to Texas (at least to East Texas), a variety imported from China.

CHAPTER TWO

7. *Epigraph.* The Dagara people live in Burkina Faso in West Africa and have a rich cosmology. In an interview, Sonbufu explained the Dagara perspective on the ongoing relationship of the Ancestors with the living. To the layperson, their cosmology, like that of many indigenous peoples the world over, can sound remarkably like Buddhist philosophy, modern physics, and string theory. The Dagara world is seamless and includes both the living and the dead. Also see Karen McCarthy Brown's classic work of anthropology on the African-based Voudon tradition of Haiti, *Mama Lola: A Voudon Priestess in Brooklyn* (Berkeley: University of California Press, 1991).

8. The dogs were brought by individual owners. They were not dogs that belonged to the Marshall Police or Fire Department, it turned out.

9. Joe C. Truet and Daniel W. Lay, *Land of Bears and Honey: A Natural History of East Texas* (Austin: University of Texas Press, 1984).

CHAPTER THREE

10. *Epigraph.* Robert Pinsky's June 13, 1999, commencement address at Stanford.

11. *The Love/Bennett Family Tree, 1830–1998,* "The Love Line," by Joyce Mack Parks, a descendant of Della Love (self-published, 1998). Courtesy of the Harrison County Historical Society Library.

CHAPTER FOUR

12. *Epigraph.* Randolph B. Campbell, *An Empire for Slavery: The Peculiar Institution in Texas, 1821–1865* (Baton Rouge: Louisiana State University Press, 1989), 1. Campbell's use of the phrase "the burden of Southern History," comes, as he notes, from C. Vann Woodward, *The Burden of Southern History* (Baton Rouge: Louisiana State University Press, 1960).

13. Interview with the dean of the Temple School of Forestry, Prof. Scott Beasley, Stephen F. Austin College, Nagodoches, Texas.

14. I consulted a variety of sources to piece together the picture I present here of the Caddo and the land. *The Southwestern Historical Quarterly*'s article on Thomas Jefferson's 1806 exploratory expedition up the Red River (the second exploratory journey that he commissioned during his presidency, the Lewis and Clark expedition being the first) was particularly helpful. Dan L. Flores, "The Ecology of the Red River in 1806: Peter Custis and Early Southwestern Natural History," Southwestern Historical Quarterly 88, no. 1 (July 1984), 1–42. Gary Endsley of the Jeffersonian Institute's Cypress Valley Education Center in Jefferson, Texas, generously shared this paper and others. Joe C. Truett and Daniel W. Lay's classic *Land of Bears and Honey: A Natural History of East Texas*, was lent to me by Francis E. Abernathy. Randolph Campbell's history of the state, *Gone to Texas,* and *The Conquest of Texas: Ethnic Cleansing in the Promised Land, 1820–1875,* by Gary Clayton Anderson, helped fill in more information on the Caddo. Also see the Web site for the Caddo Nation, headquartered in Binger, Oklahoma (www.caddonation-nsm.gov). The Caddo Lake Institute (www.caddolakeinstitute.us) and various Web sites on the Gulf Coast Plain and the ancient seas that covered East Texas were especially helpful in understanding the landscape of East Texas (www.csc.noaa.gov/beachnourishment/html/geo/index.htm; www.tsha.utexas.edu/handbook/online/articles/GG/swgqz.html; www.emporia.edu/earthsci/student/salley3/). Dean Scott Beasley of the Temple School of Forestry at Stephen F. Austin College in Nagodoches, Texas, kindly took the time to read this material for factual accuracy.

15. Adam Hochschild, *Bury the Chains: Prophets and Rebels in the Fight to Free an Empire's Slaves* (New York: Houghton Mifflin, 2005), is an excellent book that recounts the successful rebellion of over 100,000 people in slavery in Haiti.

16. Benjamin Braude's "The Mistranslation of Ham," was presented at Yale University's Guilder Lehrman Center on Slavery, Resistance, and Abolition's annual fall conference, 2004. Also see the article by Felicia R. Lee on the conference, "From Noah's Curse to Slavery's Rationale" (*New York Times*, Nov. 1, 2003), which sums up the thinking of many contemporary scholars on the sleight of hand in biblical translation that made it possible for people to justify the institution of slavery. Also see David Brion Davis's Pulitzer Prize–winning book, *Inhuman Bondage: The Rise and Fall of Slavery in the New World* (New York: Oxford, 2006).

17. See Adam Hochschild's extraordinary account of the British movement to outlaw the slave trade and ultimately to outlaw slavery: *Bury the Chains*. The British abolitionist movement, begun by a handful of Quakers led by William Wilberforce, was an important influence on the U.S. abolitionist groups, and there was a great deal of interchange between them. American abolitionists, including Frederick Douglass, traveled to England, and British abolitionists visited the South, including Texas. Also see Robert Metaxis's *Amazing Grace* (San Francisco: HarperSanFrancisco, 2007), and the movie by the same name.

18. Campbell, *Empire*, 14.

19. Campbell, *Empire*, 35.

20. Campbell, *Empire*, 4.

21. Campbell, *Empire*, 4.

22. See David Brion Davis, *Inhuman Bondage* (New York: Oxford, 2006). Davis is also the director of Yale University's Gilder Lehrman Center for the Study of Slavery, Resistance, and Abolition. "Throughout the antebellum period cotton accounted for over half the value of all American exports, and thus it paid for the major share of the nation's import and investment capital." For more on the critical role that southern cotton played in the Industrial Revolution and world trade, see pp. 181–84.

23. Davis, *Inhuman Bondage*, 18.

24. Named after a minstrel show stereotype, the term "Jim Crow laws" was used for a wide range of antiblack legislation enacted in the 1880s.

25. Pete Daniels, *The Shadow of Slavery: Peonage in the South, 1901–1969* (Urbana: University of Illinois, 1972). Daniels tells how debt peonage survived and fed off the corruption of local law enforcement and the laxity of federal law enforcement. For example, in the 1920s if a worker tried to escape the dreaded turpentine camps in the Florida woods, or the sawmills of the South, his "boss" could go to local law enforcement to find, beat, and arrest the man or woman and have him or her dragged back to work until the "debt" was paid. Debts could rarely be paid off because they were always being increased—for example, when a worker tried to attend a voter education class. Many paid with their lives.

As with Hurricane Katrina in New Orleans today, Daniels points out that "natural disasters had a way of exposing the unnatural caste system of the South." Whether it was the flood from the 1917 hurricane in Texas City, or the infamous 1927 Great Flood of the Mississippi, African Americans generally lost the most. In 1927, African Americans were herded into "refugee camps" under the control of armed National Guardsmen. After the NAACP reported on the existence of the camps and the impossibility for blacks to move in and out, Herbert Hoover, who was in charge of the rescue effort, invited interested parties to visit "any of the negro concentration camps in Arkansas, Mississippi, or Louisiana."

In the 1927 flood, as white women and children escaped in cars, black women and children rode away from the river in boxcars. Four hundred black men, pressed into service by the government to shore up the levees, were reportedly abandoned atop the levees and drowned. (pp. 151–56).

26. Daniels, *Shadow of Slavery*, 180.

27. Daniels, *The Shadow of Slavery*. Daniel's book is essential reading on this subject. Debt peonage is as vicious today as it was in the Old and New South, only today it devours refugees and immigrants—men, women, and children alike—not only African Americans and people of color but whites too. According to *Enslaved: True Stories of Modern Slavery*, edited by Jess Sage and Liora Kasten, foreword by Gloria Steinem (New York: Palgrave, 2006), which was published by the American Anti-Slavery Group, 27 million people remain enslaved today.

28. See www.usconstitution.com/40Acres.htm and other sites. Special Field Order No. 15, issued by General Sherman on January 16, 1865, did indeed give formerly enslaved people forty acres of land per family. See the website for the entire order. I excerpt this material because many have claimed that being given 40 acres and a mule was wishful thinking on the part of African Americans. It was not. The order begins:

"I. The islands from Charleston, south, the abandoned rice fields along the rivers for thirty miles back from the sea, and the country bordering the St. Johns river, Florida, are reserved and set apart for the settlement of the negroes now made free by the acts of war and the proclamation of the President of the United States...." and continues. [See also "What About My 40 Acres & a Mule?" Gerene L. Freeman, Yale-New Haven Teachers Institute: www. yale.edu/ynhti/curriculum/units/1994/4/94.04.01.x.html]

In sum, by June, 1865, 40,000 freedmen had been allocated 400,000 acres of land. Within a year, President Andrew Johnson broke the good faith of the freedmen and rescinded Sherman's order and instructed Brigadier General R. Saxton to take back the lands from the families living on them and farming.

Saxton was dismayed and wrote the Commissioner of the Freedmen's Bureau directly noting that the lands "have been solemnly pledged to the freedmen. The law of Congress has been published to them...It is of vital importance that our promises made to freedmen should be faithfully kept ... The freedmen were promised the protection of the government in their possession ... I cannot break faith with them now by recommending the restoration of any of these lands. In my opinion, this order of General Sherman's is as binding as a statute." Nonetheless Saxton's pleas went unanswered. The white planters, the former owners of the land demanded their property back and President Johnson gave it to them. Saxton was ashamed. The families were devastated but had no choice but to move on. Saxton had military orders to evacuate them and he had the U.S. Army behind him. Though the freedmen were removed, many still felt entitled to the land. Between 1865-1869 countless alternatives were proposed.

Still, "President Johnson ... mercilessly vetoed any proposal having to do with providing land to the freedmen that reached his desk. Finally, Congress overrode his veto and passed a bill to extend the life of the Freedmen's Bureau. However, it contained no provision for granting land to the Freedmen, other than to provide them access to the Southern Homestead Act at the standard rate of purchase.

"The issue of reparations refuses to die...."

29. Daniels, *Shadow of Slavery*, 170–92.

30. R. P. Littlejohn, "A Brief History of the Days of Reconstruction in Harrison County, Texas" (Marshall, Texas: n.p., 1936). A well-known outrageous 9½-page paper that has been a subject of study for some time.

31. Steven Hahn, *A Nation Under Their Feet: Black Political Struggles in the Rural South from Slavery to the Great Migration* (Cambridge, MA: Harvard University Press, 2003), 327. Steven Hahn's Pulitzer Prize-winning *A Nation Under Their Feet* and Randolph Campbell's books lay out an important, different history of this period than most schoolbooks recognize.

32. Whether they ever debated Harvard University remains a question.

33. Gail Beil, *The Banquet of My Years* (unpublished manuscript), a biography of James Farmer Jr. and James Farmer Sr.

34. I interviewed Rev. Hamilton Boswell in 2005 and 2006 at his home in California.

35. Chris Moseley Jr., "The History of Scottsville, Harrison County, Texas, and Its Relation to the Land" (term paper, Baylor University, 1985). Courtesy of the Harrison County Historical Society Library.

36. Hahn, *A Nation*.

37. Todd Lewan and Dolores Barclay, "Torn from the Land," Associated Press, 2001. Associated Press writers Woody Baird, Allen G. Breed, Shelia Hardwell Byrd, Alan Clendenning, Ron Harrist, David Lieb, and Bill Poovey, and investigative researcher Randy Herschaft contributed to this report. Dolores Barclay wrote and let me know that their series was read into the Congressional Record. Spencer Wood assisted and helped train the writers and showed them how to research old records. "A follow-up Associated Press

story by Bruce Smith that appeared October 15, 2006, "Heirs Defy History of Blacks Losing Land," tells of the Jones family who, rather than letting their land get sold off in increasingly smaller parcels, formed a corporation and are developing their valuable property on Hilton Head in South Carolina. See Associated Press, www.ap.org.

38. "New Study Shows Impact of Mercury Pollution: $8.7 Billion Lost Annually Due to Poisoning in the Womb," *Environmental Health* (Feb. 28, 2005), available at http://ehp.niehs.nih.gov/members/2005/7743/7743.pdf. The article concludes that 600,000 babies are brain-damaged *in utero* from mercury poisoning, before they even take their first breath. Studies show that "mercury pollution is directly attributable to mercury emitted by coal-fired power plants.... The EPA has identified coal-fired power plants as the largest industrial emitters of mercury...." The highest concentration of mercury in the United States is in the lignite coal mined and burned in the Caddo area.

39. Joe Nick Patosi, "The Only Honest Lake in Texas," *The Texas Observer*, July 8, 2005.

CHAPTER FIVE

40. Will Coleman, cofounder of BT, the Black Theological think tank, and author of *Tribal Talk: African Ancestral Spirituality as a Resource for Wholeness,* in *Teaching African American Religions* (Oxford: American Academy of Religious Studies, 2005), and several other works, introduced me to this understanding and to the work of other fine scholars and books on this subject.

Afro Caribbean scholar and author Gerard Pigeon, professor emeritus and former chair of the Black Studies Department at University of Santa Barbara, and anthropologist of religion Karen McCarthy Brown, professor of sociology and anthropology of religion at Drew University, author of *Mama Lola: A Voudon Priestess in Brooklyn,* have especially opened my eyes to the rich, complex world of Africa that's been carried by the Black Diaspora throughout the world.

CHAPTER SIX

41. Brian Swimme, *The Hidden Heart of the Cosmos* (New York: Orbis, 1996), 108.

CHAPTER SEVEN

42. Moseley, "The History of Scottsville, 54."

43. Sabine Farms was a federal project in the 1930s that helped black farmers buy 10,000 acres of farmland. A vestige of Sabine Farms remains today.

44. Spencer D. Wood, Ph.D., professor of sociology and a board member of the Black Farmers and Agriculturalists Association.

45. Telephone interview with Spencer Wood on his research for a forth-

coming article on the subject of black land loss, January 10, 2006. Wood's fellow professor, Jess Gilbert, a professor of rural sociology from the University of Wisconsin–Madison, is the coauthor, with Wood, of the article, "Experiments in Land Reform and Racial Justice: The New Deal State and Local African Americans Remake Civil Society in the Rural South, 1935–2004."

46. Originally the land belonged to Monsanto, then the Department of Defense. Currently it's being transferred to the Fish and Wildlife Service to be made into a National Wildlife Refuge.

47. In 1991, construction workers digging a foundation for the new Federal Building in New York City found themselves in a seventeenth- and eighteenth-century cemetery for slaves and freedmen in downtown Manhattan. The African Burial Ground Project continues to be an enormous, ongoing work of great historical significance. The burial ground itself encompassed an estimated five acres and held roughly 20,000 burials. Because of its location and the unique challenges of the site, only 419 remains were reinterred in 2003.

Since the site was designated a National Monument in February 2006, its administration has been taken over by the National Park Service and is managed in part by the Schomberg Center of the New York Public Library. ABGP is a magnificent work, which has given us a new understanding of the role that New York and the Northeast played in the history of slavery; indeed, it provides a broader, more accurate, and more complicated understanding of the history of the United States as a whole.

48. The book was published by the African American Museum in Dallas. The video, "Freedman's Cemetery Memorial: A Place of Healing," was produced by KERA television in Dallas, the local PBS station.

49. From the multitude of sources on this subject, I've chosen to rely on Adam Hochschild's book on the British abolitionists, *Bury the Chains* (Boston: Houghton Mifflin, 2005); as well as Johnson, Smith, and the WGBH Series Research Team, *Africans in America*.

50. Linda Tillery's "From Slave Ships to Sanctuary," a course on African American spirituals taught with Rev. Ann Jefferson at the Graduate Theological Union, used scholarship and song to deepen our understanding of the experience of people in slavery and the genesis of the black gospel tradition. Linda Tillery's comment in a class sparked my reflections at the Dallas Freedman's Cemetery. As we gathered in our classroom, designed for sixty people, she suggested that, before we sang, we take a minute to imagine four hundred people in the room, in chains, very few of whom could communicate with one another because of differences in tribe and language.

CHAPTER EIGHT
51. *Epigraph.* Martin Luther King Jr., "Great, but" (Ebenezer Church, Atlanta, Georgia, July 2, 1967), audiotape recording, MLKP-GAMK, 474. Cited in Stewart Burns, *To the Mountaintop: Martin Luther King's Sacred*

Mission to Save America 1955–1968 (San Francisco: HarperSanFrancisco, 2004), 345 n. 52.

52. "Mosaics of Mary, the Many Faces of the Divine Feminine Around the World," held at the Sophia Center at the Phoebe Pembrook House, with myself, Sue Monk Kidd, Peggy Rubin, Emily Devine, Janet McKenzie, and Carolyn Rivers.

53. This is how people in Brazil who go into trance in Candomble ceremonies are treated; they are upheld as they are taken over by the Spirits, saturated with their living God. Both traditions—Black Baptist and Candomble—are rooted in Africa, no matter how far apart they might seem on the surface.

CHAPTER NINE

54. *Epigraph.* The Biblical quotes at the beginnings of this chapter are taken from *The New Jerusalem Bible Pocket Edition*, edited by Henry Wansbrough, pp. 1400, 695.

55. The Antiquities Act of 1806 made it a crime to steal Indian artifacts or deface ancient and historical sites on federal land. The state of Nebraska has been the national leader in protecting Indian remains on private land and has created model legislation for this.

56. Available at http://www.texasbeyondhistory.net/timberhill/index.html.

57. Louise Levathes, "A Geneticist Maps Ancient Migrations," *New York Times*, July 27, 1983, reported on the work of Dr. Cavalli-Sforza of Stanford University Medical School and his colleagues, and their then forthcoming "publication of a genetic atlas called 'The History and Geography of Human Genes,'" by Princeton University Press. In sum, "Europeans are a mixed population that ... appear to have 65% Asian ancestry and 35% African.... All races or ethnic groups now seem to be a bewildering array of overlapping sets and subsets that are in a constant state of flux."

Also in 1983, Dr. Cavalli-Sforza and Dr. Mary-Claire King, a geneticist at the University of California at Berkeley, appeared at a hearing of the Senate Committee on Government Affairs to report on their project and the implications of their findings. "They called racism 'an ancient scourge of humanity' and expressed the hope that the[ir] extensive study of world populations would 'undercut conventional notions of race and underscore the common bonds between all humans.'"

Dr. Lucia Chiavola Birnbaum, a generous author, scholar, and intrepid cultural historian, introduced me to the work of Dr. Cavalli-Sforza and the Human Genome Diversity Project.

58. Manning Marable's *The Great Wells of Democracy: The Meaning of Race in American Life* is an invaluable examination of the double narrative in the United States and the burning need for a national conversation. I return

to him repeatedly, especially his words, "To find a common future together, we must reconstruct our common past" (xii).

59. Fairness demanded that I telephone the minister to hear his perspective, but for whatever reason, my calls were not returned. The demands of ministering are immense, and I was not a member of his church.

LOVE CEMETERY BURIAL MAP LIST

60. List was current as of April 2006.

EPILOGUE

61. As of January 2007.

62. Known especially for her painting "Jesus of the People," Janet was inspired to paint Nuthel and Doris after hearing only a fragment about Love Cemetery. See www.janetmckenzie.com.

63. With the support of the William Winter Institute, the Alliance for Truth and Racial Reconciliation (ATRR) has emerged and consists of a number of groups working for racial justice and reconciliation. www.olemiss. edu/winterinstitute. For the Alliance, see www.olemiss.edu/winterinstitute/atrr.

64. Caroline Senter writes about this Louisiana Creole community of writers and poets. Her account of them and their commitment to envisioning America was so arresting that I've drawn in large part on her essay "Creole Poets on the Verge of a Nation." Though their poetry was not especially meaningful out of context, some of it is in Senter's account. See *Creole: The History and Legacy of Louisiana's Free People of Color*, edited by Sybil Kein (Baton Rouge: Louisiana State University Press, 2000), 176–294.

65. See E. L. Doctorow's powerful fictionalized account of history, *The March*, on this brutal, chaotic period in the history of the United States following the Civil War.

Bibliography

———◆———

Anderson, Gary Clayton. *The Conquest of Texas: Ethnic Cleansing and the Promised Land, 1820–1875*. Norman: University of Oklahoma Press, 2005.

Armstrong, Karen. *Holy War: The Crusades and Their Impact on Today's World*. New York: Anchor Books, 2001.

Ball, Edward. *Slaves in the Family*. New York. Ballantine Books, 1999.

Barasch, Marc Ian. *Field Notes on the Compassionate Life: A Search for the Soul of Kindness*. New York: Rodale, 2005.

Beecher, Jonathan. *Charles Fourier: The Visionary and His World*. Berkeley: University of California Press, 1986.

Berry, Jason. *The Spirit of Black Hawk: A Mystery of Africans and Indians*. Photographs by Sydney Byrd. Jackson: University Press of Mississippi, 1995.

Berry, Thomas. *The Dream of the Earth*. San Francisco: Sierra Club Books, 1988.

Berry, Wendell. *Another Turn of the Crank*. Washington, D.C.: Counterpoint, 1995.

Bresenhan, Karoline Patterson, and Nancy O'Bryant Puentes. *Lone Stars: A Legacy of Texas Quilts, 1836–1936*. Vol. 1. Austin: University of Texas Press, 1986.

———. *Lone Stars: A Legacy of Texas Quilts, 1936–1986*. Vol. 2. Austin: University of Texas Press, 1990.

Brown, Karen McCarthy. *Mama Lola: A Voudon Priestess in Brooklyn*. Berkeley: University of California Press, 1992.

Buechner, Frederick. *Telling Secrets: A Memoir*. San Francisco: HarperSanFrancisco, 1991.

Burns, Stewart. *To the Mountaintop: Martin Luther King Jr.'s Sacred Mission to Save America, 1955–1958*. San Francisco: HarperSanFrancisco, 2004.

Campbell, Randolph B. *An Empire for Slavery: The Peculiar Institution in Texas, 1821–1865*. Baton Rouge: Louisiana State University Press, 1989.

———. *Gone to Texas: A History of the Lone Star State*. New York: Oxford, 2003.

———. *A Southern Community in Crisis: Harrison County, Texas, 1850–1880*. Austin: Texas State Historical Association, 1983.

———. *Grass-Roots Reconstruction in Texas, 1865–1880*. Baton Rouge: Louisiana State University Press, 1997.

Carybé, Jorge Amado. *The Illustrated African Gods in the Candomble of Bahia*. Salvador, Bahia: Bruno Furrer, 1993.

Cohen, William. *At Freedom's Edge: Black Mobility and the Southern White Quest for Racial Control, 1861–1915*. Baton Rouge: Louisiana State University Press, 1991.

Coleman, Will E. *Tribal Talk: Black Theology, Hermeneutics, and African/American Ways of "Telling the Story."* University Park: Pennsylvania State University Press, 2000.

Coles, Robert. *Doing Documentary Work*. New York: Oxford University Press, 1997.

Daniel, Pete. *The Shadow of Slavery: Peonage in the South, 1901–1969*. Urbana: University of Illinois, 1990.

Davis, David Brion. *Inhuman Bondage: The Rise and Fall of Slavery in the New World*. New York: Oxford University Press, 2006.

Ereira, Alan. *The Elder Brothers: A Lost South American People and Their Wisdom*. New York: Random House, 1993. Originally published in Great Britain as *The Heart of the World* by Jonathon Cape, 1990.

Faulkner, William. *The Wild Palms [If I Forget Thee, Jerusalem]*. New York: Vintage Internationals, 1939.

Flinders, Carol. *Enduring Lives: Portraits of Women and Faith in Action*. New York: Tarcher, 2006.

Gates, Henry Louis, Jr. *Loose Canons: Notes on the Culture Wars*. New York: Oxford University Press, 1992.

Geiser, Samuel Wood. *Naturalists of the Frontier*. Dallas: Southern Methodist University, 1948.

Gobodo-Madikizela, Pumla. *A Human Being Died that Night: A South African Story of Forgiveness*. New York. Houghton Mifflin, 2003.

Govenar, Alan, and Phillip Collins. *Facing the Rising Sun: Freedman's Cemetery*. Exhibition catalogue. Edited by Alan Govenar and Phillip Collins. Dallas: African American Museum and Black Dallas Remembers, 2000.

Hahn, Steven. *A Nation Under Our Feet: Black Political Struggles in the Rural South from Slavery to the Great Migration*. Cambridge, MA: Belknap Press of Harvard University Press, 2003.

Harrison County Genealogical Society and Historical Museum. *Ancestor Issues*. Vol. 12, no. 3 (March 2006).

Hirshfield, Jane. *Given Sugar, Given Salt*. New York. Harper Collins, 2001.

Hochschild, Adam. *Bury the Chains*. New York: Houghton Mifflin, 2005.

Johnson, Charles, and Patricia Smith, and the WGBH Series Research Team. *Africans in America: America's Journey Through Slavery*. New York: Harcourt Brace, 1998. (Companion book to the PBS series by the same name.)

Kasher, Steven. The *Civil Rights Movement: A Photographic History, 1954–68*. New York. Abbeville Press, 1996.

Kein, Sybil, ed. *Creole: The History and Legacy of Louisiana's Free People of Color*. Baton Rouge: Louisiana State University Press, 2000.

Lane, Belden C. *The Solace of Fierce Landscapes: Exploring Desert and Mountain Spirituality*. New York. Oxford University Press, 1998.

Lewis, Thomas, M.D., Fari Amini, M.D., and Richard Lannon, M.D. *A General Theory of Love*. New York. Vintage Books, 2000.

Lindqvist, Sven. *"Exterminate All the Brutes": One Man's Odyssey into the Heart of Darkness and the Origins of European Genocide*. New York. New Press, 1996.

Marable, Manning. *The Great Wells of Democracy: The Meaning of Race in American Life*. New York. Basic Civitas Books, 2002.

McBride, James. *The Color of Water: A Black Man's Tribute to His White Mother*. New York. Riverhead Books, 1996.

McGill, Adam, and Tim Rogers, eds. *D Magazine's Dallas: The 30 Greatest Stories Ever Told*. Dallas: Magazine Partners, L.P., 2004.

Metaxas, Eric. *Amazing Grace*. San Francisco: HarperSanFrancisco, 2007.

Morrison, Toni. *Playing in the Dark: Whiteness and the Literary Imagination*. New York. Vintage Books, 1993.

Neihardt, John G. (Flaming Rainbow). *Black Elk Speaks: Being the Life Story of a Holy Man of the Oglala Sioux*. Lincoln: University of Nebraska Press, 1961.

Neuman, Yeshi Sherover. "The Role of European Americans in Healing the Wounds of Slavery: A Pilgrimage to the Sites of the Slave Trade." *Revision* (June 1999).

O'Reilley, Mary Rose. *The Barn at the End of the World: The Apprenticeship of a Quaker, Buddhist Shepherd*. Minnesota. Milkweed Editions, 2000

Olmsted, Frederick Law. *A Journey Through Texas, or A Saddle-Trip on the Southwestern Frontier*. Lincoln: University of Nebraska, 2004.

Paiewonsky, Isidor. *Eyewitness Accounts of Slavery in the Danish West Indies, also Graphic Tales of Other Slave Happenings in Ships and Plantations*. New York. Fordham University Press, 1989.

Parks, Joyce. *Love Line: the Love/Bennett Family Tree, 1830–1998*. Self-published. Copy in Harrison County Historical Society Library, Marshall, Texas.

Robinson, Randall. *The Debt: What America Owes to Blacks*. New York. Dutton, 2000.

Rybczynski, Witold. *A Clearing in the Distance: Frederick Law Olmsted and America in the Nineteenth Century.* New York: Touchstone, 2000.

Sante, Luc. *The Factory of Facts.* New York. Pantheon Books, 1998.

Senter, Caroline. "Creole Poets on the Verge of a Nation." In *Creole: The History and Legacy of Louisiana's Free People of Color,* ed. Sybil Kein. Baton Rouge: Louisiana State University Press, 2000.

Smith, F. Todd. *The Caddo Indians: Tribes at the Convergence of Empires, 1542–1854.* College Station: Texas A & M University Press, 1995.

Smith, Griffin, Jr. *Forgotten Texas: A wilderness portfolio.* Photographs by Reagan Bradshaw. Austin: Texas Monthly Press, 1983.

Somé, Malidoma Patrice. *Of Water and the Spirit: Ritual, Magic and Initiation in the Life of an African Shaman.* New York: Penguin Arkana, 1994.

Somé, Sobonfu E. *The Spirit of Intimacy: Ancient African Ways in the Teaching in the Ways of Relationship.* New York: HarperCollins, 2002.

Swimme, Brian. *The Hidden Heart of the Cosmos.* New York: Orbis Books, 1999.

Tileson, Mary W., ed. *Daily Strengths for Daily Needs.* Boston: Roberts Brothers, 1896.

Tobin, Jacqueline T., and Raymond G. Dobard. *Hidden in Plain View: A Secret Story of Quilts and the Underground Railroad.* New York. Doubleday, 1999.

Truett, Joe C., and Daniel W. Lay. *Land of Bears and Honey: A Natural History of East Texas.* Austin: University of Texas Press, 1984.

Tucker, Mary Evelyn. *Worldly Wonder: Religions Enter Their Ecological Phase.* Chicago: Open Court, 2003.

Tyler, Ronnie C. *Santiago Vidaurri and the Southern Confederacy.* Austin: Texas State Historical Association, 1973.

Wansbrough, Henry, ed. *The New Jerusalem Bible*, *Pocket Edition.* London: Darton, Longman, and Todd, 1990. See also *The New Jerusalem Bible.* New York: Doubleday, 1990.

Weiner, Brian A. *Sins of the Parents: The Politics of National Apologies in the United States.* Philadelphia, PA: Temple University Press, 2005.

West, Cornell. *Democracy Matters: Winning the Fight Against Imperialism.* New York. Penguin, 2004.

Yetman, Norman R., ed. *Voices from Slavery: 100 Authentic Slave Narratives.* Mineola: Dover Publications, 2000.

Resources

—— • ◆ • ——

African American Museum
3536 Grand Avenue
P.O. Box 150157, Dallas, TX 75315-0157
214-565-9026
www.aamdallas.org
The African American Museum in Dallas is devoted to the preservation and display of African American artistic, cultural, and historical materials. It has one of the largest African American folk art collections in the United States.

African Burial Ground Project
Office of Public Education and Interpretation
290 Broadway, New York, NY 10007
212-637-2039
www.africanburialground.gov
In 1991, the remains of more than 400 seventeenth- and eighteenth-century Africans and African Americans were discovered during while digging the foundation for the construction of a new federal building in downtown Manhattan. Digging further, archaelogists discovered a five-acre burial ground with an estimated 20,000 burials of Africans and African American slaves from the seventeenth and eighteenth centuries. The African Burial Ground was designated a National Monument in February 2006.

Alliance for Truth and Racial Reconciliation (ATRR)
www.olemiss.edu/winterinstitute/atrr
under the umbrella of the

William Winter Institute for Racial Reconciliation
Dr. Susan M. Glisson, Director
The University of Mississippi
P.O. Box 1848, 102 Vardaman Hall, University, MS 38677

662-915-6734
glisson@olemiss.edu
www.olemiss.edu/winterinstitute
"The William Winter Institute for Racial Reconciliation fosters reconciliation and civic renewal wherever people suffer as a result of racial discrimination or alienation, and promotes scholarly research, study and teaching on race and the impact of race and racism." The Institute now functions as an umbrella organization, and supports the emergence of a new regional group, **The Alliance for Truth and Racial Reconciliation** formed in 2005, at a gathering of groups based in the Deep South who met to talk about helping communities confront issues of racial violence and reconciliation. Out of this grew the regional alliance, a network of organizations dedicated to similar ideals, who could serve local community needs throughout the South. A growing list of members of the Alliance are listed on the ATRR Web site within the Winter Institute site. The list includes the Philadelphia Coalition in Neshoba County, Mississippi (www.neshobajustice.com/); STAR, Southern Truth and Reconciliation in Atlanta, Georgia (www.southern-truth.org/); the Moore's Ford Committee, Moore's Ford, Georgia (www.mooresford.org/); and the Keepers of Love Project (www.thekeepersoflove.com).

American Anti-Slavery Group
198 Tremont St., #421, Boston, MA 02116
800-884-0719, 617/426-8161, 270-964-2716
www.iAbolish.com
While many believe that the slave trade ended some time ago, there are still over 27 million people held in bondage today. In addition to chattel and sex slaves throughout Africa, parts of Asia, and many other parts of the world, cases of human trafficking have been documented in affluent neighborhoods in the United States. Slavery isn't history. *Enslaved: True Stories of Modern Day Slavery* (Palgrave, 2006), edited by Jesse Sage and Liora Kasten, (introduction by Gloria Steinem), is a collection of firsthand accounts of slavery in the twenty-first century. All proceeds from the sales of this book go toward the programs of the American Anti-Slavery Group. Also see *Not For Sale*.

Ancestor Divination
Reda Rackley
www.ancestordivination.com
Reda Rackley, M.A., is a cultural mythologist, storyteller, and shamanic counselor. She lectures and facilitates women's retreats bridging mythology, depth psychology, and spirituality. Reda was initiated into the indigenous

medicine of the Dagara tribe in Burkina Faso, West Africa. She teaches ancient shamanic traditions through storytelling, ritual, and divination.

Bioneers
Old Lamy School House
6 Cerro Circle, Lamy, NM 87540
1-877-246-6337 (1-877-BIONEER)
info@bioneers.org
www.bioneers.org
Bioneers are "biological pioneers who are working with nature to heal nature and ourselves." Founded in 1990, Bioneers promotes practical environmental solutions and innovative social strategies for restoring the earth and communities. They conduct programs in the conservation of biological and cultural diversity, traditional farming practices, environmental restoration, and sustainability. Bioneers sponsors a dynamic annual gathering in San Rafael, California, of scientific and social innovators who have demonstrated visionary and practical models for restoring the earth and communities.

Black Farmers and Agriculturalists Association
P. O. Box 70, Covington, TN 38019
901-522-8880
www.bfaa.net
This group works to support black farmers and agriculture. They provide legal counsel and bring class action lawsuits for compensatory relief to African American farmers and those who were denied the right to make a living from agriculture, including losses incurred because of discriminatory practices within the U.S. government.

Blessed Unrest: *How the Largest Movement in the World Came into Being and Why No One Saw It Coming,* by Paul Hawken (Viking, 2007)
www.blessedunrest.com and WISER: www.wiserearth.org
This book shows us humanity's collective genius and the spontaneous movement that has arisen to reimagine our relationship to the environment and to one another. Growing out of this body, WISER is an interactive Web site that exists to support a new system of awareness, support, communication, and collaboration.

Botanical Research Institute of Texas (BRIT)
509 Pecan Street, Fort Worth, TX 76102
817-332-4441
www.brit.org
The Botanical Research Institute of Texas (BRIT) is a global institute for the conservation and preservation of botanical heritage through education, research, scientific publications, and collections.

Caddo Lake Institute
44 East Avenue, Suite 101, Austin, TX 78701
512-469-6000
info@caddolake.us
www.caddolakeinstitute.us
The Caddo Lake Institute is a private operating foundation whose role is to
act as an ecosystem-specific sponsor and technical support entity, under-
writing local wetland science and conservation expertise and training, as
well as cultural and ecological research and monitoring. Its mission is to
protect and improve the ecological and cultural integrity of the Caddo Lake
ecosystem.

The Caddo Nation
P.O. Box 487, Binger, OK 73009
405-656-2344
www.caddonation-nsn.gov
The ancestors of the Caddo Indians were agriculturalists whose distinctive
way of life and material culture emerged by A.D. 900, as seen in archaeological sites in Arkansas, Louisiana, Texas, and Oklahoma. In 1542, de Soto's
expedition encountered thriving Caddo communities along the Brazos, Trinity, Neches, Sabine, Red, and Ouachita rivers. Twenty-first century Caddos
have renewed their efforts to revitalize the economic, social, political, and
religious institutions that preserve their heritage.

Center for the Arts, Religion and Education (CARE)
Graduate Theological Union
Pacific School of Religion
1798 Scenic Road, Berkeley, CA, 94709
800-999-0528
www.careartandreligion.us
CARE's mission is to encourage and develop programs and scholarship that
bring together the arts and religion. The Keepers of Love, the outgrowth of
the work at Love Cemetery, is a project of CARE. CARE's programs, faculty,
and their course offerings emphasize the dynamic, transformative role of the
arts in theological education.

Dallas Freedman's Cemetery Memorial
Southwest corner of North Central Expressway and Lemmon Ave., Dallas, TX
The Freedman's Cemetery, which dates back to 1869, was a vital part of
Freedman's Town, a community of former slaves and their descendants. Des-
ecrated from the early 1920s by various public projects, more than 1,600
gravesites were discovered in 1986 during the widening of Central Express-

way. The African American community and the preservationists joined forces to stop the destruction and to create a powerful memorial, the Freedman's Memorial Park. More than 1,000 burials were reinterred. The striking memorial marks the reconstitution of a sacred place and celebrates the contributions of African Americans to the city of Dallas.

Forum on Religion and Ecology
www.environment.harvard.edu/religion
The Forum on Religion and Ecology
P.O. Box 280, Lewisburg, PA 17837
The environmental crisis, global in scope and local in impact, requires major changes in how we think about our world and its future. Multidisciplinary efforts are needed to produce solutions to our interconnected environmental problems. The Forum on Religion and Ecology highlights the important roles that religions play in constructing moral frameworks for interacting with other people and the environment.

Foundation for Facing History and Ourselves
16 Hurd Road, Brookline, MA 02445-6919
617-232-1595
Ten regional offices: www.facinghistory.org
Since 1976, Facing History and Ourselves has offered in-depth professional development services; curricular resources; and ongoing support to educators and students in the areas of history, social studies, and language arts. They are dedicated to helping teachers around the world lead their students in a critical examination of history, with particular focus on genocide and mass violence.

Gilder Lehrman Center for the Study of Slavery, Resistance & Abolition
Yale University
P.O. Box 208206, 34 Hillhouse Avenue, New Haven, CT 06520
203-432-3339
Gilder.Lehrman.Center@yale.edu
www.yale.edu/glc
The center is dedicated to the investigation and dissemination of knowledge concerning all aspects of chattel slavery and its destruction. While the primary focus has been on scholarly research, they also seeks to bridge the divide between scholarship and public knowledge by opening channels between the scholarly community and the wider public. The center facilitates a locally rooted understanding of the global impact of slavery through programs, publications, and annual conferences.

Harrison County Genealogical Society and Historical Museum
Temporarily housed at 707 N. Washington, Marshall, TX 75670
P.O. Box 1987, Marshall, TX 75671
903-938-2680
museum@marshalltx.com
www.harrisoncountymuseum.org
The museum library is open to all interested individuals and is recommended for researchers who have ancestors who lived in Harrison County. The museum houses a collection of Caddo Indian artifacts, Civil War memorabilia, a Tuskegee airman display, and mementos of James Farmer Jr., Lady Bird Johnson, Bill Moyers, and others.

Janet McKenzie Studio
www.janetmckenzie.com
Janet McKenzie's strong, arresting style of painting celebrates the spirit of women and breaks down racial barriers. McKenzie's "Jesus of the People," depicts an androgynous black Christ and won *The National Catholic Reporter*'s competition for a 21st century Jesus. She writes, " 'The Keepers of Love' is a visual reminder of the sorrow of America's ongoing racial inequality."

The Keepers of Love
For more information about the ongoing Keepers of Love Project, go to www.thekeepersoflove.com and www.chinagalland.com

Land Loss Fund (LLF)
CCT's Land Loss Fund
P.O. Box 61, Tillery, NC 27887
http://members.aol.com/tillery/llf.html
This is a grassroots educational and charitable organization begun in 1983 that seeks to improve the social, educational, and economic welfare of people whose lives are being affected by the continued loss of family-owned land, especially in rural African American communities. LLF is a racially mixed group composed of farmers, educators, social workers, businesspersons, and other interested individuals. The fund provides educational, organizing, networking, research, and other technical assistance to small economically disadvantaged landowners in rural North Carolina counties in the effort to keep the land in the hands of the black community.

Linda Tillery and the Cultural Heritage Choir
P.O. Box 11195, Oakland, CA 94611
510-891-0454, Fax: 510-891-0453
www.culturalheritagechoir.com
Linda Tillery heard field recordings of traditional African American music and uncovered a treasure trove of spirituals, work songs, field hollers, and slave songs in 1992. A master performer, veteran vocalist, percussionist, producer, cultural historian, teacher, and scholar whose international career has spanned thirty-four years, Tillery then assembled the Cultural Heritage Choir—Rhonda Benin, Elouise Burrell, Melanie DeMore, and Simon Monserrat—to perform the music that kept black people alive.

Museum of the African Diaspora
685 Mission Street, San Francisco, CA 94105
415-358-7200
www.moadsf.org
MoAD's goal is to promote, explore, and appreciate the contributions people of African descent have made across the globe, and to foster a greater understanding of human history and promote cross-cultural communication. The museum seeks to capture the essence of the African Diaspora experience.

Rock Rose Institute — The Art of Non-Violent Conflict Resolution
1009 General Kennedy, 1st Floor
P.O. Box 29317, San Francisco CA 94129-0317
415-561-3232
info@rockroseinstitute.org
www.rockroseinstitute.org
Founded in 2004 by four women attorneys committed to peace building, the institute supports, promotes and advances non-violent conflict resolution through education, improved communication and a deeper understanding of justice.

Schomburg Center for Research in Black Culture
515 Malcolm X Boulevard, New York, NY 10037
212-491-2200
www.ny.com/museums/schomburg.center.for.research.in.black.culture.html
The Schomburg Center for Research in Black Culture in New York has invaluable resources for researching African American history. The center, part of the New York Public Library system, also has a new interpretation and Web site for African-American history, on the self-motivated migrations of people of African descent: *In Motion: The African-American Migration Experience* with a companion book by the same name.

Sobonfu Somé
Ancestors Wisdom Spring
5960 South Land Park Drive #200, Sacramento, CA 95822
sobonfu@sobonfu.com
www.sobonfu.com
Author and teacher Sobonfu Somé, one of the foremost voices in African
spirituality to come to the West, travels the world to share the rich spiritual
life and culture of her native Burkina Faso and the Dagara tradition.

The Sophia Institute
26 Society Street, Charleston, SC 29401
843-720-8528
www.thesophiainstitute.org
The Sophia Institute offers retreats with authors and teachers such as Sue
Monk Kidd, Marion Woodman, Jean Shinoda Bolen, China Galland, Dr. Gus
Speth, Angeles Arrien, Rick Brown, Jean Houston, Janet McKenzie, and
others, "transforming people who transform the world." Modeling spiritual
partnership and integration between feminine and masculine values, the institute fosters a spirit of co-creative wisdom.

Spirit Riders
www.spiritridersmovie.com
Ron His Horse Is Thunder
Sitting Bull College, Fort Yates, ND 58538
701-854-3861
www.sittingbull.edu
Spirit Riders is an international award-winning documentary film about an
American Indian peace movement begun in 1990 by the Lakota Nation, and
its growth over the subsequent years. The thirteen-day winter horseback ride
through the snows from Chief Sitting Bull's assassination site to Wounded
Knee was created to honor and memorialize the massacre at Wounded Knee
on December 29, 1890. The "Wiping Away the Tears" ceremony performed
inspires Lakota leaders to continue the rides annually for the sake of Lakota
youth, now called "Future Generation Riders."

Texas Center for Documentary Photography
2104 E. Martin Luther King Blvd, Austin, TX 78702
512-478-8387
alanpogue@mac.com
www.documentaryphotographs.com
Alan Pogue's photographs focus on issues of social justice the world over:
from Iraq to Guatemala and New Orleans. Pogue is the staff photographer for
The Texas Observer, and a friend of Love Cemetery.

Texas Historical Commission
P.O. Box 12276 , Austin, TX 78711-2276
512-463-6100
thc@thc.state.tx.us
www.thc.state.tx.us
The Texas Historical Commission works with citizens and organizations to preserve Texas's architectural, archeological, and cultural landmarks, as well as Texas's cemeteries.

Texas Observer
307 West 7th Street , Austin, TX 78701
512-477-0746
800-939-6620 toll-free
business@texasobserver.org
www.texasobserver.org
The Texas Observer writes about issues ignored or underreported in the mainstream press. Molly Ivins was a former editor of this independent monthly. Their goal is to cover stories crucial to the public interest and to provoke dialogue that promotes democratic participation and open government, in pursuit of a vision of Texas where education, justice, and material progress are available to all.

U.S. National Slavery Museum
Vonita W. Foster, Ph.D. Executive Director
1320 Central Park Boulevard, Suite 251, Fredericksburg, VA 22401
540-548-8818
www.usnationalslaverymuseum.org
Construction on the United States National Slavery Museum in Fredericksburg, Virginia, began in 2006 and is scheduled for completion in 2008. The museum will offer 100,000 feet of permanent and temporary exhibit space. Exhibits will take visitors on a journey through time, beginning with Africa as the cradle of civilization through the Middle Passage on slave ships, to the slave resistance movement, the Civil War, and the continuing struggle for equality today. The library and archives at the museum will serve all those seeking information pertaining to slavery in America. Through a vast and ever-growing collection of materials in all formats—oral histories, maps, rare editions, film, and video—it will tell the individual and collective story of a people and their pursuit of freedom.

Wilberforce Institute for the Study of Slavery and Emancipation (WISE)
Oriel Chambers
27 High Street, Hull, HU1 1NE, United Kingdom
+44 (0)1482 305176
www.hull.ac.uk/wise/
WISE is named after William Wilberforce, a British statesman and reformer from the early part of the nineteenth century who led a successful twenty-year fight to abolish the British slave trade. He was also instrumental in passing legislation to abolish slavery in the British colonies, just three days before his death in 1833. The institute sponsors conferences and carries on academic research and learning that shed new light on slavery and modern human rights abuses. *Amazing Grace*, a feature film by Ken Wales, chronicles William Wilberforce's extraordinary contributions to the world. A companion biography, *Amazing Grace: William Wilberforce and the Heroic Campaign to End Slavery* by Eric Metaxas, was published simultaneously (HarperSanFrancisco, 2007). The film sparked "Amazing Change," a modern-day campaign "to carry on Wilberforce's vision of justice and mercy" and to end slavery today. See also *Not For Sale* by Eric Metaxes, www.theamazingchange.com.

Credits

———•◆•———

Photos on pages 19, 53, 58, 90, 101, and 206 by Madelon Gallard.
Photos on pages 56, 119, 131, 142, 149, and 207 by the author.

ENDPAPERS
New Map of Rebublic of Texas, 1836. Cartography by J. II. Young.
Courtesy of the Harrison County Historical Society Library.

FRONTIS PIECE
"The Keepers of Love" Oil on canvas by Janet McKenzie © 2005. Courtesy
of Janet McKenzie.

CHAPTER THREE
Photograph of Della Love Walker from *Love Line: Love/Bennett Family 1830–
1998,* by Joyce Parks. Courtesy of the Harrison County Historical Association Library.

CHAPTER FOUR
Illustration 17th Century Texas and Mississippi Valley map from *The Caddo
Indians: Tribes at the Convergence of Empires, 1542–1854* by F. Todd
Smith. Courtesy of Texas A&M University Press. Reconstruction by Topuz
Maps.
Photograph of the Era No. 10 paddle steamer, photographer unknown. Cour-
tesy of Northwestern State University of Louisiana, Watson Memorial Li-
brary, Cammie G. Henry Research Center (Dellnon Collection).
Photograph of 1935 Champion Debate Team from Wiley College 1936 year-
book in Marshall Texas, photographer unknown. Courtesy of Gail Beil.

CHAPTER SEVEN
Photograph of Sabine Farms, by Russell Lee. Courtesy of the Library of Con-
gress, Prints and Photographs Division, FSA-OWI Collection, [LC-
USF33-012185-M3 DLC].
List of enslaved people of Mimosa Hall plantation. Courtesy of the Harrison
County Historical Association Library.

CHAPTER NINE
Photograph of Chief Show-e-Tat. Courtesy of the National Anthropological
Archives, Smithsonian Institution. (Negative no. 1373-B)

LOVE CEMETERY BURIAL MAP
Illustration by Kate Danaher and David Ziegler.